# Then All Hell Broke Loose

*The Odyssey of a Marine Corps Photographer in Vietnam*

## Dennis I. Fisher

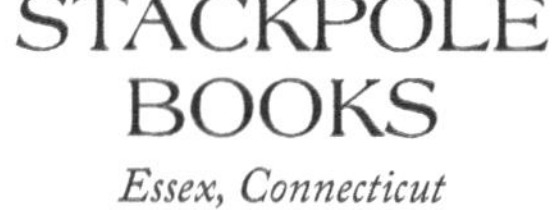

STACKPOLE
BOOKS

*Essex, Connecticut*

## STACKPOLE BOOKS

An imprint of The Globe Pequot Publishing Group, Inc.
64 South Main St.
Essex, CT 06426
www.GlobePequot.com

Copyright © 2025 by Dennis I. Fisher
Maps by Dennis I. Fisher

*All rights reserved.* No part of this book may be reproduced in any form or by any electronic or mechanical means, including information storage and retrieval systems, without written permission from the publisher, except by a reviewer who may quote passages in a review.

British Library Cataloguing in Publication Information available

Library of Congress Cataloging-in-Publication Data available

ISBN 978-0-8117-7760-5 (paperback)
ISBN 978-0-8117-7761-2 (ebook)

*This book is dedicated to my friend and fellow Marine combat photographer, Corporal John C. Pennington, who was killed in action on June 9, 1968.*

# CONTENTS

# Preface

Providing my family, especially my children, with a narrative of my service in the US Marines and experiences in Vietnam has been weighing on me for some time. I was recently asked to participate in an oral history project, bringing to mind the realization that when I'm gone, the story of my time in Vietnam dies with me. Like my father's World War II experiences in the Pacific, or my grandfather's World War I service in France, or my great-grandfather's Civil War service, mine too would be lost in the sands of time. How I wish they had committed their stories to paper, or at least in my father's case, told me more about them. This narrative is my attempt to break the chain of silence so that my family will never have to wonder what I experienced in Vietnam. In a broader sense, this is a tribute to all the Marines who fought in Vietnam, memorialized with images of their bravery, captured and preserved for all eternity.

Drawing on a number of sources—including a folio of letters I sent to my parents; journal entries, photographs, and audio recordings; copies of orders, medical records, after-action reports, and unit command chronologies; along with photo captions and news accounts—I've endeavored to reconstruct as accurately as possible my tour of duty in Vietnam as a combat photographer. The narrative follows in chronological order and is given in the first person. Any thought of doing otherwise seemed to detract from what is, after all, a personal account. These are my recollections, and no attempt has been made to mold them into an academic treatise on the Vietnam War. They are the thoughts and experiences of a twenty-year-old, told with the authenticity of one who was there, dimmed but little by the passage of time.

Marines speak in a language of jargon, abbreviations, and acronyms that to the uninitiated seems like some sort of code. This "milspeak" is meant to convey both complex and ordinary military thoughts and actions as quickly as possible. Reading the transcript of my oral history session, too much time was spent trying to explain the terms and acronyms, which only served to break the continuity of the narrative. Terms evolved during the war, and those used here were in vogue during my time in country. All the definitions and explanations of the jargon have been placed in a glossary at the end.

Many of the books I've read on Vietnam are illustrated with photographs that were sourced from the National Archives and Records Administration (NARA), or from stock photo companies. While there is nothing wrong with that, these photos are generally captioned with brief, one-line descriptions, lacking the full backstory or context that only the photographer could provide. Some were only representative of what was being discussed and were actually from other events.

The photos I present in this book are woven into a narrative to provide a complete picture of my personal experiences. With few exceptions, the photos were taken by me during my eighteen months of service as an infantry rifleman and as a combat photographer in Vietnam with the 1st Marine Division. A number of the original negatives and slides contained in this narrative are on file at NARA. The majority come from my personal collection, until now, unpublished.

So saddle up—we're ready to move out on a mission to a place and time that exist only in my mind. My own mental time machine, powered by the aforementioned materials, stands ready to bring forth the events of my youth, transporting the reader back to the 1960s and the Vietnam War as seen through the lens of a newly minted Marine combat photographer.

# INTRODUCTION

EVERY VETERAN WILL EVENTUALLY BE ASKED ABOUT THEIR WAR EXPERIENCES BY THEIR children, friends, or relatives, especially if they were known to have participated in combat operations. This is true for all armed conflicts, and answering should be a straightforward declaration of the facts. But for those who slugged it out with the enemy in the rice paddies, jungles, rivers, and mountaintops of Vietnam, it's not quite that simple. Attempts to answer even simple questions about service in combat frequently devolve into a struggle for words. Sometimes it's easier to just say nothing, or gloss over the truth with feel-good stories. In this narrative, however, I present an unvarnished account of my war experiences in both words and photographs, from a "boots on the ground" view of the action.

This is my story—Marine sergeant Dennis Irwin Fisher—from my transfer out of the infantry to the 1st Marine Division Combat Photo Section; my participation in combat operations, hospitalization after being wounded, return to Vietnam, and my eventual return to the States. Over the course of my three-year enlistment, I would rise from a buck private right out of boot camp to a battle-hardened sergeant. The accounts are true, and the people mentioned are real, not fictional creations. The story of each Marine who served in this conflict is unique, and this one is true to form. The simple transposition of four digits on my orders would send me down a path that no Marine rifleman could have ever anticipated. This mistake would ultimately affect not only my service in the Marine Corps, but the rest of my life.

Once in Vietnam, the day-to-day routine would soon give way to steady participation in combat operations during 1967 and 1968. These years saw the most intense fighting of the war for Marines. Battles like Hue and Khe Sanh in I Corps headlined the news and proved deadly for the Marines during the Tet Offensive. This would soon be followed by Mini-Tet, or Tet II, as the North Vietnamese tried to sweep across South Vietnam for a second time. Back in the States, big battles garnered most of TV airtime, along with magazine and newspaper headlines, but small unit actions interspersed with multi-battalion "named" operations were the norm for most of the Marine rifle companies.

After ten months in country, on September 29, 1967, I'd find that my luck had finally run out when I was taken down with shrapnel from a 60mm mortar near Dai Loc. So began a fifty-nine-day hospitalization at the US naval hospital on Guam before returning to duty. (The irony of this was that twenty-one years earlier, my father had served in the army on Guam during World War II.) I would return to Vietnam on January 18, 1968, just in time for the Tet Offensive, where I would spend the next seven months covering Marine combat operations in I Corps.

In the middle of August, 1968, my extended tour in Vietnam would finally come to an end, and I returned to Camp Lejeune, North Carolina, to finish my enlistment. I was released from active duty a few months early, and returned to civilian life, where I began a career as a professional photographer. My time as a Marine may have ended, but I would never stop being a Marine. The lessons learned so hard in combat never go away. The men you served with are never forgotten, the things you saw never leave you, and certain sounds and smells still trigger memories of those events from long ago.

To fully understand my story, it's necessary to begin with a brief look into my early life, and a series of events that led me down the path to the US Marine Corps recruiting office. Let's step back to 1965, the year before my enlistment, and pick up the narrative as I prepared for college.

I graduated from Ligonier Valley High School in 1965, in the small town of Ligonier, Pennsylvania. The town was named after Fort Ligonier, a French and Indian War fortification built by the British in 1758 during the Forbes Campaign to capture Fort Duquesne from the French, at what is now Pittsburgh. It was, and still is, a small town of under 1,500 people, nestled in a beautiful valley between Chestnut Ridge and Laurel Mountain in western Pennsylvania. It is officially called the Borough of Ligonier, which is larger than a village and smaller than a town in the Commonwealth of Pennsylvania.

Glancing around the town square—or the Diamond, as it is called—transports one back to the late 1800s, with its prominent bandstand in the center, large shade trees, park benches, and monuments to fallen soldiers from conflicts past. Surrounding the Diamond is the Methodist church with its clock tower, and retail businesses to supply the necessities of small-town life.

Growing up in this town, I was surrounded by veterans who were living testaments to the spirit of patriotism and love of the country for which they had sacrificed so much. Bear in mind that this was only twenty years after the end of World War II, and the activities of local veterans' organizations and parades kept that spirit alive. To serve in the military, either in the reserves or on active duty, was not only considered honorable, but almost a rite of passage for young men at that time.

The values of the veterans of World War II and the Korean War were my values, and they would certainly influence my later decision to join the Marines, but that was still a year off in the future. Their exploits, especially as portrayed in numerous films, further cemented in my mind the notion that military service was a noble and patriotic pursuit. Images of the infantry slugging it out with the enemy in hard-fought battles were utmost in my mind. No one who volunteered for military service was seeking glory as a cook, supply clerk, or typist; they wanted to take the fight to the enemy as machine-gunners, riflemen, mortarmen, automatic riflemen, tankers, or artillerymen. Of course, I can't speak for the draftees, who may have viewed military service in another light.

We didn't have a Pearl Harbor or Twin Towers to rally behind, but the Cold War was heating up, and fighting communism in Vietnam was the current flashpoint. Had the local vets or my dad been more forthcoming about the reality of combat, they may have steered my decision to serve in the military service in another direction, but at eighteen years old, probably not.

They say that you make your own luck by being prepared with the right skill set when opportunity comes knocking. The following illustrates how I gradually acquired the knowledge, skills, and abilities that prepared me for a career as a Marine Corps combat photographer when the opportunity came along.

After high school graduation, I converted the job I had at Fort Ligonier from part-time to full-time, assisting in the archaeological excavation of the site. I wanted to build up my savings before heading off to the University of Miami in Coral Gables, Florida, to study chemistry. My ultimate goal was to combine my love of scuba diving and chemistry into a degree in chemical oceanography. I had enrolled in advanced placement classes in chemistry to get a head start on college. My family was of modest means, and attending any university would put a strain on the family finances, even with what I could make at various jobs.

My parents, Paul and Bettie Fisher, grew up within twenty-five miles of Ligonier and had six children, of which I was the oldest. Both of my parents had a big influence on my life. They raised all of us to have a good work ethic, to be frugal with our money, and to have faith in God. They were from the Great Depression generation, and knew how to make do under the worst of circumstances. My dad, who served in the army during the Pacific Campaign in World War II, could fix or repair anything, and I will be forever grateful for the hands-on training he gave me in that respect. He was also an avid photographer, and when I showed a similar interest, he helped me to equip and set up a darkroom at home.

My mom was more the academic of the house, and a lifelong learner. She had her hands full raising us, as my dad's work would keep him on the road a lot. I don't know how she did it. I will never forget coming home on a cold winter day to the smell of fresh-baked cinnamon rolls and hot cocoa. During World War II, she served as a civilian rifle instructor, and with my dad being an army infantry vet, there was no lack of marksmanship training in my life. This served me well when hunting small game and deer and competing on the high school rifle team. I had no idea how much these skills would serve me in years to come.

Funding college for all six of us was not in the cards, but being the oldest child and showing promise in the sciences, my parents did their best to support my education. With high hopes and our Ford station wagon packed full of everything I needed for my first year of college, my mom and I headed for sunny south Florida and the University of Miami. Our departure was delayed by a few days, as television and radio news reported that Hurricane Betsy was poised to come ashore around Fort Lauderdale, or Miami. The storm was estimated to be over 600 miles across, so there was bound to be a lot of damage. But once the storm had moved on, we began our 1,200-mile drive down the East Coast, arriving amid a massive cleanup following the hurricane. My mom stayed for a couple of days before driving back to Ligonier, and I settled in to college and life in the dorm at Eaton Hall.

You may be wondering what this has to do with a decision to join the Marines. Well, a lot. Three people I met and worked with at the university would influence my decision to join the Marines, and to pursue my passion for photography. I've always subscribed to the idea of giving credit where credit is due, so to that end, I would like to recognize the following people.

The first was Ron Sarron, who served as our floor advisor in the Eaton Hall dorm. Ron was small in stature but a muscular powerhouse. I can still see him outside our dorm doing pull-ups with an ease that made me envious. I could barely knock out ten while he seemed able to go on indefinitely. He was enrolled in the Marine Corps Platoon Leaders Class (PLC), which was the Corps version of the Army's ROTC (Reserve Officers' Training Corps). In essence, it was a commissioning program for Marine Corps officers.

Ron and I had many talks about the Marines and met with Major St. Clair and others in the program; soon, he encouraged me to sign up, too. I assured him that I was interested and would give it some serious thought over the summer break. I was a bit torn between the army and the Marines, as both my father and grandfather were army veterans. My grandfather, Paul C. Fisher, served with the American Volunteer Ambulance Corps during World War I in France, and my father served with the army in the Panama Canal Zone before the war, and in the Pacific during World War II.

At this point I still had hopes of earning enough money during the summer to return to the U of M for my sophomore year. While that would never happen, the impression that Ron made on me about the Marine Corps would overcome my adherence to family tradition of army service, and was a deciding factor in joining the Marines.

Ron would later serve as a helicopter pilot in Vietnam and attain the rank of captain before being struck down by multiple sclerosis and medically discharged from the Corps. I kept in touch with him until his death, years later. Having survived his tour in Vietnam, Ron was soon engaged in a much tougher battle against the effects of MS at his home in Miami. His battle would end on a warm Wednesday afternoon, May 10, 1989, when he slipped beneath the water while exercising in his pool at home. The crippling effects of MS had robbed this once-powerful man of his strength and the ability to keep his head above water.

The next influencer was Mr. Wilson Hicks, the former executive editor of *Life* magazine. After his retirement from that publication, he was hired at the U of M, where his photojournalism and editorial talents were brought to bear in a number of different visual communications disciplines. I met him in his role as advisor to student publications, primarily the *Ibis* yearbook, *Tempo* magazine, and *Hurricane* newspaper. The Miami Conference on Communication Arts was also his baby, drawing professionals from all over the country.

After reviewing some of my work, Mr. Hicks was very complimentary of my action news photography and urged me to pursue a career in photojournalism. Encouragement from such a respected professional gave me the confidence to do just that when the time was right. However, at that time I looked on photography more as a hobby than a career choice, and more importantly, as a way to earn some extra money while at college, shooting for the school newspaper and yearbook.

There was more to it than just the money, however. Mr. Hicks presented me with two press passes: one for the U of M *Hurricane* newspaper, and another for the *Ibis* yearbook. These gave me access to everything going on at the U of M, from backstage meetings with big-time performers to prominent speakers to sporting events. I was hooked. Little did I know then that I would spend the rest of my life recording history through the viewfinder of a camera.

I had planned on returning to the U of M after I got out of the Marines, but events would send me down another path. Returning from Vietnam, I wanted to take a portfolio of my work to show Mr. Hicks, thanking him for where his advice had led me, but he'd passed away before I had a chance to get down there.

This brings me to the last influencer from the U of M, Mr. William "Bill" Retskin. Bill was a zoology major with a passion for photography. When I met him he was serving as the photo editor for the school newspaper, yearbook, and student magazine. I had approached him about shooting for the *Hurricane*, the school paper, with zero appreciation for what was considered the proper way to apply for a photo job. I had no portfolio, no references, no nothing. Still, we hit it off with our mutual love of the sciences and photography. He engaged me in a discussion about photography as an informal interview and sent me out on an assignment to see what I came back with. This was a big incentive for me to not only shoot the assignment, but to get back, process the film, and make prints to meet the publication deadline.

Bill liked my work, became a mentor to me, and helped to refine my shooting techniques and darkroom procedures, to learn the jargon of news photographers, and to gain an understanding for how the news business works. He soon enlisted me as his assistant for off-campus jobs, shooting weddings and social events, giving me entrée to the local Jewish community in Miami, Coconut Grove, and Coral Gables. After these jobs we would retire to his parents' home in Coral Gables where he had a full darkroom setup to process and print the film. His mom, Mimi, would always ask me to stay for dinner, where she lavished us with good home-cooked meals and advice on dating Jewish girls.

At the time I was dating Donna Sellinger, a Jewish girl from Long Island, New York. Her advice was not to get serious with her, because I was a gentile, and her parents would never let her marry outside the faith. I had read about gentiles in the Bible, of course, but never really thought of myself that way. Living in a big city was a new experience for me, but I fully embraced campus life and all the activities with enthusiasm, and my camera.

I lost track of Bill within a few years, but I've always wondered how his life unfolded. In 2021 I finally tracked him down when a Google search turned up his obituary from 2016, noting his passing at age seventy-four. It turns out that he had indeed had a full life as a professional photographer, musician, and herpetologist, and a number of business ventures. The irony of this discovery was that he lived in Asheville, North Carolina, a place I had visited many times over the years to meet with "Del" Del Vecchio, my Marine combat photographer buddy and best friend from Vietnam who resided there.

All three of these friends and mentors have passed on without ever knowing the influence they had on my life. When I decided to enlist in the Marines, Ron's advice was there in the back of my mind. When I decided to try and get transferred out of the infantry in Vietnam and into the Photo Lab, Mr. Hicks was there, encouraging me to pursue photojournalism. When my transfer to Photo was finally approved, Bill was there as I applied many of the skills he'd taught me about photo craft.

Back in those days, while the ranks of the army were filled primarily with draftees, the Marines depended on volunteers, although some draftees were pulled in when recruiting goals fell short. Those of us who volunteered for military service did so for various reasons. The first would be the loss of their draft deferment, as happened to me when I left college. Next would be that they had received their draft notice and wanted to enlist in something other than the army. A third reason would be that they didn't have any good job prospects and looked to the military for job training, regular pay, and perhaps some world travel. One more factor that I weighed was the GI Bill's educational benefits. I still had three years of college to finish, and by enlisting in the Marines with their three-year active-duty program, I would be entitled to three years of educational benefits. That sealed the deal.

Of course, this was all happening against the backdrop of the Vietnam War. There was always the possibility that I would never live to collect on the college assistance program, but I was young and didn't give that outcome the serious thought it deserved.

The writing was already on the wall with regard to funding my sophomore year at the U of M, so I decided to start making plans early. My actual enlistment in the Marines has all but faded from my memory. As best I can recall, I signed up during the Christmas break when I was home for the holidays in 1965. I joined under a six-month-delayed enlistment program that put off my reporting date until the end of June, 1966. This gave me time to finish my freshman year and work for a month or so before shipping off to boot camp.

I remember talking with the recruiters in Pennsylvania and going over various options at their office. The sergeant said that my test results at boot camp would determine what career fields would be open to me, and that having a year of college would definitely be an advantage in that respect. What he failed to mention was that the Marine Corps' needs outweighed my wants and qualifications. We also talked about the GI Bill's educational benefits, which were foremost in my mind. I had little appreciation for the vast number of job skills that were needed in addition to the infantry, to keep planes flying or tanks running or supplies flowing, or keeping all the personnel records up to date. He explained that there were nine basic career fields and each one was divided into many subcategories, for 1,182 different jobs. There was even an MOS (military occupational specialty) for band members, which had 29 subcategories. But like Forrest Gump's box of chocolates, you never knew what MOS you would get until graduation from boot camp.

My return to campus after the Christmas break was anticlimactic. I continued with my studies and photo assignments, but my mind was now focused on my upcoming induction into the Marines. My relationship with my girlfriend Donna was sort of on again, off again, and I began dating Tammy Newbold. Trying to pursue any sort of meaningful relationship with her when both she and I knew I'd be shipping out in a few months was tough. Long-distance relationships among young people are hard to maintain under the best of circumstances, and I knew that the chances of Tammy putting her dating life on hold and awaiting my return were pretty slim. Had we been engaged I might have been more optimistic, but as boyfriend and girlfriend, not so much. Still, we continued to date and enjoy the time we had left. Thoughts of those last few months together certainly helped keep my morale up through the training and early portion of my tour in Vietnam, but her letters came less and less often, until I too had one to post on our "Dear John" bulletin board.

I returned home after the school year ended and went to work for A. H. Sweeney Construction Company in Ligonier. The company was owned by Archie Sweeney, the father of Darcy Sweeney, one of my classmates in high school. The construction work paid much better than the job at Fort Ligonier, and with only a little over a month before I left for boot camp, I had to "make hay while the sun shines." Time passed quickly, and before long I was on a bus to Pittsburgh for my induction physical.

So that was how I came to enlist in the Marine Corps. Little did I know at the time that the photography skill set I had developed would be the catalyst that enabled me to transfer from the infantry to the Combat Photo Section in Vietnam. Some would say I was just lucky, but luck will pass you by if you're not prepared to exploit it. I was prepared.

# Chapter 1

# Security Platoon

"If your pictures aren't good enough, you aren't close enough," said Robert Capa, a famous civilian combat photographer who covered five different wars. He died following his own advice during the First Indochina War when he stepped on a land mine while trying to get closer to the action. As a Marine Corps combat photographer in Vietnam, his words still rang true as I ran to the sound of the guns to capture photos of our men in action.

Looking at those photos today, they take me back to a time and place that no longer exists but is forever etched in my mind. This drive to get the best possible photos frequently led me into the heart of the action in I Corps from June 1967 until August 1968, a time period that encompassed the heaviest fighting of the Vietnam War. But before I ever picked up a camera at 1st Division Photo, destiny led me down a most unconventional path of administrative errors, happenstance, and good luck that ended up at the door of the 1st Marine Division Photo Lab.

The USNS *Hugh J. Gaffey* dropped anchor at 1430 hours on December 27, 1966, under an overcast sky in the harbor at Da Nang, Vietnam. Making my way topside with anxious anticipation to get a look at the country I had heard so much about ended in disappointment as the Marine haze blocked the view beyond the immediate harbor area.

There were ten or more ships resting at anchor in the harbor, three of which were tankers from Shell and Esso. The word was passed to pack our sea bags in preparation for being taken ashore the next morning. Orders were handed out and we headed belowdecks to our berthing area for the last night aboard ship. There would be no amphibious landing for us, no storming the beaches under withering enemy fire, just a short ride in a vintage LCM "Mike Boat" as they took us ashore, seventy or eighty at a time.

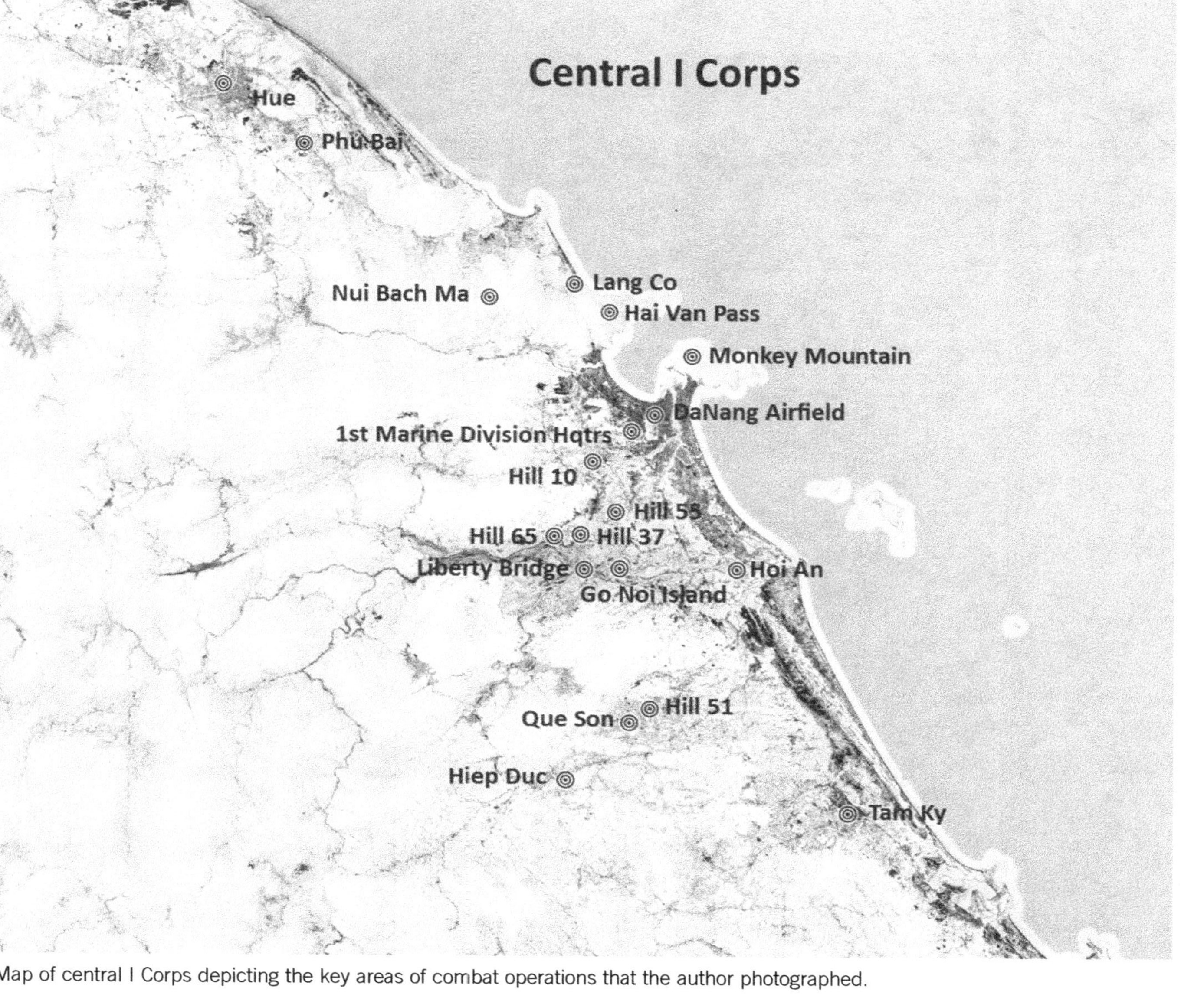


Map of central I Corps depicting the key areas of combat operations that the author photographed.

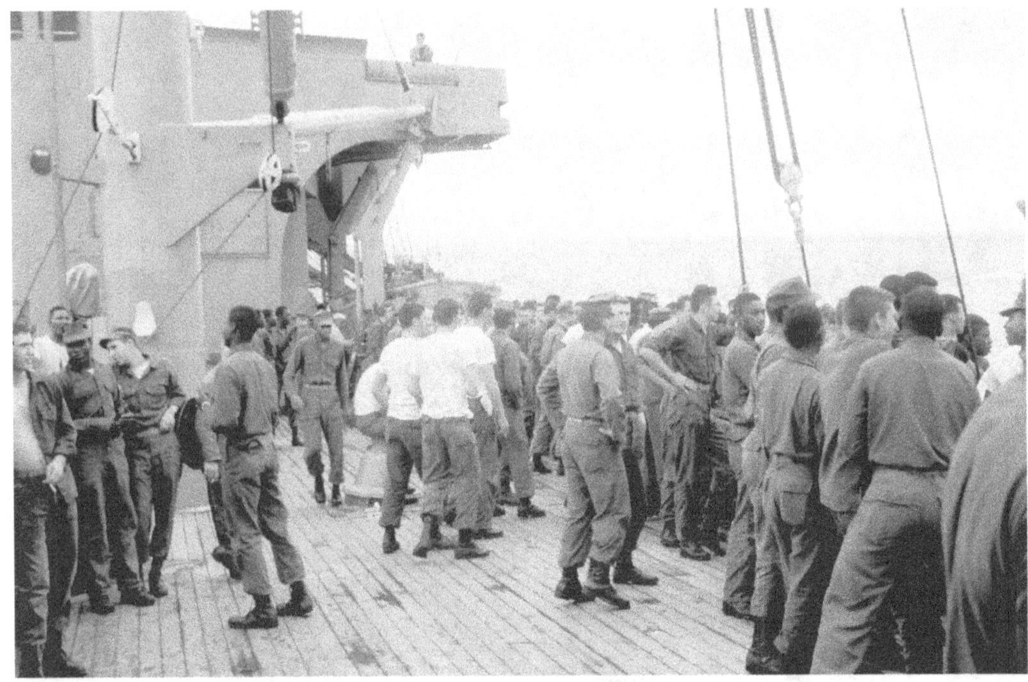

Marines line the rail of the USNS *Hugh J. Gaffey* to get their first look at Vietnam while approaching the harbor at Da Nang, RVN, on December 27, 1966. PHOTO BY PFC DENNIS FISHER

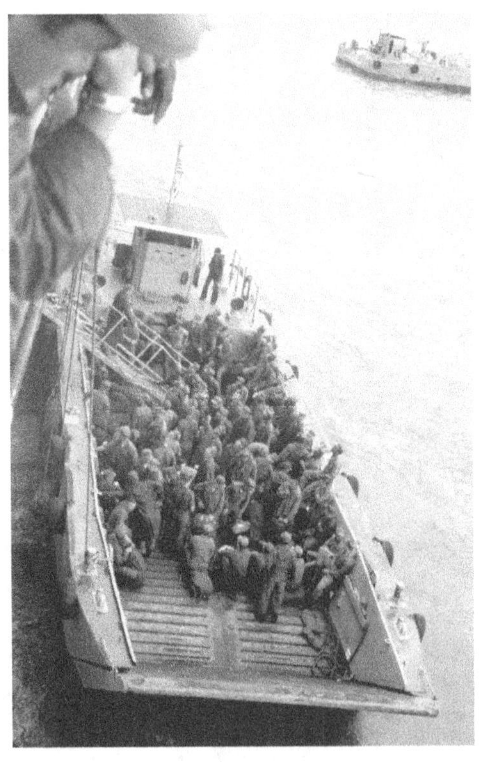

Everyone began comparing their orders to see which units they were destined to serve with. Most of us had an infantry MOS and expected to be assigned directly to line companies. However, a snafu in the MOS on my orders resulted in me being listed as unassigned. The admin clerk had mistakenly transposed the 3026 unit number of my training company at Camp Pendleton for my actual 0311 infantry rifleman MOS. Bringing this to the attention of our sergeant proved fruitless, and he said it was too late to do anything about it now. It would have to be resolved at the 1st Division Headquarters personnel office after we disembarked.

Marines from the 1st Division disembarking from the troop transport ship USNS *Hugh J. Gaffey* to an LCM for transport to shore on December 28, 1966, at Da Nang harbor, RVN. PHOTO BY PFC DENNIS FISHER

That night I lay in my bunk reflecting back on my time in the Marine Corps thus far. The next day, December 28, 1966, would mark six months since I'd enlisted. That time had been a never-ending series of training exercises that began with boot camp at Parris Island, South Carolina, then continued with advanced infantry training at Camp Geiger in North Carolina, and concluded with more pre-deployment infantry training at Camp Pendleton in California. I pondered how this mix-up in my orders would play out. Mistakes happen, but little did I know the one that happened that day would end up changing not only my service in Vietnam, but the rest of my life. The simple transposition of those four digits by an admin clerk sent me down an uncharted course and changed everything.

The next morning, we disembarked from the *Gaffey* and were deposited dockside on the quay, awaiting transportation to our various units as local street vendors besieged us with all types of things for sale. A number of us who were bound for 1st Division Headquarters were picked up by a deuce and a half and driven to the personnel office. The ride took us through part of Da Nang, past the airstrip, and through "Dog Patch," a rather shabby-looking collection of bamboo and corrugated-steel huts that catered to the various needs of the airfield personnel. If you wanted to get your laundry done, your truck washed, buy some souvenirs, get a beer, or get laid, this was the place—at least for the enlisted troops.

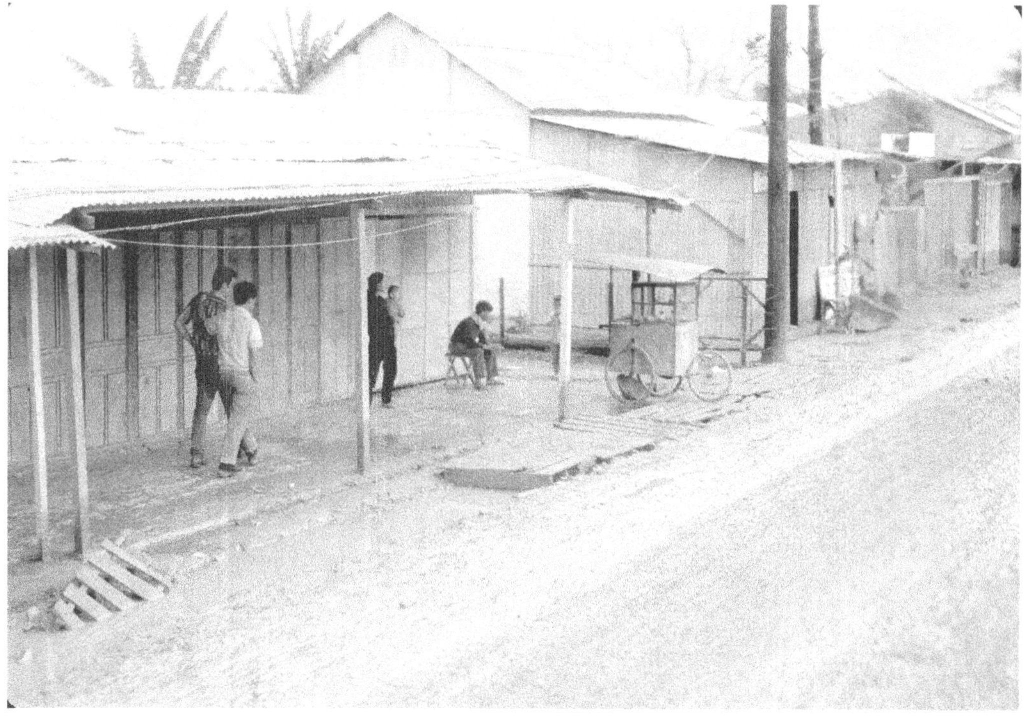

"Dog Patch," as it was called by the Marines, after a location in the *Li'l Abner* comic strip, was situated along the route leading from the Da Nang harbor to the 1st Marine Division Headquarters area.
PHOTO BY PFC DENNIS FISHER

There was a big crowd on hand to watch *The Bob Hope Christmas Show* as we passed the Freedom Hill PX complex. Our driver had orders to take us straight to Personnel, so there was no show for us. The whole drive took about twenty minutes. Approaching our destination, we passed 1st Medical Battalion and 1st Force Recon hooches off to our right, nestled next to an expanse of rice paddies. The MPs waved us through the gate and we entered into the main part of Division Headquarters.

Jumping down from the truck, I thanked the driver and took a look around. The muddy dirt road that had brought us here more or less bisected the headquarters area, which had been cut into the side of a large hill. The actual headquarters building, officers' quarters, mess hall, generals' quarters, and other administrative offices were terraced into the hill on the left side of the road, while others sloped down on the right side. The S1 personnel office was among the latter.

We shouldered our sea bags, made our way to the office, and lined up outside as the admin clerks called us in a couple at a time. There were sixteen of us in all, and it took some time for the clerks to process everyone. When my turn came, I turned in my personnel file and a copy of my orders, quickly explaining the mix-up. The clerk told me they would get things squared away with my orders; in the meantime, since I had a 0311 MOS, he assigned me to the Security Platoon.

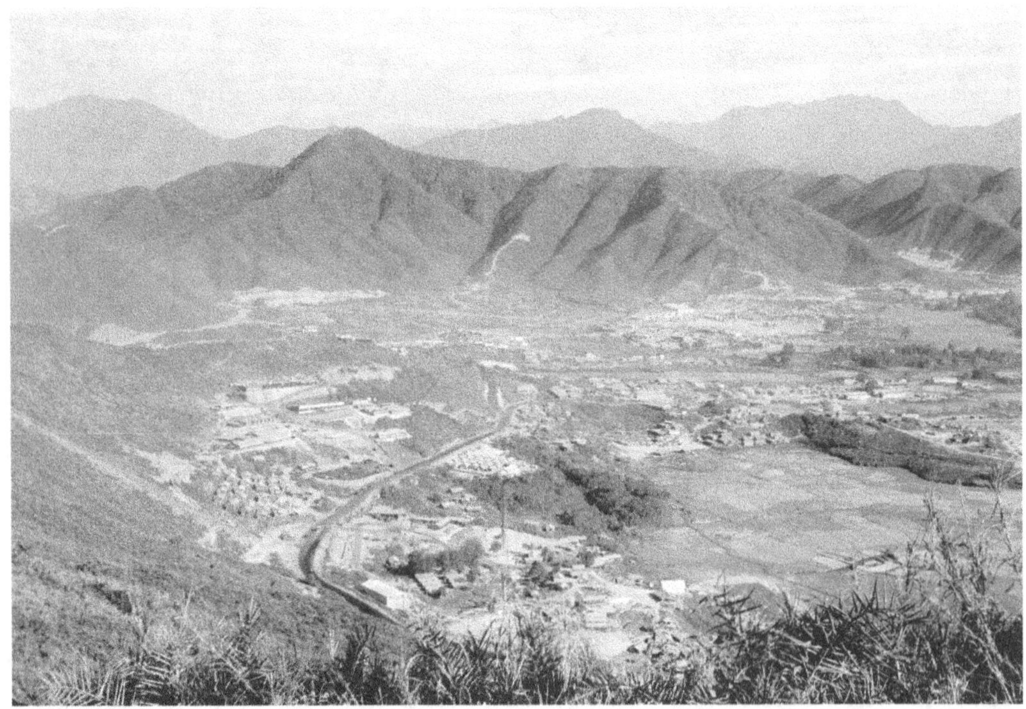

The view of the 1st Marine Division Headquarters area as seen looking north from atop Hill 327 during the spring of 1967. PHOTO BY PFC DENNIS FISHER

A battered-looking EE-8 field phone in a green canvas case sat on his field desk, and after a few cranks of the handle he reached the operator, who patched him through to the Security Platoon. I could only hear his side of the conversation as he asked them to send their driver down to pick me up. He slid the handset back in the phone case and told me to wait outside, where someone would be down to pick me up. Doing as he said, I went outside, and in about fifteen minutes a Marine arrived in a mud-splattered Mighty Mite to transport me up the hill to my new home.

The Security Platoon was located about two-thirds of the way up the hill near the general's house, overlooking much of the 1st Division area, as well as the countryside that stretched off in an easterly direction toward the ocean. A quick look around revealed a number of wood-framed hooches with sandbag fighting holes scattered between the buildings. They weren't laid out in any particular order, but instead were situated wherever the land was level enough to build them.

A short walk brought me to the orderly room, where I handed off my service records and a copy of my orders. The orderly then assigned me to one of the hooches and pointed me in the direction of the next check-in stop. The remainder of the day was spent going through more of the check-in process and exchanging my greenbacks for MPC and twenty dollars' worth of piasters/dong, the local currency. I hadn't been able to complete the check-in process by the end of the duty day, so that was put on hold for a while. I spent all of the next day, December 29, in orientation lectures to prepare me for my tour of duty there. December 30 was spent finishing my check-in process, drawing my weapon (a brand-new M14) and magazines, and some of my 782 gear. Supply was out of a lot of things, but I got all the essentials.

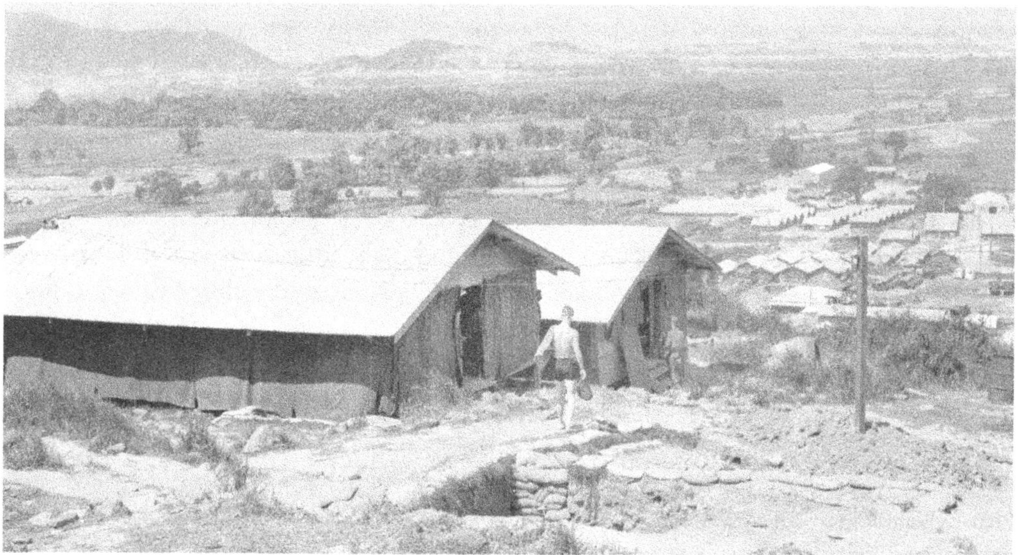

Security Platoon hooches in the 1st Marine Division Headquarters area were the living quarters for the platoon's enlisted men. PHOTO BY PFC DENNIS FISHER

The Security Platoon was there to provide protection for the Division Headquarters area, and particularly, for Major General Herman Nickerson and his staff. A series of sandbag bunkers had been constructed behind a barrier of concertina wire to establish a pretty secure defensive perimeter. During the day we worked on improving the defenses and running patrols out into the surrounding hills, valleys, and villages. At night we manned the bunkers and sent out night ambushes. All the bunkers were connected to the CP with EE-8 field telephones, and we also had PRC-25 radios ("Prick 25s," as we called them) to call in fire missions or illumination at night. The duties were rotated so that no one was doing the same task every day. The routine soon became familiar as the steady monsoon rains pounded out a loud racket on the corrugated-steel roofs of our hooches and bunkers.

I served in the Security Platoon for six months, from my arrival in Vietnam until my transfer to the Photo Lab on June 22, 1967. Looking back on it, the administrative mistake with my orders was a blessing in disguise.

First off, it was a soft introduction to the war. Many of the Marines who arrived with me were assigned directly to combat units, and being killed or wounded in the first few months of their tour was not uncommon. There was a lot to learn about conducting yourself under combat conditions, and it's sad to say that most of it was learned on the job. In spite of all the training we had received, there weren't any classes that could prepare you for all the idiosyncrasies of this war. You needed to watch, listen, and learn from the grunts who had been in the bush for a while. Second, the Security Platoon was right up the hill from the Photo Lab. Although my inquiries about being transferred there were initially rebuffed, my frequent visits and persistence eventually paid off. This would not have been possible if I had been assigned to a field unit. Third, when the personnel office assigned me to the Security Platoon, they considered the problem with my orders resolved, and unless there was some pressing need for my services elsewhere, there I would stay.

I quickly found out that the accommodations we enjoyed at the Security Platoon meant we were "living the good life" compared to the field units. The hooches we lived in were two-by-four wooden-framed structures with corrugated-steel roofs. The walls were screened in and covered with the remnants of green canvas squad tents to keep out the rain. On hot days you could roll up the canvas and get a little airflow. The floors were four-by-eight-foot sheets of plywood laid out to make a sixteen-by-thirty-two-foot floor which accommodated eight men along each side. You had one sheet of plywood floor space per person. This provided room for a fold-up cot and a place to stow your sea bag and gear. In rear areas like this, there was electricity that powered one or two lightbulbs that hung from the ceiling rafters. Some also had a duplex outlet at either end to plug in anything electrical you might have. We had a communal shower but no hot water. The latrine was a two-hole outhouse. The waste was captured in fifty-five-gallon drums that were cut in half. These were removed daily, liberally soaked in diesel fuel, and set on fire until only ashes remained.

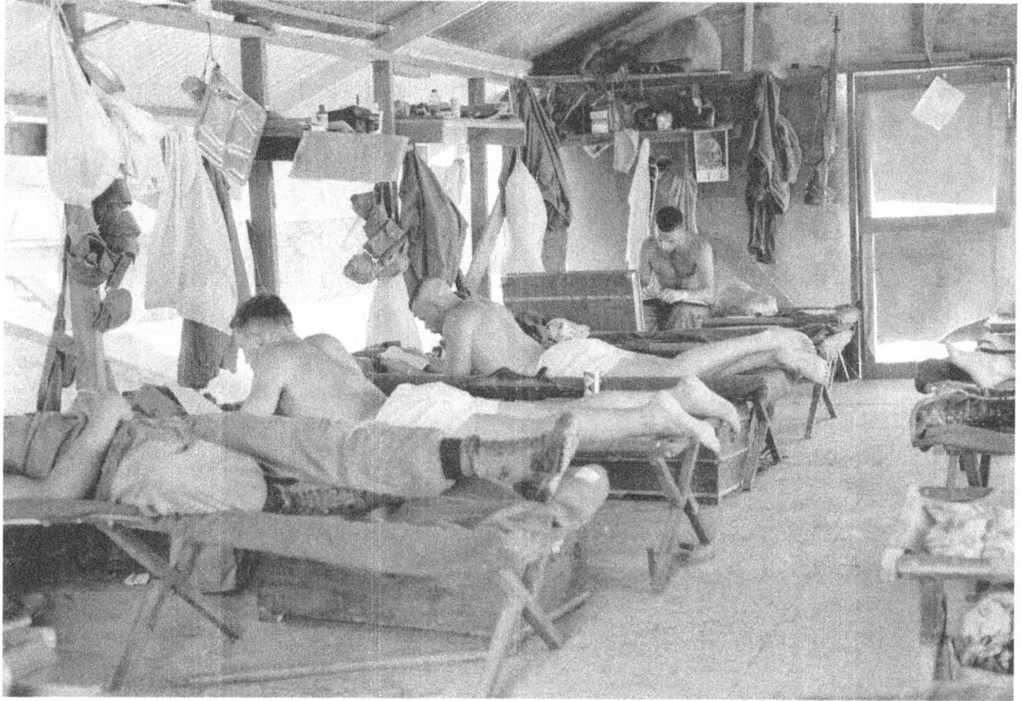

Marines of the 1st Marine Division Security Platoon resting during downtime before going on guard duty. These spartan living conditions were luxurious compared to field units. PHOTO BY PFC DENNIS FISHER

A mess hall provided three hot meals a day and prepared "midrats" consisting of sandwiches and beverages for men on guard duty at night. Short for midnight rations, these were taken around to men in the bunkers on night guard duty by the corporal or sergeant of the guard.

The mess hall food left a lot to be desired, and wasn't what we were used to getting stateside. It was better than C-rations, but chowing down on reconstituted powdered eggs and powdered milk for breakfast garnered many complaints. A bakery had been established by the time I arrived, so we had fresh bread and rolls. It was a typical mess hall with several serving lines, and you brought your own mess kit, utensils, and canteen cup to eat with. After the meal you went outside to a line of big metal trash cans filled with water and immersion heaters. The procedure was to scrape off any leftover food into a garbage can, then dip everything into the first can full of hot soapy water, finally rinsing it all in the next can of clear hot water. While complaining about the chow was a common theme of discussion, humble as it was, it was still better than what the field units had.

It had been raining nearly every day since my arrival, and many of the areas we normally patrolled were either deep in thick red mud or underwater. It was the monsoon season, after all. On New Year's Day I had a little time off and made a run down to the nearby PX to get some writing paper and other odds and ends. Upon exiting the building, I ran right into Sergeant Lucien "Butch" Moscinski. Butch had lived just two houses up the street from me in Ligonier, Pennsylvania, dropping out of school in his junior year to join the Marines.

I couldn't believe it—here I was, halfway around the world in a war zone, and after only four days in country, I ran into my neighbor. What are the odds!

Butch had been in Nam for a while and was looking like a real seasoned warrior. He was the commander of an M48 Patton tank and was assigned to the 1st Tank Battalion. If I recall correctly, their unit had been deployed to Vietnam in the spring of 1966. We didn't talk too long, as both of us had to get back to our units, but we did meet a couple days later over at 1st Tanks to get caught up. This was the first of three surprising encounters I had while in the Security Platoon.

The next occurred on January 31. I had the day off and went down to the Freedom Hill PX complex to get a burger and fries at the cafeteria. As I moved through the line, one of the Red Cross ladies who was helping serve looked at me and said, "Well, Dennis, aren't you even going to say hi?" I was dumbstruck. It was Alice Voytco, or Miss Voytco as I knew her in Ligonier, as my sophomore English teacher. I had a great chat with her and stopped by a number of times over the following months to share news from back home, or to play a little ping-pong. I had been in the country a month and had already run into two people from my hometown, a pretty small hometown at that. Who would have ever thought it possible?

The last encounter involved a celebrity. On the evening of February 15, two of us had been selected for general's guard and were being questioned by the OD (officer of the day) on a number of military topics prior to going on post. I think he just wanted to make sure the Marines who were guarding the general were at the top of their game. I and another Marine were walking our post at his house just around dusk when, as I noted in my journal for that date:

*Jayne Mansfield came in by helicopter with the general [Nickerson] for dinner. I got a*
*real close look at her in her mini-dress. Wow!*
(Journal entry, February 15, 1967)

We had no idea that she—or the general, for that matter—were coming. As we saw his helicopter landing, we prepared to look our best. Imagine our surprise when we saw that there was a woman with him, and not just any woman! The path to his house led Jayne Mansfield within a foot of us. She paused and said hi to us, along with giving us a kiss on the cheek as she passed. I told her how much we all appreciated her taking the time to visit us over here. She replied that this was just a short visit, and she would be returning home in a few days. That was the extent of my Jayne Mansfield contact, and it seemed rather surreal. Little did she or any of us know that she would be dead by the end of June in a tragic car accident.

On Saturday, March 12, my friend LeBlanc got orders for 1st Battalion of the 5th Marine Regiment (1/5). We had become pretty close during my time in the Security Platoon, and I hated to see him go. I didn't know it at the time, but in August of that year I would be assigned to photograph Operation Cochise with Delta Company 1/5. I wasn't able to meet up with him in the field and concluded that he must have been with another company. Later in March, another good friend, George Dougherty, got orders for 1/1. The writing was on the wall as men were slowly being rotated out to line companies. This would only increase as the fighting intensified during the summer months.

As the weather improved we began running patrols into areas beyond our perimeter, with only sporadic enemy contact. This area was on the reverse slopes of the ridges behind the 1st Division Headquarters area and the valley beyond. Our biggest enemy was the terrain. The area was heavily overgrown with elephant grass and low jungle canopy, making

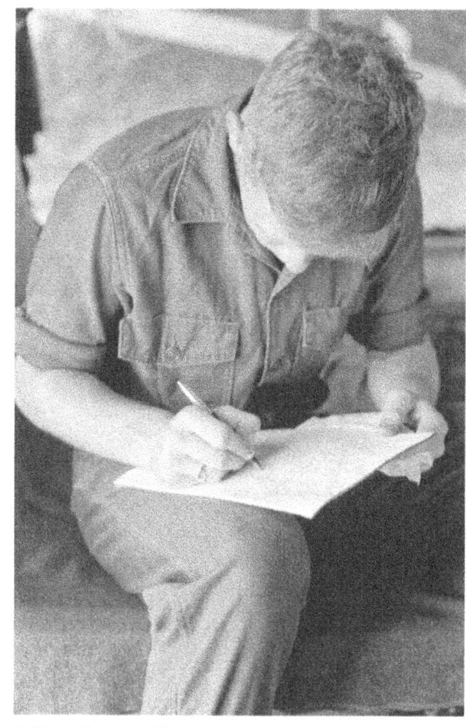

L/Cpl. George Dougherty writing a letter home while serving with the 1st Marine Division Security Platoon at Da Nang, RVN.
PHOTO BY PFC DENNIS FISHER

travel very difficult, with the heat and humidity. This was especially true of the steep slopes leading down to the villages below. Once down on the flatlands, movement became much easier.

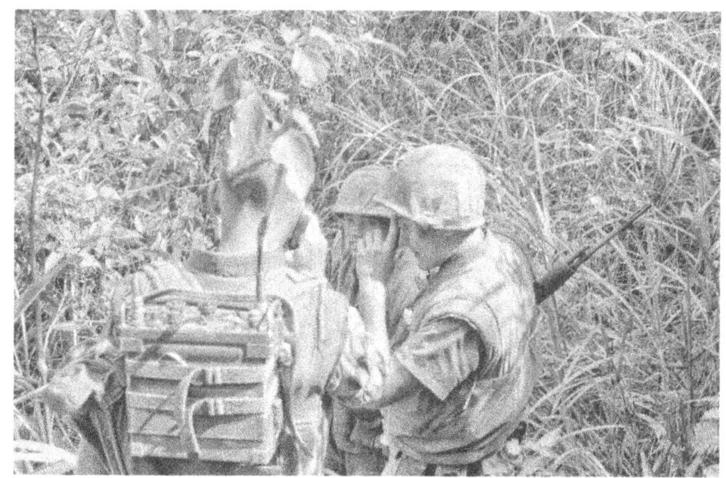

Marines from the 1st Marine Division Security Platoon conducting area denial patrol west of Da Nang during the spring of 1967. The RTO is seen here radioing in checkpoints as the patrol makes its way through heavy undergrowth.
PHOTO BY PFC DENNIS FISHER

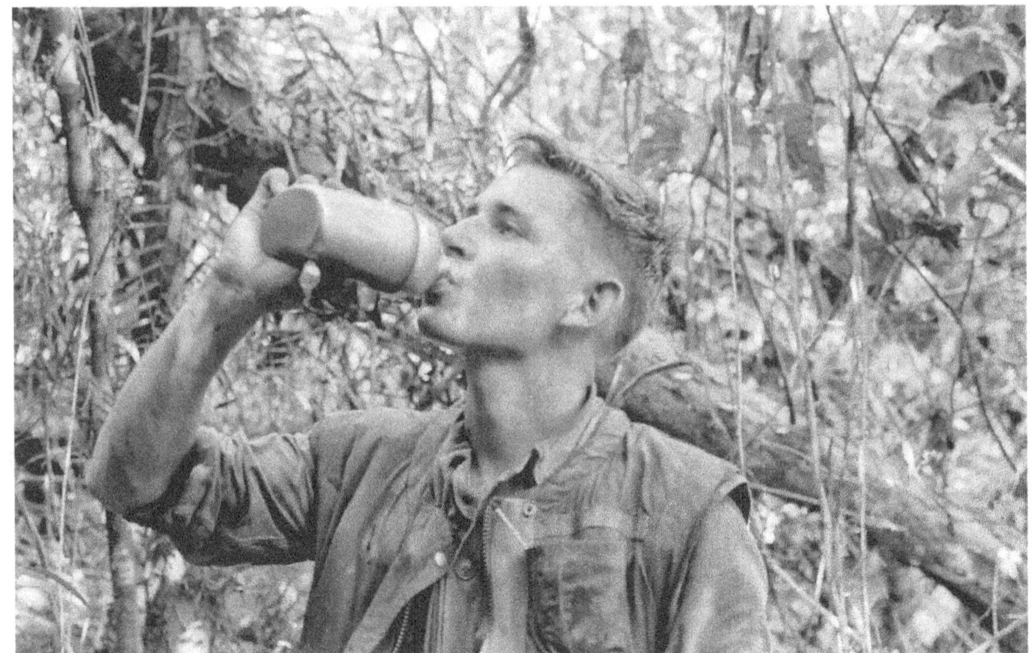

A Marine takes a canteen break amid high-temperature and humidity conditions during an area denial patrol. PHOTO BY PFC DENNIS FISHER

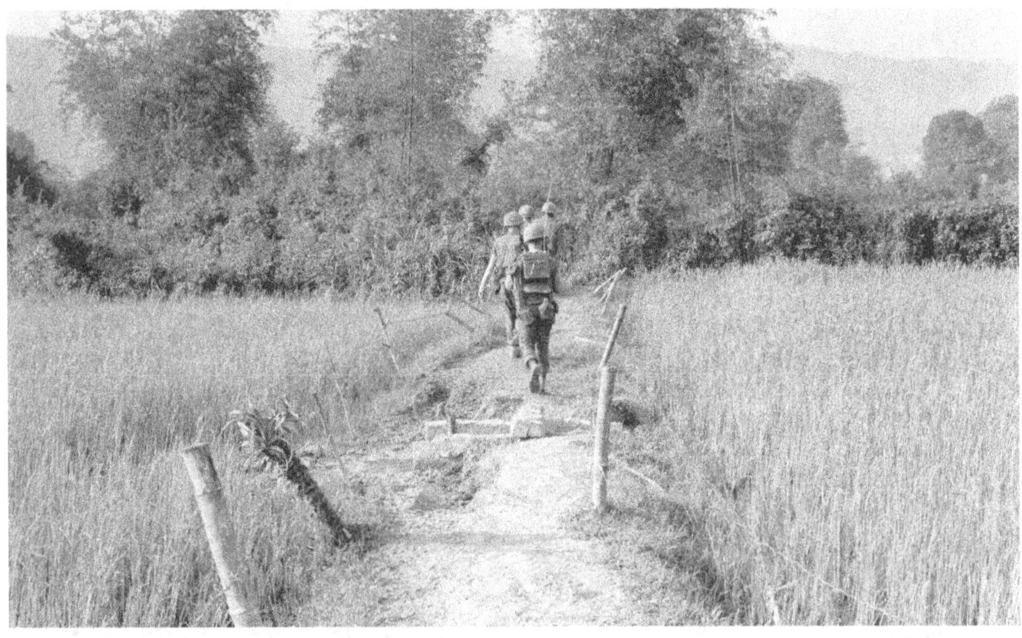

Lead elements from a patrol approach a tree line searching for signs of recent enemy activity. PHOTO BY PFC DENNIS FISHER

The people in this area were generally friendly, and our corpsmen were frequently imposed upon for medical assistance. You could hear the word being passed among the villagers that a *bac si* ("doctor") was there. The corpsmen were not doctors, but their medical training was good, and they could handle most complaints. The Vietnamese as a rule didn't speak English, and we didn't have an interpreter, so an improvised version of sign language was used to indicate the problem. This was adequate for most maladies. The larger Marine units would conduct MEDCAP (medical civic action program) visits, but ours was a small unit, so we did the best we could to help with the resources available.

I took a short walk down to the Photo Lab in the beginning of April, to try my luck once again for a transfer to that unit. I had a nice talk with Lieutenant McKay, and he informally interviewed me to gauge my photo knowledge, lab skills, and knowledge of the cameras and equipment they used. The visit went well, and I was encouraged with his comments. He was what we called a "mustang"—an officer who came up through the enlisted ranks before being commissioned—so he had been around the Marine Corps for some time, and knew how things worked. He suggested that it would be very difficult to get transferred out of the infantry and into Photo, as they needed riflemen a lot more than they needed photographers. His best advice was to submit an AA (administrative action) form, requesting a transfer to the Photo Lab, and if it made it to him, he would endorse it and support my transfer.

With that faint glimmer of hope I told him I would head to the personnel office and do just that. On Sunday, April 9, I went down to Personnel and worked with Gunnery Sergeant Romero to prepare the AA form. He told me that I would have to extend my tour in Vietnam an additional six months in order to have the transfer considered. Even then, Marine Corps needs might scuttle the whole deal. My original tour was thirteen months, and an additional six months would make for a long time over there.

While pondering whether or not to go through with this, the gunny was looking over my personnel record. He reminded me that I had been selected for OCS (Officer Candidate School); since I was now twenty years old and met the age requirement, he asked if I would rather head back to the States for officer training. All I had to do was extend my enlistment for a six-year commitment, and he could have the paperwork ready in a few days.

I had put OCS on the back burner and hadn't given it much thought since landing in Vietnam. Suddenly I felt like I was trapped in an episode of *Let's Make a Deal*. Should I pick door number 1—finish out my tour and go home?—or pick door number 2, transferring to Photo Lab and extending my tour for an additional six months? Or, door number 3, extending my enlistment for six years and going to OCS? If I picked the wrong one, what would happen? Door number 1 meant I would probably be sent out to a line company very soon. With number 2, I would end up out in the field, photographing combat operations and essentially starting my tour in Nam all over again. Finally, with number

3, I would go back to the States for training, in all likelihood, returning to Vietnam as an infantry platoon commander.

Ultimately, my love of photography won out. I took the completed AA form down to Lieutenant McKay for his endorsement and waited to see what would happen. There was no guarantee that it would be approved, but they said I should hear something within a month or so.

In the meantime, life went on at the Security Platoon. I received my PC (M37 personnel carrier) license, and was given the job of platoon driver, a much better job than what I had been doing, and before I knew it, we were into May. As the middle of the month rolled around, I still hadn't heard anything on my AA form. Lieutenant Tomlinson, our new platoon commander, told me that my name had been submitted for transfer, and he seemed confident it would come through. However, one of my friends in the orderly room told me he had seen a list of guys who were getting orders for 2/5, and I was on that list. I wasn't too surprised, and thanked him for the heads-up. Even though this wasn't official, I wrote to my dad to let him know what was coming.

*I just found out that I'm being sent to a line company and the Nikonos [camera] will take most any punishment you can hand out. About going to the field. The 2nd Battalion, 5th Marine Regiment was hit pretty hard and they are pulling all of us 0311s [infantry riflemen] out of Headquarters Company and sending us to the field, where we are badly needed. So much for Photo Lab. Maybe some other time.*
(Excerpt from letter to my dad, June 5, 1967)

At the Security Platoon, things had been spookily quiet for several weeks when out of nowhere, the VC (Viet Cong) penetrated the perimeter on Hill 327 on June 14 and blew up four Hawk antiaircraft missiles. It was about a thousand meters from our portion of the perimeter and lit up the night. The quick reaction force rapidly cleared the site of the enemy, but the damage was already done.

By now it was into June, and I still hadn't heard anything about the AA form. The wheels grind slowly in the military, but in this case they seemed to have stopped. Then, on June 17, our company gunny called me over after a mail call and said, "Hey, Fisher, you finally got your orders." I thought it was about time as he handed them to me. I was so excited they had finally come through, but much to my surprise, they were not orders transferring me to the Photo Lab. Instead, I was directed to report to the commanding officer, 2nd Battalion, 5th Marine regiment, the infantry regiment in the thick of the fighting.

The orders indicated a reporting date of June 25, which left me more than a little heartbroken, as I was really counting on going to Photo. But heavy fighting during the summer had created a big demand for riflemen.

The next day I walked down to the Photo Lab and told Lieutenant McKay I'd received orders for 2/5 and would be heading out in a week. I thanked him for all he'd done to try and get me a transfer to Photo. He looked surprised, and told me not to give up hope yet; he would look into it. Back at the Security Platoon I began out-processing and packing, which doesn't take all that long when everything you own will fit in a duffel bag. It was time to get ready to head for 2/5.

A few days later, on June 22, I was coming back from chow and one of my buddies said that Gunny White wanted to see me. So it was off to the admin hooch to find out what was going on. I assumed he was just checking to make sure my out-processing had been completed and I was ready to ship out.

When I entered the gunny just smiled and held up a new set of orders, saying, "Someone must really like you, Fisher. Here's your orders for Division Photo." In addition was another set of orders assigning me a secondary 4631 MOS as a still photographer. I was only three days away from leaving for the grunts. Lieutenant McKay had worked some sort of magic.

This is the unconventional route I took to become a combat photographer. It was a unique path, to be sure, and I know of no other Marine combat photographer who trod one even close to it.

# Chapter 2

# Division Photo

I wasted no time, quickly saying good-bye to all my friends in the Security Platoon and asking Chris, who I shared platoon driver duties with, to give me and my gear a lift down the hill to the Division Photo Lab. Tossing my sea bag in the back of the PC, I reflected back on my time in country as we drove down the hill. Despite being there for six months, I had not been involved in any heavy fighting. Most of our patrols were uneventful, except for some occasional sniper fire.

I was also pondering the six-month extension of my tour of duty and what that would mean. In the most basic sense, it seemed like I was beginning again from ground zero. Having already completed about half of my original tour and being on the downhill slope toward going home, I was now starting all over again. Then there was the talk I'd had with Lieutenant McKay and his description of the role of a combat photographer, which was both exciting and scary. That was especially true when he told me that two Marine photographers had been killed in action (KIA) since the landing in 1965, and many more wounded. One of them, with 3rd Division, had been KIA just a few months ago.

Chris dropped me off at my new hooch, which was just like the one I'd left, and I stowed my gear in one of the unused areas. The rest of that day and the next were spent checking in and getting an in-depth tour of the Photo Lab. It was a pretty basic operation, with a film-processing room, print rooms, a finishing area, a small studio, a camera repair section, supply room, chemical mix area, an E-3 Ektachrome slide-processing room, and an administrative area.

The darkrooms were accessed via a revolving door that allowed entry and exit from the darkroom without interrupting the work that was under way. The rooms were equipped with contact printers and Omega D2-V enlargers. Prints were made on both Kodak and Dupont polycontrast, single-weight paper and hand-developed in trays. The prints were then run through a Pako washer and dried glossy on a Pako drum dryer. Once the prints came off the dryer, they were collected and taken to a finishing table to be sorted, stamped, and assembled with the original work order for delivery to the customer. Hundreds of prints went through the lab each day.

Film was developed by hand using Nikkor stainless-steel reels and tanks of various capacities. Once the film was developed, fixed, and washed, it was treated with Photo-Flo and hung up in a drying cabinet. There was a mobile Photo Lab truck, but all the equipment had been stripped out and placed in the building. The studio area was used primarily for taking ID photos and portraits. As I recall, the portraits were for officer promotions. Out back there was a small assembly area with a couple picnic tables and a homemade barbecue grill. This area had wooden bleacher-type seats to accommodate the whole section for roll call, or when the OIC wanted to speak with everyone.

Gunny Dietz told me he wanted to keep me in the lab for the first month, and gave me the opportunity to work in each area, except camera repair. This was so I could become familiar with the equipment and get a feel for the work flow and how things were done. He also sent me out on shooting assignments in and around the Division area. During this time, I was learning how the Marine Corps trained photographers. I was the only photographer in the Photo Lab that had not been to the photo school at Fort Monmouth, New Jersey. I was self-taught, and could see from the prints coming through the lab that these photographers knew what they were doing. While I was going through advanced infantry training (AIT), these guys were going to photo school. Others had been in the Marines for a while and had a lot of practical experience, too. Regardless, I began applying all that I had learned at the U of M, working for Bill Retskin and Wilson Hicks. The gunny kept an eye on my work for the first couple of weeks, but once he was confident that I knew what I was doing, he added me to the assignment rotation with everyone else.

Da Nang was being rocketed on a pretty regular basis, and about a month after I joined Photo, in the early-morning hours of July 15, the airfield was hit again. This was the worst attack on the Da Nang Air Base during the entire war. The sound of explosions woke me up a little after midnight. I was about to go back to sleep, but the explosions continued, so I pulled on my boots and headed up the hill to my old Security Platoon, where I could get a better view. The sounds were coming from the direction of the airfield, which was about five miles away as the crow flies.

I had just reached the Security Platoon area when a huge fireball lit up the night sky, followed about half a minute later by the sound of a big explosion. In the midst of all this our artillery started returning fire. Although the attack only lasted for five or ten minutes, the full extent of the damage and casualties wouldn't be known till much later in the day. First reports indicated that a number of aircraft had been destroyed or damaged, a dozen or more barracks hit, 8 men killed, and another 175 wounded. The big fireball I saw turned out to be the bomb dump exploding. As rocket attacks go, this was a really bad one, and although the airfield seemed to be the main target, Red Beach and other areas were hit, too. The rockets aren't that accurate, but they were good enough when shooting at a large base.

The gunny sent me over in the morning to get some photos of the damage. While waiting for a ride, a call from Intel came in requesting a photographer to accompany one of their teams out to the launch site in the afternoon. So it was off to the airfield to take photos of the damage there and then out to the field with the Intel team to cover the launch site. The grunts that had swept the area and secured the site right after the attack were now waiting for our arrival.

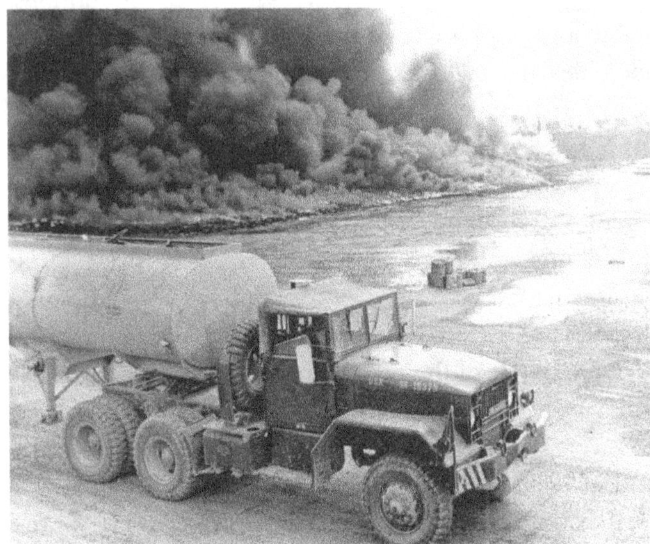

Aftermath of a barrage of 122mm rockets on the Da Nang Air Base flight line on the morning of July 15, 1967, causing extensive damage to infrastructure and the loss of 8 men killed and 175 wounded. PHOTO BY L/CPL. DENNIS FISHER

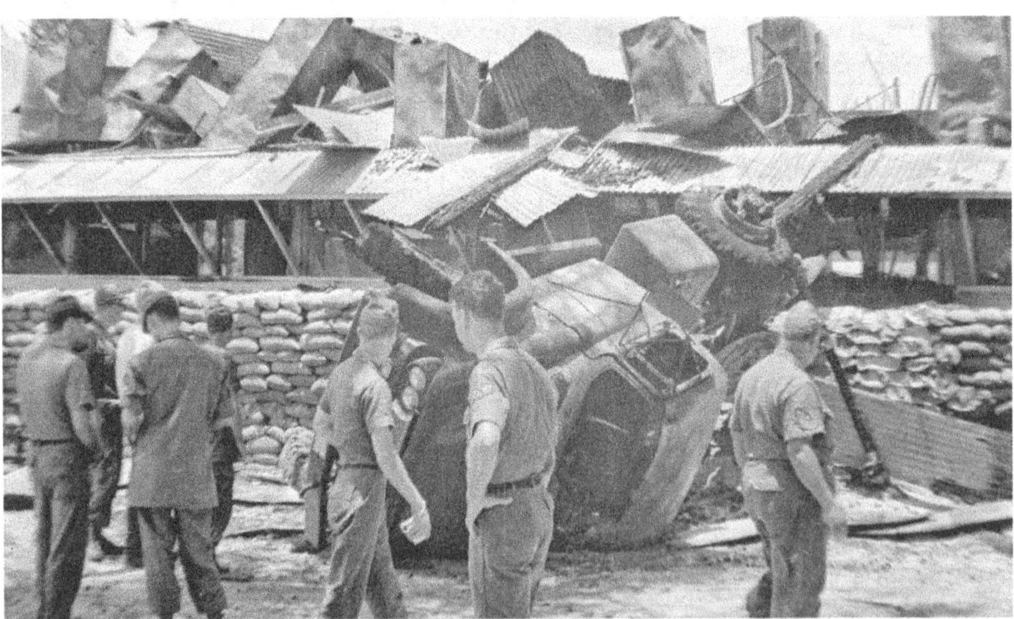

US Air Force personnel survey the damage to their barracks following the rocket attack on the Da Nang Air Base on July 15, 1967. PHOTO BY L/CPL. DENNIS FISHER

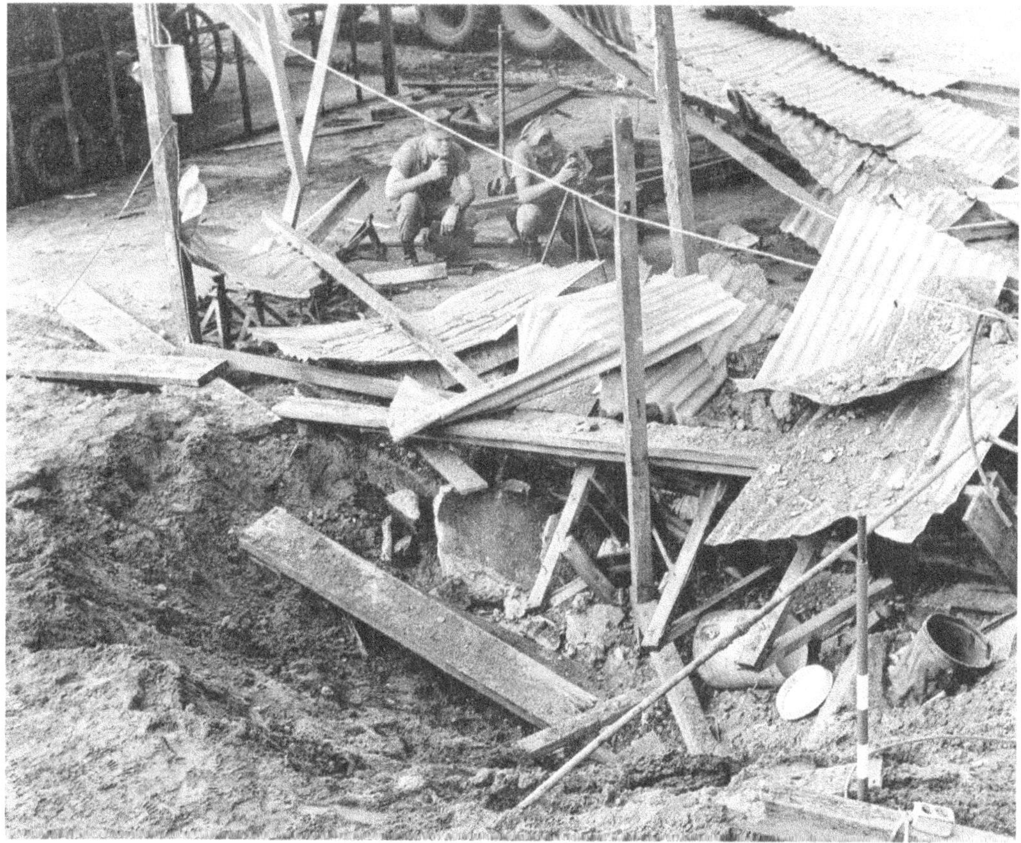

Marines examine damage to a supply building following the attack of July 15, 1967, at the Da Nang Air Base. PHOTO BY L/CPL. DENNIS FISHER

Approaching the launch site from the air, it was plain to see that the counter-battery fire had been not only timely but right on target. These launch sites were generally thrown up overnight and abandoned moments after the rockets were launched. This was because we used counter-battery MPQ-4 radar that could pinpoint the location of a launch site in as little as twenty seconds and direct artillery fire on it. The response to this attack had been quick, and the enemy left behind one of their dead, a number of rockets, and some other gear. Leaving those 122mm rockets unfired was a sure sign that they were driven off the site quickly.

I photographed general shots of the site as well as detailed photos that were called out by both the Intel and EOD teams. The 122mm rockets were new in the country at the time, and finding some unfired was a significant coup for the team. One puzzling thing that was noted on the rockets was the presence of a round cylindrical protrusion about a half-inch in diameter and a half-inch high, attached to the rocket body just forward of the fin assembly. The Intel team pondered the purpose of this, because at first glance it seemed the rocket would not completely fit in the launch tube. It wasn't until sometime later, when one of the launchers was captured, that the purpose was revealed. The launch tube had a spiral groove, which the protrusion engaged. This served much like the rifling in a gun, imparting spin to the rocket as it sped down the launch tube, stabilizing it as it took flight.

After photographing everything, EOD checked to make sure the rockets weren't booby-trapped, and then loaded them on a three-quarter-ton PC to take them back for study.

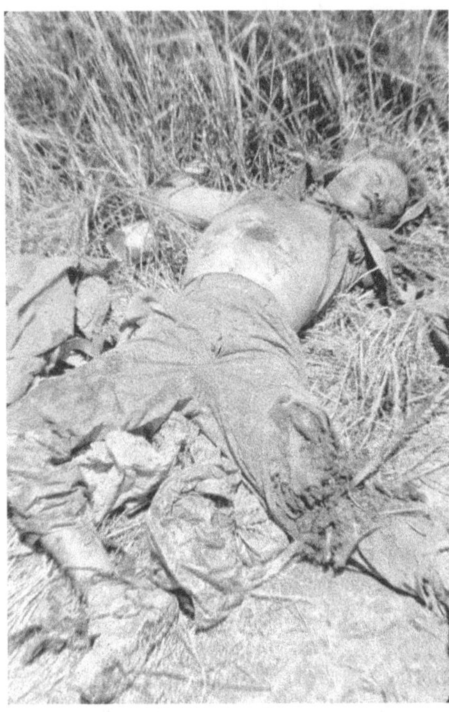

Enemy soldier killed with counter-battery artillery fire while engaged in conducting the rocket attack on Da Nang Air Base, July 15, 1967. PHOTO BY L/CPL. DENNIS FISHER

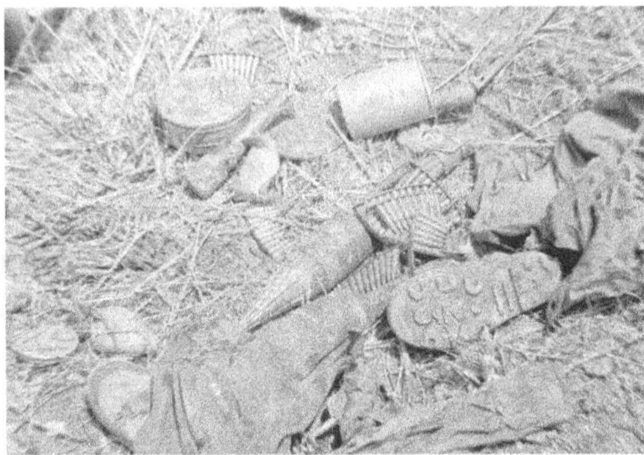

Enemy equipment left behind at a rocket launch site south of Da Nang. The enemy was forced to make a hasty retreat while conducting the attack on Da Nang Air Base, July 15, 1967. PHOTO BY L/CPL. DENNIS FISHER

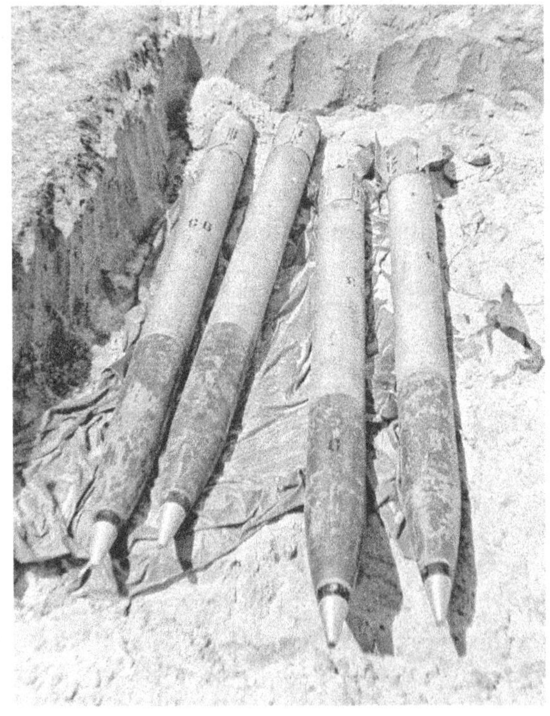

These 122mm rockets were abandoned by the enemy launch team during the July 15 attack on Da Nang Air Base, when their location was discovered and counter-battery artillery fire drove them off. PHOTO BY L/CPL. DENNIS FISHER

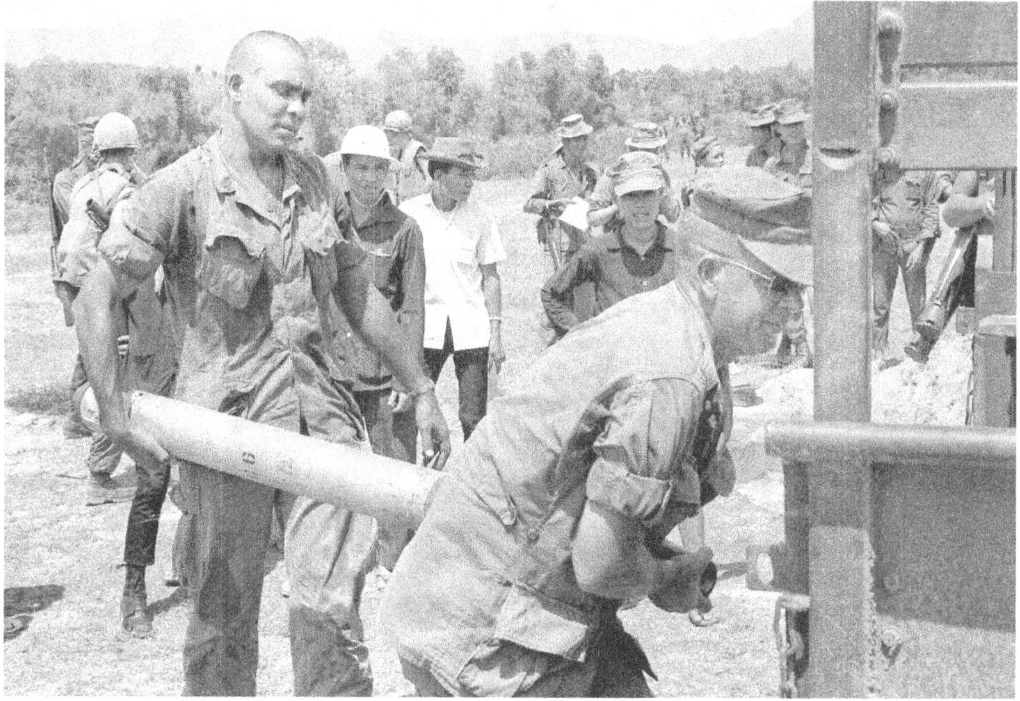

Captured 122mm rockets being loaded on a three-quarter-ton personnel carrier by EOD personnel. EOD gunnery sergeant Russell Curtis is seen on the left, supporting the rear of the rocket. PHOTO BY L/CPL. DENNIS FISHER

With our job there done, the EOD team left by truck, and a CH-46 was called in to transport everyone who was left. The grunts were getting a little nervous about being in one spot for so long, as it gave the enemy a chance to get close enough to take shots at the helicopter. Sure enough, as we were boarding the chopper, Charlie opened up with small arms. You could barely hear the sound of the firing over the noise of the helicopter, but Corporal Mot Keltner, the door gunner, spotted the muzzle flashes and returned fire with his Ma Deuce.

In an instant I realized what was happening, made a quick adjustment to my camera settings, and began taking photos. Spent brass poured out of the gun and the one-hundred-round ammo can was quickly emptied. Mot removed it and replaced it with a full can in one deft motion. He reloaded the gun and continued firing as the helicopter began to lift off. He kept up this suppressing fire until everyone was aboard. The whole event was over in fifteen or twenty seconds. His quick response ended the shoot-out, and the helicopter quickly climbed out of their range. Other than a few bullet holes in the fuselage, we escaped unharmed, thanks to the keen eye and excellent shooting skills of the crew's gunner.

One of the EOD members who worked the site and helped load the rockets was Gunnery Sergeant Russell Curtis. The following month he was severely wounded while

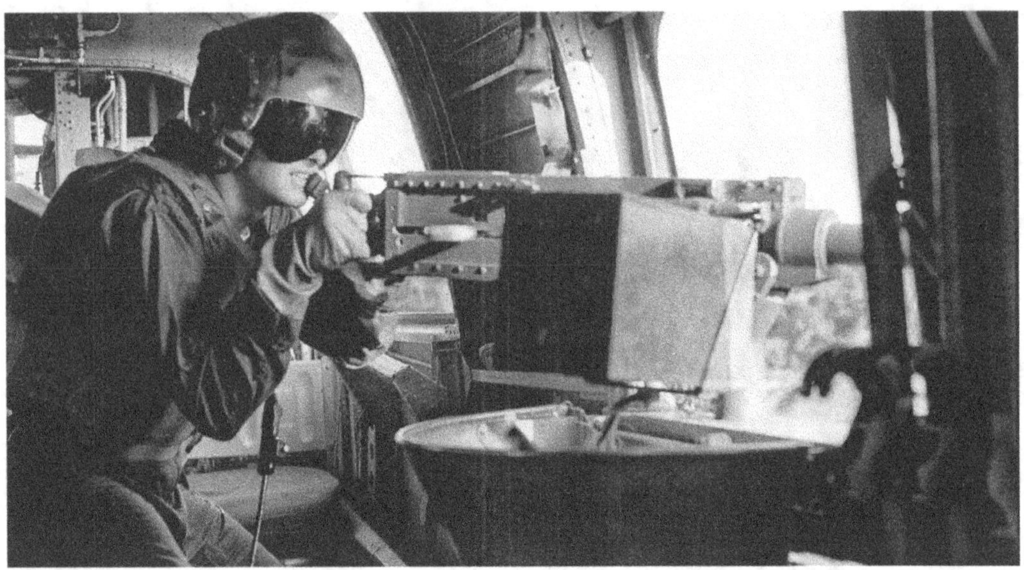

Cpl. Mot Keltner opens fire on the enemy with his M2 .50 caliber machine gun as his CH-46 Sea Knight helicopter was taken under fire by the Viet Cong on Go Noi Island near Da Nang in July 1967.
PHOTO BY L/CPL. DENNIS FISHER

removing a road mine that was booby-trapped with an M26 fragmentation grenade. He threw himself between the grenade and his fellow Marines, with his body absorbing most of the blast. He survived and was awarded the Navy Cross for his heroism.

Returning to the lab to process the film, I was starting to feel my decision to pursue photography was the correct one. At least it felt right, and I didn't have any misgivings. The familiar smell of the chemicals and of the hot prints coming off the dryer still remain in my mind. Beyond the familiarity of the lab, there was an unspoken camaraderie and esprit de corps among the photographers, proud of the work they did in capturing for posterity the scenes of Marines at war. This was especially true for our coverage of the grunts, whose hardships and sacrifices would receive little recognition except by those who fought with them. Our photos ensured that what they did would not be forgotten.

One thing was for sure: It wouldn't be long before I finally got to cover a big named operation. The action around Da Nang was heating up in the A Shau, Que Son, and Hiep Duc valleys with the 5th and the 7th Marines. Operation Arizona near An Hoa was in progress when I joined the Photo Lab, wrapping up around the end of June. This op was talked about for some time, and the area where it was conducted would from then on be known as Arizona Territory.

On a daily basis I would see our photographers returning from the field looking all grungy and heavily suntanned. Others—like Sergeant Jim Colton, who had been wounded and was returning from the hospital—were a bit pale, but ready to get back in the action. The Division Photo Lab was a beehive of activity, and things were about to pick up for me, too.

# Chapter 3

# Operation Cochise

## *Que Son Valley*

At the beginning of August, word came down that a big operation was coming up in the Que Son valley and would involve multiple Marine battalions, ARVN forces (Army of the Republic of Vietnam), and army units. It was called Operation Cochise, and I was assigned to cover the 1st Battalion of the 5th Marine Regiment (1/5), which was located on Hill 51, at the Que Son combat base. Corporal Bill Page went out on this op, too, and was with Kilo 3/5. I'm not sure, but I think we were the only two covering the op.

This would be my first named operation as a combat photographer, and I wanted to come back with some good images. I knew roughly where Hill 51 was, but had never been there. It is about twenty-five miles south of Da Nang and fifteen miles inland from the coast. The North Vietnamese Army (NVA) had been using the hills surrounding the Que Son and Hiep Duc valleys as staging areas for attacks in southern I Corps. Que Son and Hiep Duc were adjoining districts within Quang Nam province that ran in a southwesterly direction from the coastal city of Hoi An. The 2nd NVA Division was operating in a mountainous area bounded roughly by Thang Binh, Tam Ky, and Hiep Duc. This operation was meant to drive them out.

Lieutenant McKay passed on the information he had gleaned from a briefing at Division to give us an idea about the scope of the operation. He said that recent intel had placed the 3rd NVA Regiment in the vicinity of Hiep Duc in the Que Son valley, and that our CG, Major General Robertson, had reactivated Task Force X-Ray to help push them out of the area. It's always nice to get an overall picture of what the operation is supposed to accomplish, because once you get there your world shrinks to the platoon you're with and what they encounter.

With word that 1/5 would be kicking off their part of the operation on August 11, Gunny Dietz suggested that I go out there a couple days early to size up the operation and figure out which platoon I wanted to travel with. Corporal Jim "Dog" Donnelly was a friend of mine and served as a squad leader with Delta Company's 1st Platoon, so that was where I would head. I started getting my gear together as the time to depart grew closer. I wanted to make sure I had everything I might need, but from previous experience in the Security Platoon, didn't want to over-pack and end up lugging around a bunch of gear I wouldn't use.

What I wore and took along on operations varied with the weather and location. For those who served in the infantry, no description is needed, but I provide the following for those unfamiliar with how Marines were equipped for combat—or in this case, for combat photography.

In general, I wore jungle utilities and boots with a flak jacket and helmet; a web belt with a .45 automatic pistol and two extra magazines; two or three canteens; a gas mask; a jungle first-aid kit; and a KA-BAR knife. I also packed a poncho and poncho liner, a towel, an extra pair of socks, insect repellent, an entrenching tool, a pack to hold everything, two or three days of C-rations and a C-ration opener, dog tags, church key, water purification tablets, salt tablets, and a small journal. The insect repellent, salt tablets, and water purification tablets were carried on my helmet and secured with a giant rubber band cut from an inner tube.

Then there was my photo equipment that included a Nikon FTN and three or four lenses. The lenses I took depended on where I was going. If I knew we were going to be primarily in a jungle environment or something like that, I knew that a long telephoto lens wouldn't do me any good because you can't see very far. I would normally take a 35mm wide-angle lens, a 50mm normal lens, a 105mm short telephoto lens, and a 135mm medium telephoto lens. Depending on how long I was going to be out, I'd carry a twenty- to thirty-roll mixed assortment of B&W and color slide film. Each roll of film held thirty-six exposures. I would also carry equipment for cleaning and maintaining my camera; brushes to remove dust; lens cleaner and lens tissue; and a set of jeweler's screwdrivers. A small pocket-size notebook for noting caption information and a slate to identify each roll of film with my name, unit, date, location, and the name of the operation was also included. A picture of the slate at the beginning of each roll was taken so you could identify it among all the other rolls of film being processed back in the lab.

I carried a lot of different weapons as a photographer, but when I first transferred down to Photo, I was issued a .45 caliber automatic pistol. It was lightweight, you could carry it on your hip, and it didn't get in the way of doing photography. When I returned to duty in January 1968, the Tet Offensive was starting, and that's when I picked up an M3A1 grease gun (.45 caliber submachine gun), which I would carry for the rest of my time in Vietnam.

The fighting was intensifying everywhere in 1968. First we had the Tet Offensive; then, a few months later, the mini Tet Offensive. It seemed that we were getting into a lot more intense fighting. Deciding that I needed a little more firepower than a pistol, I stuck with the grease gun. It hung low on the hip, didn't get in the way, and provided a little extra firepower if needed.

But I digress a little. Back to Operation Cochise.

I saddled up with my gear and walked down to the Division helipad in search of a ride down to Que Son. There were no scheduled flights; one just waited for a helicopter to land and checked with the crew to see where they were headed for next. Eventually a CH-46 Sea Knight came along that was en route to Tam Ky. While this wasn't my destination, it was a lot closer. After a short flight we arrived and set down on a big PSP (perforated steel planking) landing mat helipad. I worked my way aft to the ramp as the door gunners were clearing their weapons. The ear-piercing sound of the turbines abated as they were shut down and the rotors slowed to a stop. I went down the ramp and looked for a place to rest until the next chopper arrived to start the whole ride-sharing process over again.

It was really hot this time of the year, so I found a little shade in the lee of a supply pallet and settled down next it, pulling out my canteen for a drink of lukewarm water. It didn't exactly qualify as thirst-quenching refreshment, so I decided to see if I could find something more palatable.

The LZ was surrounded by squad tents with a variety of trucks coming and going to drop off or pick up shipments. I decided to wander around and see if I could scare up something cold to drink. As I walked between the tents I came upon a fifty-five-gallon drum that was cut in half lengthways and filled with ice and sodas. I felt like I'd reached an oasis, and looked around for the owner of these refreshments. Not seeing anyone, I decided to help myself.

I pulled out my canteen cup, filled it with ice, extracted a Pepsi from its icy bed, and with church key in hand, opened it up. Pouring the contents into the cup, I grabbed a second can from the ice and retreated to a shady spot at the LZ to enjoy the drink. In no time at all I had polished off both cans and decided to return to the scene of the crime for a refill. However, when I arrived there was a corporal sitting on a cot in the tent next to the drinks. I fessed up to my earlier theft and asked if I could pay him for the ones I took and get a few more to go. He didn't answer directly, but motioned to my camera and asked if I was with the photo unit. I said I was, and had just joined about a month ago.

Turns out he was friends with Lance Corporal Clark Thomas, one of our photographers, and asked me say hi to him when I returned. He also said there was no charge for the sodas, and to take whatever I wanted. Elated at my good luck, I stuck two cans of Pepsi in my pack, broke out my canteen cup, filled it with ice, opened up another Pepsi, poured the fizzing contents over the ice, and began drinking.

Just about then the corporal yelled out, "Drink it out of the can! That ice is made from river water and will give you the shits."

Surprised and dismayed, I thanked him for the warning, although it was a little late, and returned to the LZ as I heard another chopper approaching. I knew this op was not going to start off well as I pondered what microscopic bacteria I had introduced to my digestive system.

An H-34 landed, and as luck would have it, they were taking mail out to Hill 51. The crew chief motioned me on board after all the mail bags were loaded, and I settled in among them on the floor. This flight was also of short duration, and I was soon deposited on Hill 51.

I got out of the helicopter and immediately asked one of the Marines for directions to sick bay, where I hoped to get some preventive medicine to stave off any problems caused by the river water ice. A corpsman fixed me up with some tablets in case the worst should happen. Fortunately, I didn't get sick on this occasion, and considered myself pretty lucky.

My next stop was to find Captain Robert Morgan, the CO of Delta 1/5. He was very gracious, welcomed me to his unit, and recommended that I attend the mission briefing for Operation Cochise, to be held the next morning. He said that all the commanders would be there for a briefing on the operation, and it was the best way to find out all the details. I asked him if I could travel with 1st Platoon, and he said that was probably as good as any. So I looked up Donnelly and we spent the rest of the day talking about all the enemy activity in the Que Son valley and their seemingly unending patrols and operations. Jim assured me there would be plenty of action to photograph, as they seldom went on patrols or operations without making enemy contact. I was now more anxious than ever to see this op get under way.

The next morning, I attended the mission briefing for Operation Cochise. I don't recall the specifics anymore, except for the fact that the enemy was in the area in large numbers and heavy fighting was expected. My first photo of Operation Cochise was at that briefing. The most important takeaway from the meeting was that we would depart Hill 51 at 0230 hours the following morning.

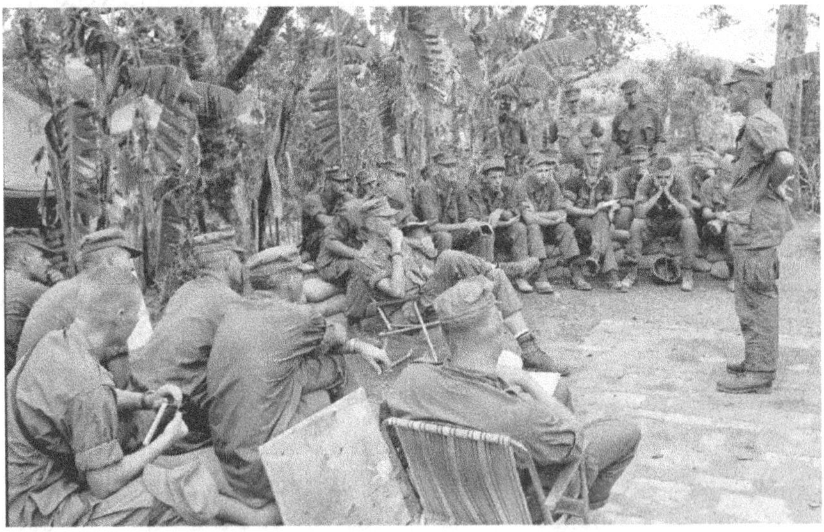

The command staff of the 1st Battalion/5th Marine Regiment attending a mission briefing on Operation Cochise at the Que Son combat base on Hill 51 on August 11, 1967, the day prior to the kickoff of the operation. PHOTO BY L/CPL. DENNIS FISHER

I returned to 1st Platoon's area and told Donnelly what I had heard in the briefing. The platoon commander arrived shortly thereafter and gave the platoon more detailed information. Everything seemed to be going smoothly. For the Marines from this company, this was just another operation. Some of the men were in their tents, writing letters, checking over their gear, or bullshitting with their buddies. No one was going to get much sleep, but some were dozing on their cots.

Jim and I decided to walk down to the line of shops that had sprung up outside the perimeter wire. Constructed mainly of bamboo, corrugated steel, and the cardboard from C-ration cases, these shops sold all sorts of things that were in demand by the Marines stationed there. There were sodas and beer, souvenirs, laundry services, sewing, and everything else that was normally seen around our more established combat bases. Shooting a few photos as we walked, Jim suggested we return to the platoon's tents and try to get some shut eye.

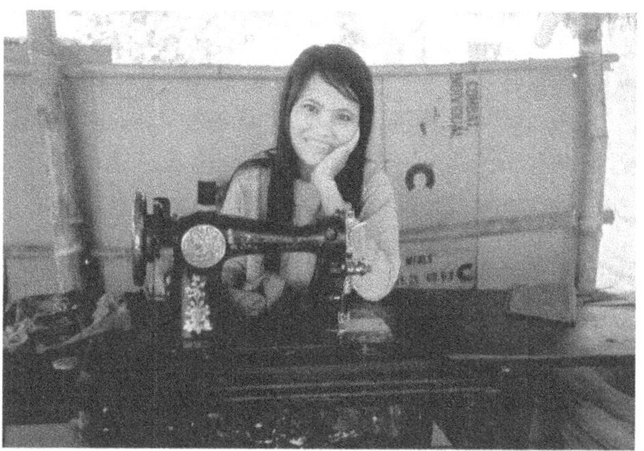

A seamstress poses with her sewing machine in a small shop in Que Son where she mended Marine uniforms and performed other sewing chores. PHOTO BY L/CPL. DENNIS FISHER

Sleep didn't come easy that night as my mind was filled with thoughts of the op and my first real trial by fire as a combat photographer.

*First day began at 0230 when we moved out of the 1/5 Battalion area. We marched under a quarter moon until 0600 in the morning. Without stopping for chow we moved immediately toward our first objective, which was a small village.*
(Journal entry, August 12, 1967)

What I didn't mention about that night in my journal—probably because I was too ashamed to commit it to writing—was that around 0330 or 0400, we stopped for a short break. Everyone sat down on the ground along the trail to rest. The next thing I know, everyone was gone and I'm sitting there in the dark by myself. I had dozed off, and was now trying to figure out how long I had been out, and how far ahead the rest of the unit could be. I couldn't call out to them and give away my position, and I didn't want to suddenly appear at the rear of the column for fear of being shot by the rear security.

After what seemed like an eternity, working my way down the trail—actually, only about fifteen minutes—I could hear the sound of people on the move and the rustle of equipment up ahead. The quarter moon didn't provide much light, and trying to keep on the trail was a challenge. Following at a distance until they stopped for a few minutes to check their maps, I finally decided it was safe to approach. The rear security spotted me in the dim light and asked what the hell I was doing behind him. He reminded me that it was a good way to get shot. I couldn't argue with that. It's a pretty scary feeling to find yourself alone in Indian country. I had been on night patrols and listening posts with the Security Platoon, but it was always with at least one other person. It gave me some appreciation for the pilots who were shot down and left alone in hostile territory.

We reached a village that was our first objective around 0600 and found it nearly deserted, except for a couple of families. After a search that yielded no information or physical evidence that the VC had been there, we moved on to our next objective. By now there was enough light to begin photographing the operation. All photography was done with available light, as a flash would have revealed our position to the enemy.

Around 1000 hours we reached another village, our second objective, and it was basically a repeat of the first one. Nothing of interest was found until we began to move out. One of the men spotted a partially exposed mine. Captain Morgan, his staff, and a dozen others had walked past it without seeing anything. Engineers were called up and it was blown in place.

The device was actually a submunition from a cluster bomb about the size of a soup can that had failed to explode. They contained explosives and pea-sized ball bearings and were meant as antipersonnel munitions. The VC retrieved them and converted them into booby traps. Each cluster bomb contained hundreds of these submunitions, many of which failed to explode, and the word was passed to keep on the lookout for more of them.

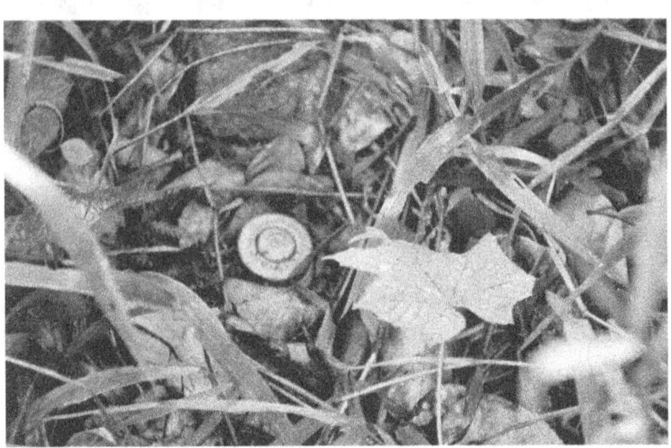

Unexploded submunition from a cluster bomb that the enemy had repurposed as a booby trap during Operation Cochise. The device was encountered by Marines of the Delta 1/5 and blown in place. PHOTO BY L/CPL. DENNIS FISHER

I would have my own close call with one of these later in the day when the Marine behind me called a rather frightened halt. I froze and asked what was the matter. He pointed to another cluster bomblet hidden on the trail. My boot had skimmed over the top, removing a big leaf that had been camouflaging it and exposing the device. We marked the location and called for the engineers, who blew it in place after we had moved out of the area.

The day continued uneventfully for 1st Platoon until the afternoon. Donnelly was telling me that they normally made a lot of contact in this area, and things seemed a little too quiet.

Then, as if on cue, a sniper round snapped by us and everyone took cover. In an instant, our platoon began returning fire with everything they had. My infantry instincts immediately kicked in, and I pulled out my .45 and began firing too. However, I quickly remembered that I wasn't in the infantry anymore, put away the pistol, and began taking photos of the action. All the photos I had taken thus far were of the locals being questioned and Marines on the move, but now we were actually engaged with the enemy. I was a little nervous at first with the sound of rifle rounds snapping by, squad leaders yelling out orders, the call for "guns up," and the grenadier lobbing rounds with his blooper. I knew whoever was shooting at us was more than likely targeting the machine-gun team.

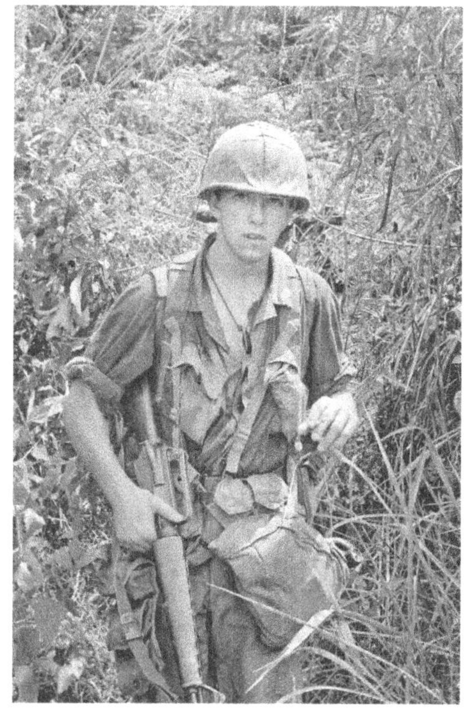

Corporal Jim Donnelly, squad leader with 1st Platoon of Delta 1/5, moving through heavy undergrowth during Operation Cochise on August 12, 1967. PHOTO BY L/CPL. DENNIS FISHER

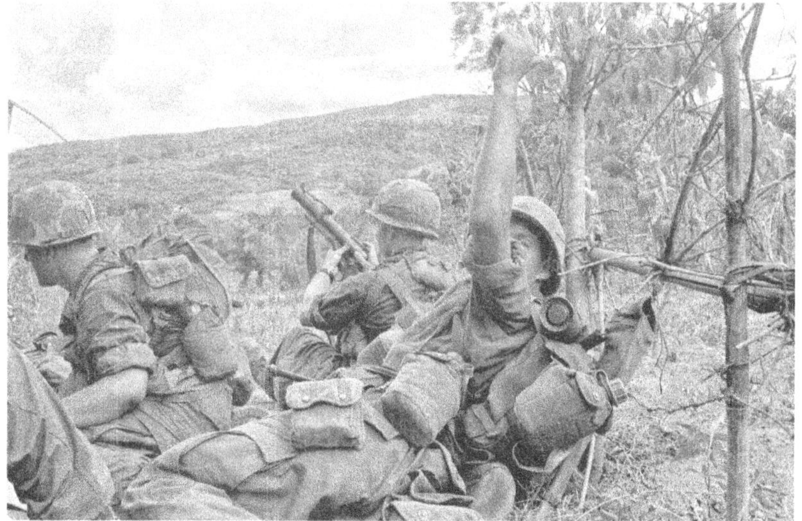

A Marine from Delta Company 1/5 signals his squad to move up during a firefight with enemy snipers during Operation Cochise, near Hill 29. PHOTO BY L/CPL. DENNIS FISHER/COURTESY OF NARA STILL PICTURE BRANCH

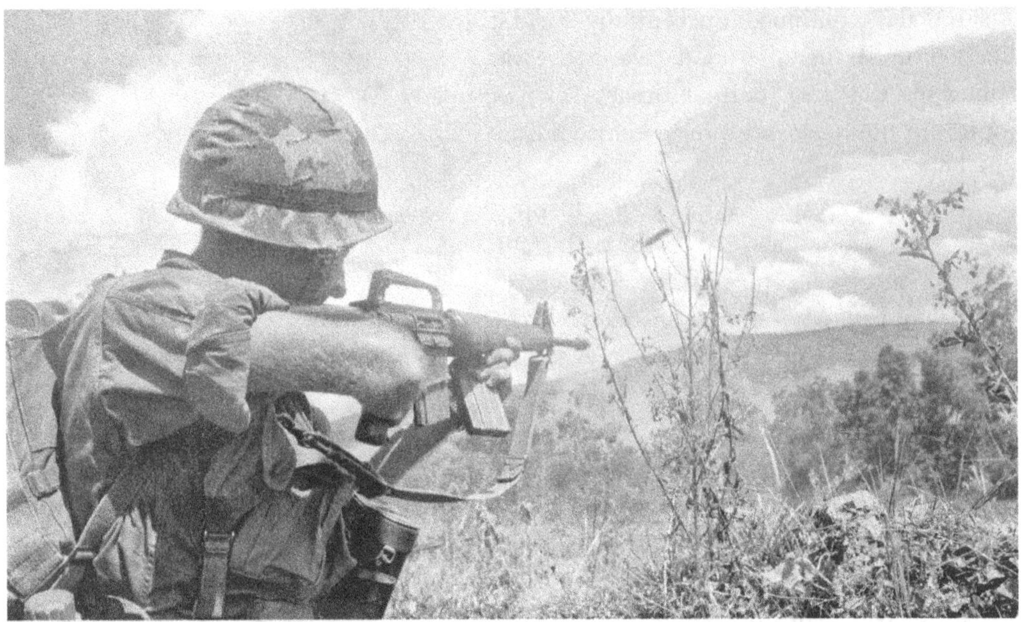

A Marine from Delta Company 1/5 lays down a base of fire while members of his squad assault a tree line during Operation Cochise. PHOTO BY L/CPL. DENNIS FISHER/COURTESY OF NARA STILL PICTURE BRANCH

This action set off an instant response by the Marines and a fusillade of fire raked the tree line that concealed the VC. My focus now, no pun intended, was on my camera settings and composition as I moved from position to position to capture as much of the action as possible. The M60 was laying down a base of fire and the platoon began advancing toward the sniper's position in the tree line. They moved forward in fire-team rushes and quickly overtook the position. The VC had gotten away with only a blood trail to mark their exit path. From the empty shell casings, it appeared there were two snipers.

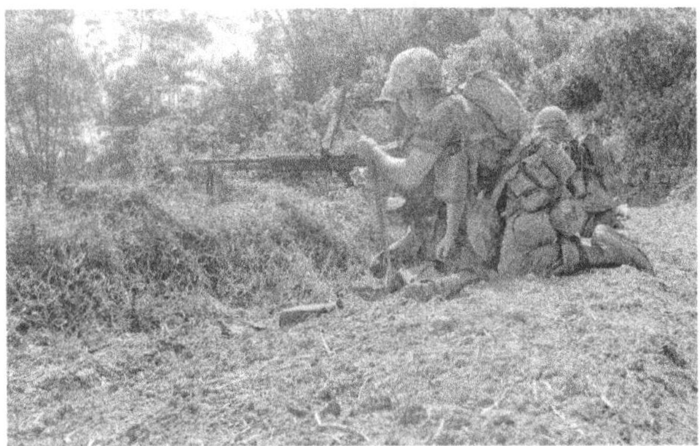

An M60 machine-gun team from Delta 1/5 reloads their weapon in a firefight during Operation Cochise. PHOTO BY L/CPL. DENNIS FISHER/COURTESY OF NARA STILL PICTURE BRANCH

We continued moving in the direction of the blood trail and came to a village nestled in the woods. Heavy and accurate sniper fire greeted us on approaching the village from an estimated four or five VC, and almost immediately we suffered a casualty when one of the Marines was shot through the cheek. Another had his M16 shot out of his hand; fortunately, although the rifle was ruined, he was not hurt.

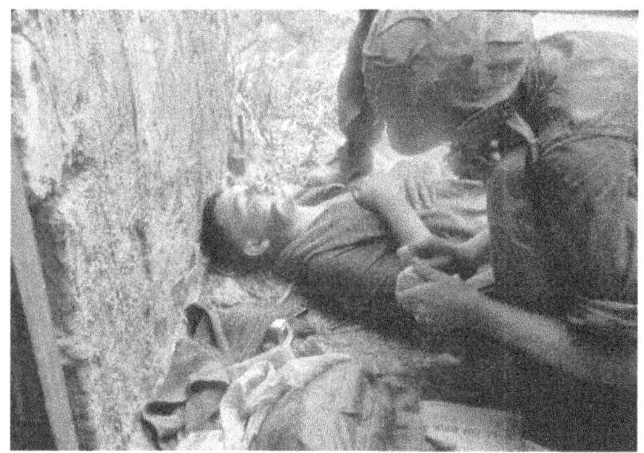

A corpsman serving with Delta Company 1/5 treats a wounded Marine who was shot through the cheek by an enemy sniper during Operation Cochise. PHOTO BY L/CPL. DENNIS FISHER

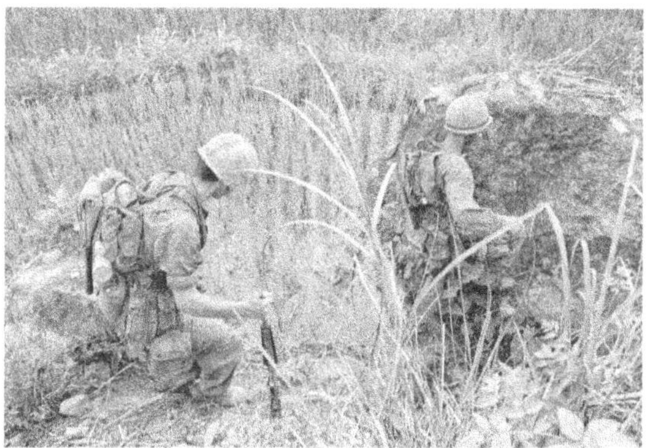

Marines from Delta Company 1/5 move through broken terrain as they pursue the enemy during Operation Cochise. PHOTO BY L/CPL. DENNIS FISHER/COURTESY OF NARA STILL PICTURE BRANCH

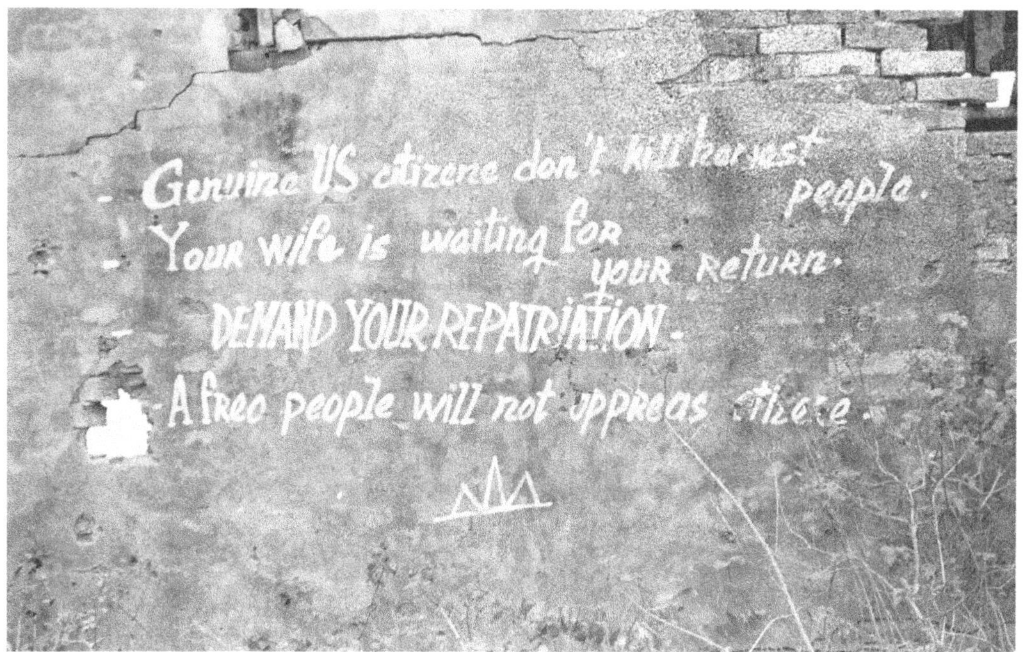


Enemy propaganda left behind to encourage Marines to desert, usually read with a chuckle and suggested improvements to grammar. PHOTO BY L/CPL. DENNIS FISHER

Firing had become pretty general by now, and I moved from one group of men to another, capturing the intensity of the firefight. The VC cleared out of the village as the Marines rushed their position, but no bodies were found.

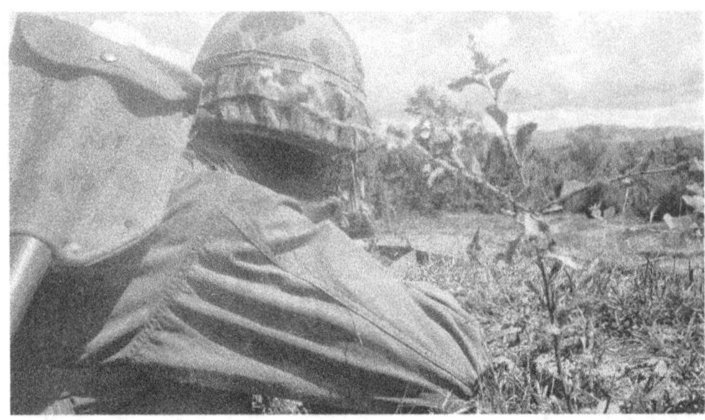

A Marine from Delta Company 1/5 engages enemy snipers during an Operation Cochise firefight. PHOTO BY L/CPL. DENNIS FISHER/COURTESY OF NARA STILL PICTURE BRANCH

The platoon moved on and selected a hill to set in on for the night. Captain Morgan laid out a defensive perimeter for the platoons, and everyone began digging in. After we had some C-rations for dinner, the company first sergeant set the watch for the night, and I believe they sent two men out to set up a listening post along the trail we had taken to the top of the hill.

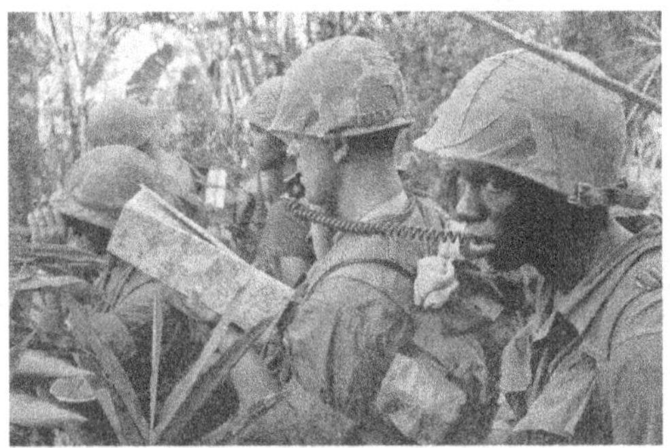

Delta Company 1/5 commander Captain Robert Morgan calls in air support during Operation Cochise. PHOTO BY L/CPL. DENNIS FISHER/COURTESY OF NARA STILL PICTURE BRANCH

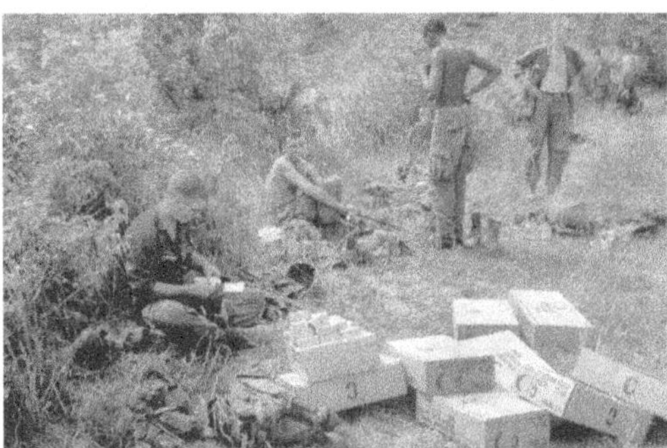

Marines from Delta Company 1/5 are resupplied with C-rations as they prepare to dig in for the night during Operation Cochise. PHOTO BY L/CPL. DENNIS FISHER

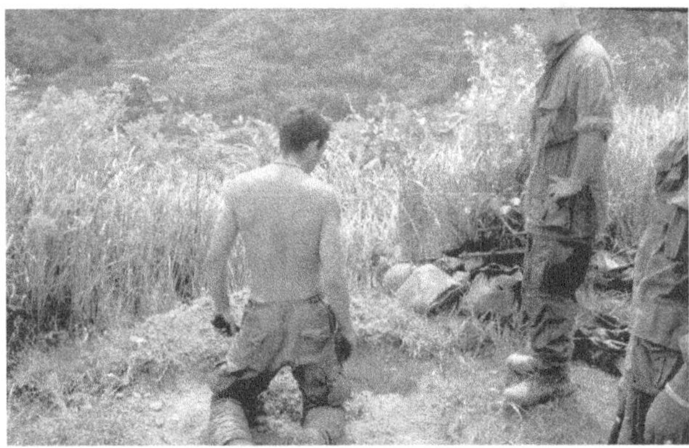

A Marine from 1st Platoon Delta Company 1/5 preparing his position on their night defensive perimeter during Operation Cochise. PHOTO BY L/CPL. DENNIS FISHER

We had definitely poked the hornets' nest, and a night ground attack or a mortar attack was a real possibility. I was with Delta Company, but began wondering where the other companies were and how they were faring. Bravo Company had been on our flank, but in this hilly and mountainous terrain, I'd lost sight of them almost immediately.

So ended my first day as a combat photographer.

The morning of August 13, 1967, we moved off the hill and headed for another one, where we were to be resupplied with ammo and rations. While waiting for the resupply choppers I met two civilian war photographers and stopped to talk with them. I figured this must be a noteworthy operation if it had attracted the civilian press. We talked briefly about the op, but were interrupted as a CH-46 arrived with our resupply. I didn't get any photos of them, assuming I would be running into them as the op continued, but they boarded the helicopter along with two wounded Marines and flew off toward Da Nang.

*Bravo Company was already occupying the hill when we arrived. I met two photographers, one named Schneider from CBS. A big red beard on his face and dressed in ARVN tiger stripe jungles [jungle utilities]. He carried what looked to be a 9mm semi-auto pistol in a Vietnamese-made holster. The pistol had ivory grips with dragons carved on them. He carried a Nikon F, a Nikkormat, and a motion picture camera. On his head he wore a bush hat and he carried a large pack with all kinds of gear. The other photographer, Al Webb, was from AP [actually UPI, as I found out recently] and looked like any other soldier or Marine.*

(Journal entry, August 13, 1967)

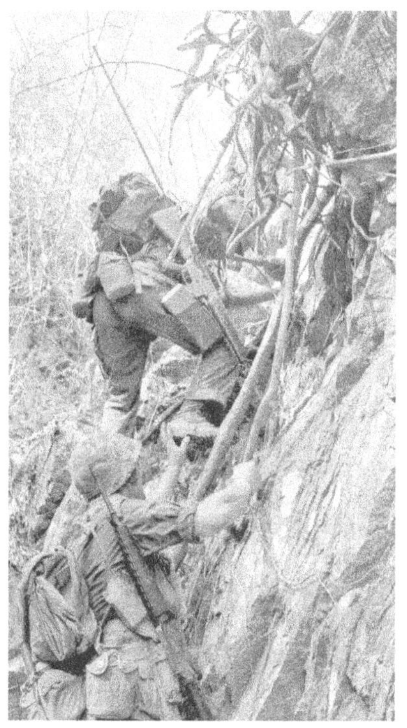

Mountainous terrain slows Marines from Delta Company 1/5 as they pursue the enemy during Operation Cochise, near Que Son, in August 1967.
PHOTO BY L/CPL. DENNIS FISHER/ COURTESY OF NARA STILL PICTURE BRANCH

The companies quickly offloaded the supplies and divvied them up as needed, and we were back on the move.

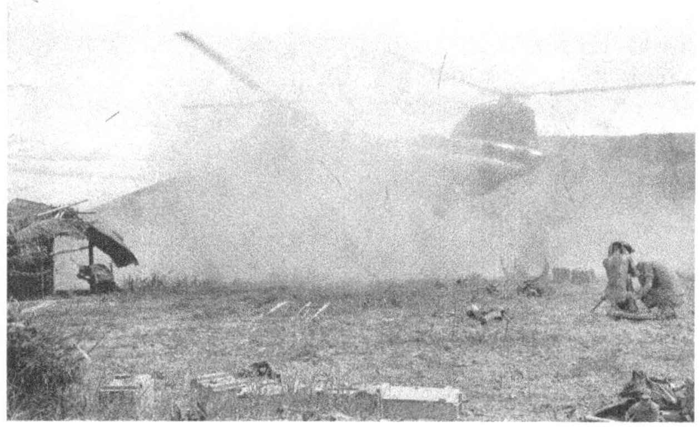

A CH-46 helicopter lands during Operation Cochise with a resupply of rations and ammunition for elements of the 5th Marines. PHOTO BY L/CPL DENNIS FISHER

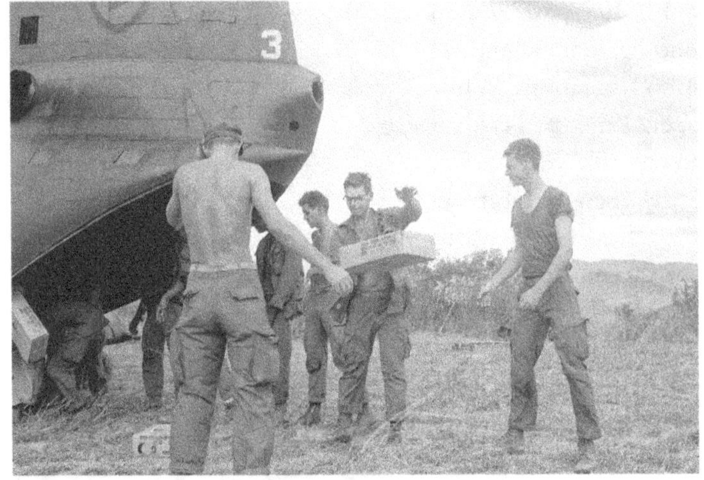

Marines offload supplies from a resupply helicopter during Operation Cochise in August 1967. PHOTO BY L/CPL. DENNIS FISHER

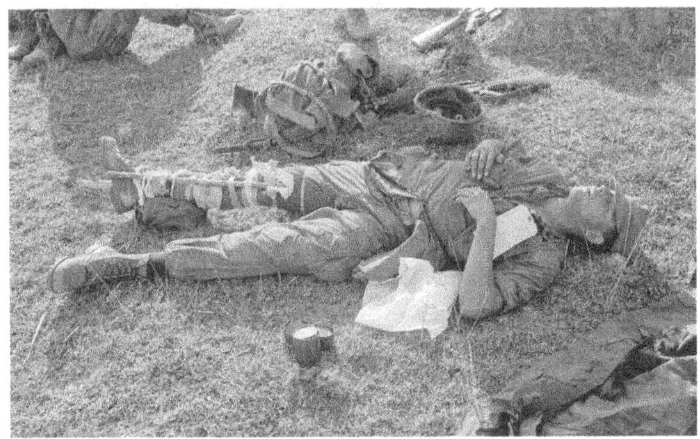

A wounded Marine awaits medical evacuation during Operation Cochise in the hills surrounding the Que Son valley. PHOTO BY L/CPL. DENNIS FISHER

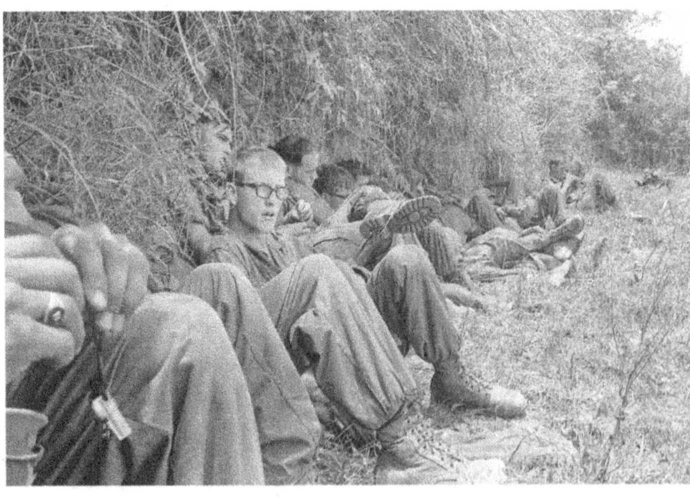

Marines from Delta Company 1/5 get a break while awaiting the arrival of a resupply helicopter during Operation Cochise. PHOTO BY L/CPL. DENNIS FISHER

About an hour later, Delta Company was tasked to set up a perimeter and secure an LZ for a UH-34 that was inbound. As the helicopter neared the ground, it suddenly seemed to lose power and fall from the sky. The chopper hit the ground hard and bounced about thirty feet back up in the air only to fall sideways off the LZ and down a twenty-foot embankment, where it came to rest on its side.

Taking pictures of the whole event as it unfolded, I hit the ground as hunks of rotor blades and debris flew everywhere. As the crew climbed out of the wreckage, I resumed my photography of the crash site. I finally put down my camera and joined other Marines to help them remove their gear from the wreckage. While the crew was shaken up, no one was seriously hurt.

Delta Company was kept on-site to secure the wreckage until a CH-53 could come in and lift it out. Two gunships remained on station to provide security for the CH-53 as it prepared to lift out the wreckage, but were themselves taken under fire by enemy ground forces. They returned fire with machine guns and 2.75-inch folding-fin rockets, effectively silencing the enemy. The retrieval of the UH-34 ultimately failed due to the location of the wreck, and it was destroyed.

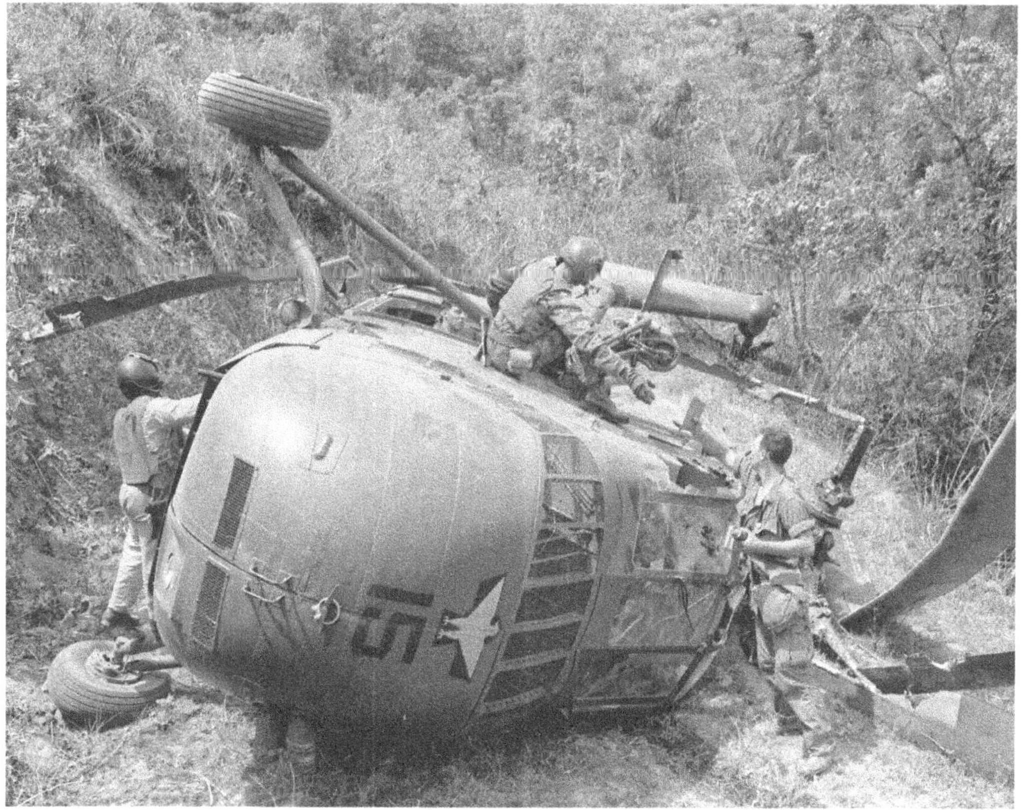

Crew members remove equipment from a downed Marine UH-34 helicopter that was lost during Operation Cochise in August 1967. PHOTO BY L/CPL. DENNIS FISHER

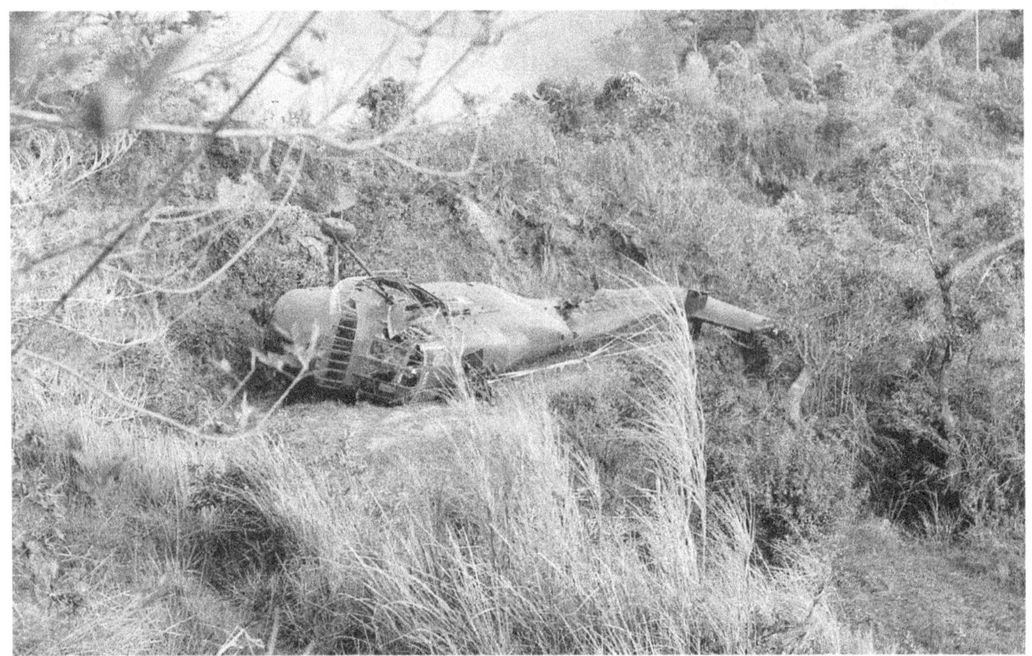

A downed Marine UH-34 helicopter that was lost during Operation Cochise, rigged and ready for extraction in August 1967. PHOTO BY L/CPL. DENNIS FISHER

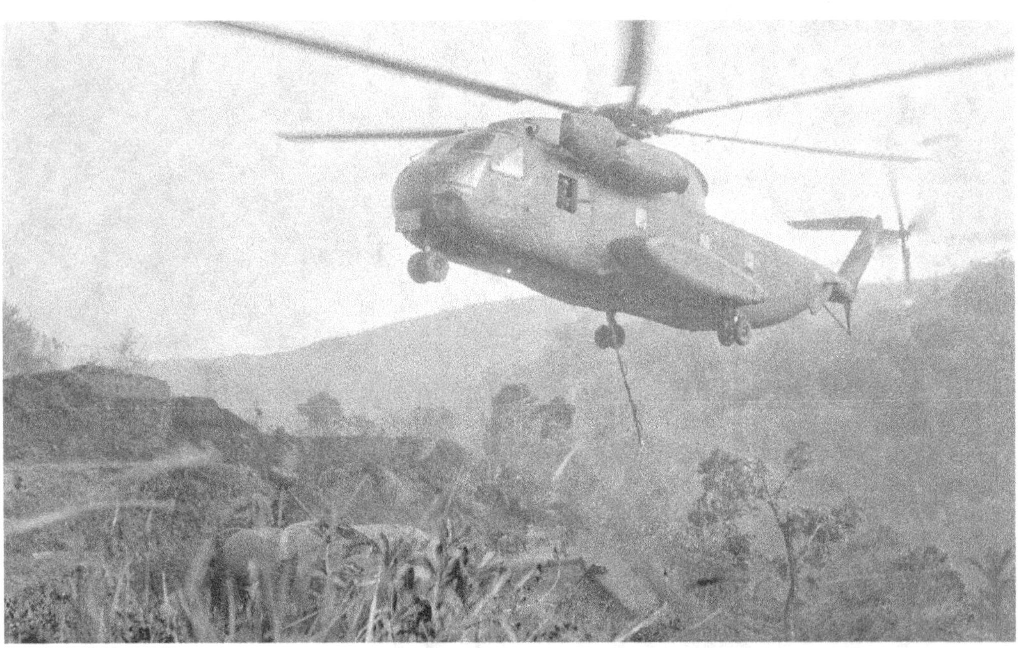

A CH-53 Sea Stallion helicopter attempts to extract a downed UH-34 helicopter during Operation Cochise in August 1967. The lift ultimately failed, and the downed helicopter was destroyed. PHOTO BY L/CPL. DENNIS FISHER/COURTESY OF NARA STILL PICTURE BRANCH

Operation Cochise continued with no major contact by the unit I was with, but as I would find out later, the ARVN Rangers made contact with the NVA on the morning of August 12, the first full day of the operation, and were engaged in heavy fighting all day and well into the night. Marine helicopters flew in emergency supplies of ammunition so they could continue the fight. The NVA finally broke contact around midnight, leaving 197 dead on the field. The Rangers took heavy casualties, too, with 81 killed and about twice that number wounded.

After returning to the Photo Lab, I heard Bill Page—who had been with Kilo 3/5 on this op—say that they were attacked on the night of August 16, which resulted in 35 or 40 enemy killed. There were a few other significant engagements in which 3/5 was involved. So, in closing out my account of Operation Cochise, I would say that the battle swirled all around us without any big engagements by Delta 1/5. We were choppered out on August 18, to begin Phase II of Cochise, which turned out to be more or less a walk in the park. Phase III officially ran from August 25 through 28, but with little enemy contact, the company was directed to return to Hill 51 on August 26.

It was time to head back to the Photo Lab and process my film, but Captain Morgan asked me to stay one more day to photograph medal presentations, Purple Heart awards, and some promotions at 1600 the next day. I readily agreed, promising to send out prints of everything after I got back to the lab. I asked him what he'd heard from the other commanders about the success of the op; while he felt we had bloodied their noses, he suggested they would be back after they had regrouped and resupplied.

As a postscript to this account, a week after Cochise had pushed them out of the Que Son valley, the NVA moved back in and attacked Delta 1/5's position on Hill 51 in the early-morning hours of September 4. Heavy fighting ensued, with the enemy getting inside the perimeter. Donnelly told me that Captain Morgan led a counterattack and drove them back. However, the enemy regrouped and attacked again, killing Morgan. This attack prompted Operation Swift to counter the renewed threat.

Back at the Photo Lab, I processed my B&W film and slides and made selections to send forward to Headquarters Marine Corps (HQMC). The negatives were numbered and captioned and prints were made to fulfill immediate requirements for Intel and the Information Services Office (ISO). A number of the photos from Operation Cochise that were sent off to HQMC now reside in the National Archives and Records Administration (NARA) Still Picture Branch in College Park, Maryland. Initially the photos were used locally to illustrate stories prepared by our combat correspondents for the *Sea Tiger* or *Stars and Stripes*. These were in-country newspapers for the military, and were used to keep the troops informed about what was happening in Vietnam. I also printed up all the photos I had taken at the awards ceremony and sent them out to 1/5, little knowing at the time that Captain Morgan was dead.

With my first operation completed, I was anxious to get back out in the field. I had been promoted to lance corporal and was pulling down a whopping $121.50 base pay,

$65.00 hostile fire pay, and $9.00 overseas pay, for a grand total of $195.00 a month. I couldn't help but wonder how much those civilian war photographers I met were making each month. In the meantime, the gunny had me shooting assignments around the Division area: promotions, medal presentations, civic action programs, and MEDCAPs.

When I heard that Delta 1/5 was back in the action on Operation Swift, I requested to be sent back out with them. The Gunny nixed that idea and instead sent me out with Staff Sergeant Maurice "Mo" Upton to cover an upcoming op with the 7th Marines, west of Da Nang, near Dai Loc.

One day at morning roll call, we were cautioned not to try to shoot any captured weapons. No explanation was given, but most of us assumed it was just a cautionary warning, as out in the field, Marines would open fire in the direction of the sound of enemy weapons being fired.

After the war I found out there was a secret unconventional warfare mission called Project Eldest Son, run by the SOG (Studies and Observation Group). The intention was to sabotage enemy ammunition, resulting in the weapons exploding when these cartridges were fired. This was done with rifle, machine-gun, and mortar shells. The mortar shell fuses were altered to cause the round to explode in the launch tube as it was being fired. The project involved taking captured ammunition and remanufacturing the cartridges with high explosives that increased the chamber pressures to five times the design limit. This altered ammunition was randomly reinserted in ammo boxes and magazines, just a few here and there when enemy weapons caches were found and left undisturbed. The idea was to have the enemy question the quality of their ammo supply. Although the senior brass probably knew about the project, we didn't, and due to its secret nature, no one was going to take the chance of compromising it by telling all the Marines about it. Instead, we received a warning to not try and fire captured weapons.

Every morning we had a unit formation where Top (Master Sergeant) Brown, the gunny, or the CO would pass on information to everyone on any number of topics related to our daily operations. At one of my first formations, the gunny came out of the lab and greeted us with the shouted command "Attitude check!" While I didn't know what he was asking, everyone else did, and they answered in unison "F*ck it!" This was followed by "Morale check," which was answered with a chorus of "I hate this f*ckin' place!" He then said "I'm glad everything is normal—get to work."

One advantage of being back in the rear was you could listen to Armed Forces Radio. Most people have heard of Adrian Cronauer, who opened his morning show with "Goooood morning, Vietnam," made famous by Robin Williams in a movie by that name. They had various programs ranging from popular music to sports, and gave us a little taste of home. I had also received some quarter-inch tapes with popular music compilations from WFUN, a Top 40 radio station in Miami, Florida. One guy in the lab had a Zenith Trans-Oceanic radio which could receive broadcasts from back in the States, but the reception was sketchy and you had to listen in his hooch, where he'd built an antenna on the roof. Of course there was always Hanoi Hannah if you wanted a good laugh. Such was our entertainment.

Remember that this was a war and there weren't any weekends off; we worked every day, but would be given an afternoon off or a day off if things were slow. On those occasions you could go to the PX or the movie down at Freedom Hill, as long as you stayed in the Division area. It was important not to stray too far, as you were always subject to immediate recall if something happened. I described some of these activities when I was with the Security Platoon, and things weren't too different in the Photo Lab, except we were busier and had less time for these leisure activities.

One-day assignments around the Division area and a run out to Hill 55 occupied my time in the middle of September. Hill 55 was the headquarters for the 7th Marine Regiment at the time, and I went there one day to find out if there were any upcoming operations that we hadn't heard about.

As a lance corporal I couldn't just walk into Operations and get a briefing on the regiment's activities, but I could speak with the enlisted admin clerks who knew what was planned. A corporal there recommended that I check with 3/7 out at Dai Loc. That unit had been conducting search-and-destroy ops in the area between their base and An Hoa.

It was too late to get to Dai Loc, so I opted to head back to the lab. With Operation Cochise under my belt, I was anxious to get back out in the field. The 7th Marines seemed like a good place to start.

CHAPTER 4

# Operation Zippo

### *Dai Loc*

STAFF SERGEANT MO UPTON AND I WERE ASSIGNED TO COVER OPERATION ZIPPO WITH Lima 3/7 near their base at Dai Loc. The operation was planned for September 28, 1967, and was to kick off from Hill 37, which overlooked the village of Dai Loc. This hill served as the combat base for 3/7 and was topped with a big brick-and-concrete bunker left over from the French occupation during the Indochina War.

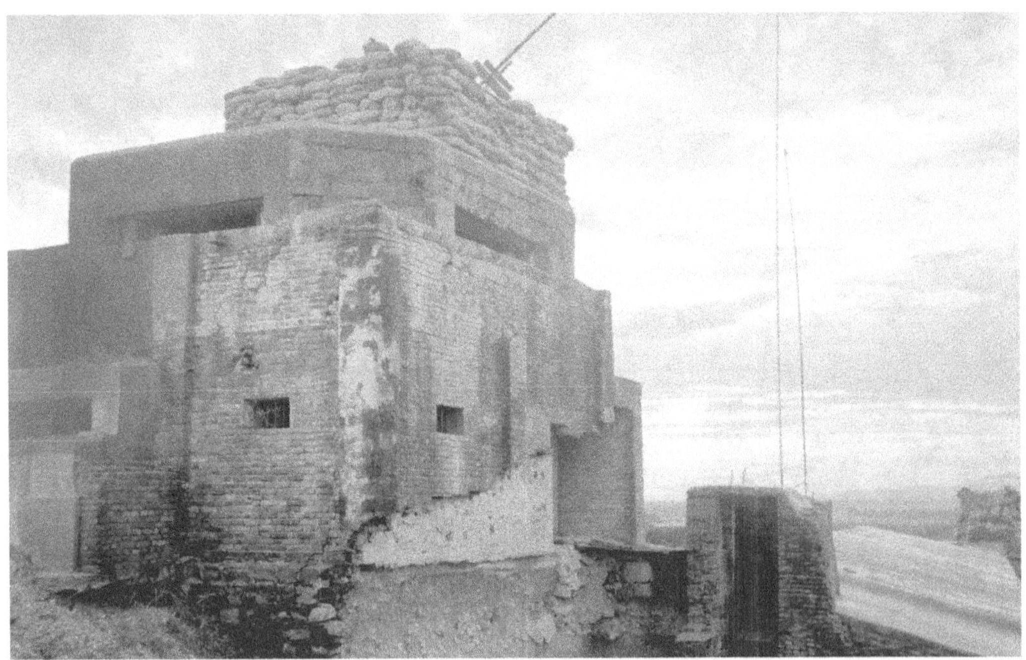

A French bunker from the Indochina War that sits atop Hill 37 at Dai Loc, repurposed by the Marines of 3/7 for use at their combat base. PHOTO BY L/CPL. DENNIS FISHER

I have not been able to find any contemporary references to this operation, but back then, search-and-destroy missions were sometimes referred to as "Zippo raids," and I think that is why 3/7 called this Operation Zippo. When enemy base camps were found they would be burned, the fires either started with flamethrowers or simply by taking out your Zippo lighter and setting them alight. Also, named operations were generally at least battalion size, and this one was only a company.

My recollection of our trip out to Hill 37 is a little foggy, but I recall hitching a ride on a deuce and a half that was hauling supplies out to Hill 55, which served as the regimental headquarters for the 7th Marines. We stopped there briefly until another ride to Hill 37 could be located.

Before too long another ride was found, and after an uneventful trip we arrived late in the afternoon. It should be noted that traveling by road was always a crapshoot. The engineers had to sweep the roads for mines every morning, and they usually remained closed until around 1000 hours. Once cleared of mines, the main threat was ambush, and on the more dangerous routes the vehicles traveled in convoys that were escorted by gun trucks. Gun trucks were two-and-a-half- or five-ton trucks that had been equipped with homemade armor and fitted with quad-50s or other machine guns. In our situation, we were traveling unescorted and alone.

Mo and I arrived without incident, checked in at the battalion command post, and received details about the upcoming op. It was suggested that we join up with Lima Company, and to look up Captain Marshall, the company CO, and inform him that we had been sent out to cover the operation. He gave us a few more details about the op and recommended that we travel with 1st Platoon. Mo knew some of the Marines out here and went to look them up while I located the 1st Platoon.

I didn't know any of the Marines with this unit, and asked the platoon commander which squad he recommended I travel with. He recommended the "Dirty Dozen" as one of squads that always seemed to end up engaged with the enemy. A full-strength squad consisted of three fire teams of four men each, a squad leader, and a grenadier, which adds up to fourteen—but this was Vietnam, and units were seldom if ever at full strength. I think there were only eight or nine men in the Dirty Dozen, their name taken from a popular war movie of that time, which had been released a few months earlier. They were accompanied by an M60 machine-gun team from the Weapons Platoon, led by Corporal Fred Angehrn, with his assistant gunner Lance Corporal Joe Miller. Actually, Fred was there as an "attachment." The gun teams, mortars, snipers, and rocket teams belonged to H&S Company/Weapons Platoon, and went where they were needed.

Locating the squad wasn't hard, and they invited me to crash on an empty cot in their hooch for the night. I dropped my pack and excess gear, and one of the Marines invited me to check out the town of Dai Loc, which was spread out along the river at the bottom of the hill. Grabbing my camera and sidearm, we went down to check it out.

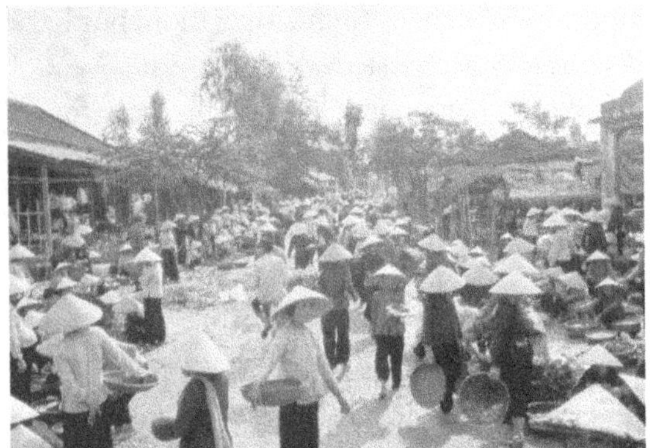

Shoppers crowd the market on the main street of Dai Loc in September 1967, outside the Marine base at Hill 37. PHOTO BY L/CPL. DENNIS FISHER

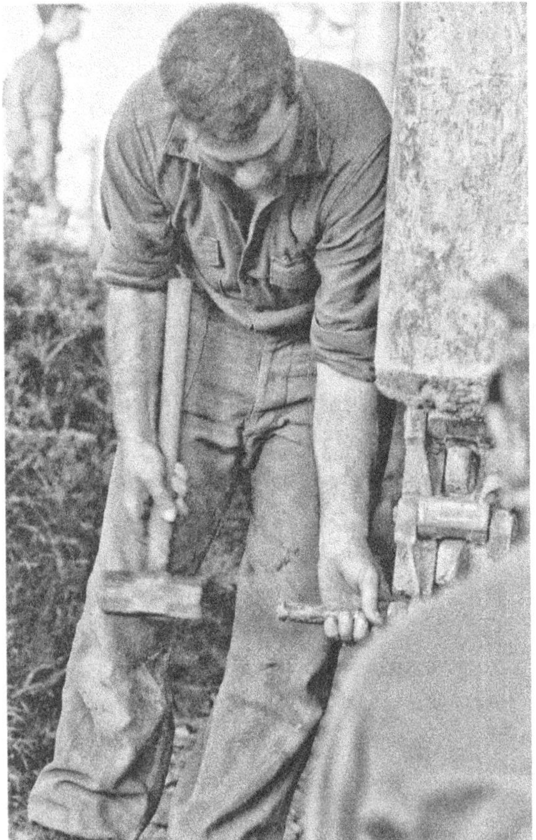

A Marine makes last-minute repairs to his Amtrac before ferrying Lima 3/7 across the Vu Gia River near Dai Loc during Operation Zippo on September 30, 1967. PHOTO BY L/CPL. DENNIS FISHER

Upon arriving at what passed for a main street, it looked like market day was in full swing, with a large crowd of shoppers, and vendors selling all sorts of fruits and vegetables. There was no electricity or refrigeration, so people bought things fresh as needed. We looked around for about a half-hour; I took a few photos, and then returned to the hill. The op kicked off early the next morning, and I wanted to grab some chow and catch a little shut-eye.

It was still dark when I was awakened on the morning of September 29 by the sounds of men shuffling around and putting on their boots. I quickly followed suit, and we headed over to the chow hall for the traditional steak-and-eggs breakfast that Marines received before heading out on an operation. We knew this might be the last good meal we'd have for a while, and for some, it might be their last meal, period.

After chow we put on our gear and formed up in preparation for leaving the hill. Dawn was upon us as we marched off the hill and headed for the river.

Operation Zippo was being conducted on the other side of the Vu Gia River, and Amtracs arrived to ferry us across. I began shooting photos of the move across the river, not knowing if we were being observed by the VC, or if they would start taking potshots at us while we were out on the water. But all was quiet and we crossed without incident. After everyone disembarked from the Amtracs, the platoon began moving toward their first objective.

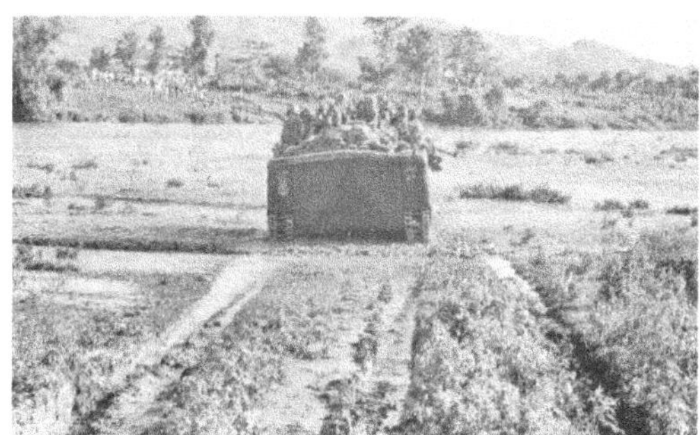

An Amtrac ferries Marines from Lima 3/7 across the Vu Gia River near Dai Loc during the kickoff of Operation Zippo on September 30, 1967. PHOTO BY L/CPL. DENNIS FISHER

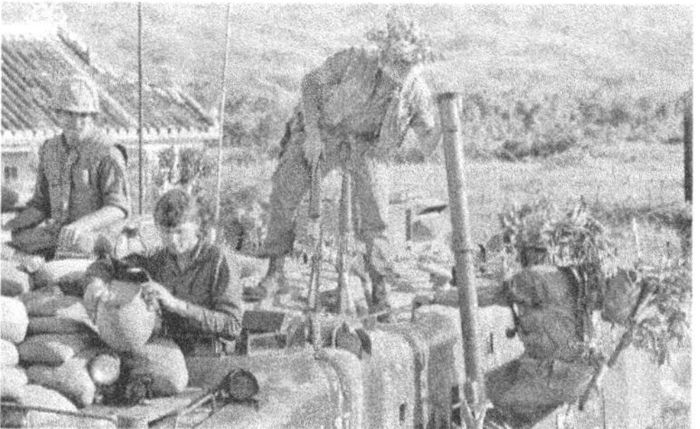

Marines from Lima 3/7 disembark from an Amtrac during Operation Zippo near Dai Loc on September 30, 1967. PHOTO BY L/CPL. DENNIS FISHER

We swept across some open area into a wood line and a village. Almost immediately we began encountering civilians attempting to leave the area before the fighting started. Marines gathered them into small groups and escorted them to the rear for their own safety. One couldn't help but feel sorry for them. The Viet Cong had a strong presence in this area, and reprisal killings of those who assisted the Americans were common.

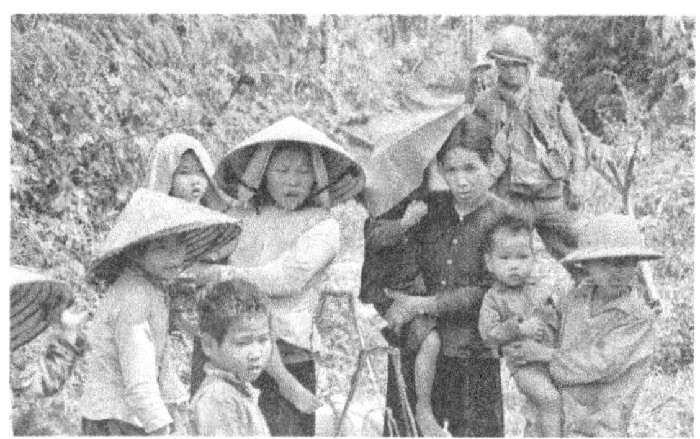

A Marine from Lima Company 3/7 escorts women and children away from the operational area to safety during Operation Zippo near Dai Loc. PHOTO BY CPL DENNIS FISHER

The men hadn't gone too far when a halt was called and we took cover along a trail in some abandoned VC trenches. It seemed our South Vietnamese allies, who were participating in this operation too, were delayed when their Otter became stuck in the river. An Amtrac was recalled to assist them and get their men across the river. This was around 0800. It took the entire day to finally get everyone over. In the meantime, we searched the village and blew up a few bunkers, but remained in generally the same area all day. This gave Charlie the whole day to start maneuvering on us.

As the afternoon wore on we started taking increased sniper fire. I heard some rather close rifle fire, which was easily discernible as 7.62x39mm enemy weapons, followed by automatic weapons fire. Almost before the sound had died away the call of "Guns up" could be heard echoing down the line to summon the M60 machine-gun team. The firing was becoming general now, with automatic weapons fully engaged on both sides. I followed Corporal Fred Angehrn and Lance Corporal Joe Miller as they quickly moved in the direction of the firing.

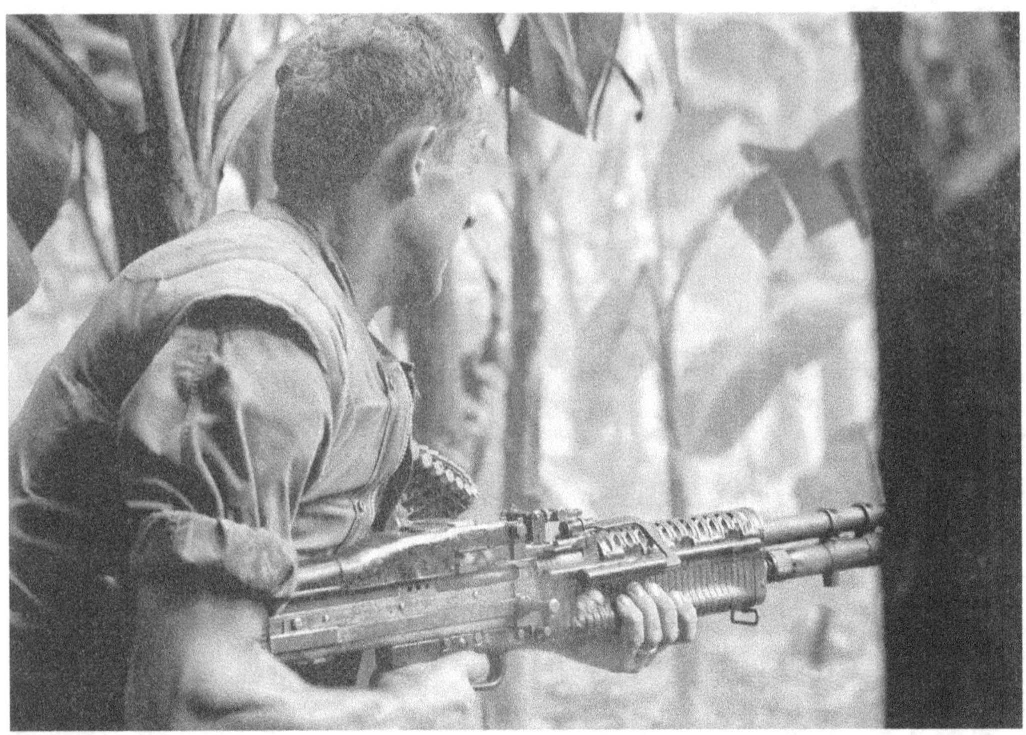

Cpl. Fred Angehrn with Lima 3/7 lays down suppressing fire on the enemy during Operation Zippo near Dai Loc on September 30, 1967. PHOTO BY L/CPL. DENNIS FISHER/COURTESY OF NARA STILL PICTURE BRANCH

The location of the action was marked by the sound of outgoing M79 rounds, exploding hand grenades, and a half-dozen or more M16s firing. The gun team swung into action, with Fred firing from the hip and laying down a grazing fire through a stand

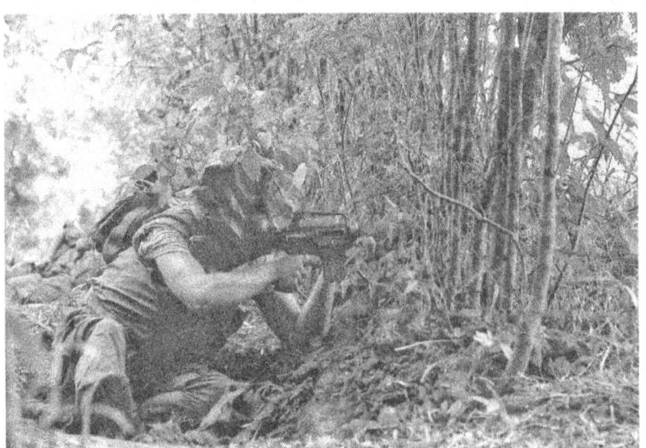

A Marine from Lima 3/7 engaging the enemy with his M16 during a firefight on Operation Zippo near Dai Loc on September 30, 1967. PHOTO BY L/CPL. DENNIS FISHER

of banana trees toward the enemy, perhaps fifty yards away.

Taking up a good position, I began photographing the action. As he burned through about 150 rounds, the barrel became very hot and he was nearly out of ammo. Miller linked up their last 100 rounds and asked if I had another assault pouch. I told him I didn't, so, he ran back to their previous position and returned with a new barrel and several more assault pouches of ammo to continue the fight.

The M60 fires at about ten rounds per second, and simple math says that it doesn't take long to shoot up a one-hundred-round belt of ammo, even when firing in short bursts of five or ten rounds. The ammunition for the M60 was packaged in one-hundred-round assault pouches. These were OD-colored cloth with a carrying strap. As the gun team couldn't carry enough ammo, many of the riflemen would carry an extra assault pouch for them until needed. I continued photographing as they changed the barrel and Fred began firing again. The air was now filled with the smell of hot metal coming from the overheated barrel and gunpowder smoke.

About this time we could hear the sound of a 60mm mortar being fired. Both the Marines and the North Vietnamese Army (NVA) used these weapons, and since the sound was coming from the same area as the rifle fire, we knew the round was headed our way. A 60mm smoke round landed very close, indicating the enemy was targeting us and an HE (high explosive) round wouldn't be far behind.

We retreated to a nearby brick building for cover and waited for the HE rounds to hit. Nothing happened, so Fred resumed his position and began firing again, and I resumed shooting photos.

Once again I heard the sound of 60mm mortars being fired.

High overhead, three HE rounds were rapidly descending on our position, in an instant, filling the air with hot shrapnel, and putting an end to our participation in Operation Zippo.

Chapter 5

# Wounded in Action

In less time than it takes to describe, three 60mm mortar rounds landed in rapid succession near us, wounding Fred, his assistant gunner Joe, and me. I was in a kneeling position when the shrapnel slammed into my foot, knee, and thigh. The initial impact was something akin to being hit with a baseball bat that produced a dull throbbing pain, nothing like I had imagined.

A quick self-examination didn't reveal any other leaks, so I turned to Fred to see how he was doing, and it wasn't good. Miller had multiple shrapnel wounds in one of his legs. He grabbed the gun and I helped Fred get back to the protection of the small brick building, calling "Corpsman up."

As the fighting continued around us, we hobbled back along the trail, helping each other along the way, trying to stay out of the line of fire. We soon encountered the corpsman who was trying to reach us and rejoined the rest of the platoon. I could hear the radioman calling for a medevac as I lay on the ground. Being the least critically wounded, I just applied pressure to the wounds on my knee and thigh to slow the bleeding until the corpsman had finished treating the others. Once he'd finished with me, there was nothing left to do but wait for the medevac. Staff Sergeant Mo Upton had arrived on the scene by this point, and I handed off my camera, film, and captions to him before the medevac arrived. This day was not turning out as I had expected.

As soon as the corpsman got everyone stabilized, he filled out medevac tags and attached them to our uniforms. A few Marines helped us move toward a clearing where the medevac chopper could set down and pick us up. We had to cross a chest-deep stream in the process, but we made it, and were taken out on a UH-34 helicopter.

The chopper touched down for a minute or so at Hill 55 to pick up a Vietnamese child who required medical treatment, and we were soon airborne again. There was no room for the mother of the child, but she didn't want to be left behind, and climbed onto the landing strut of the helicopter as we took off, hanging on for the ride back to

Da Nang. The crew didn't see her until we were airborne, and pressed on anyway—just another of those weird things that happen in war.

Within about ten minutes we were on the ground at the 1st Medical Battalion hospital, or Charlie Med, as we called it, at Division Headquarters. Stripping off my helmet, pack, weapon, ammo, and flak jacket, I was taken into triage. Corpsmen helped each of us onto stretchers and completed a preliminary examination. Fred was immediately taken into surgery while I waited my turn. By now the wounds were beginning to throb, and I was given a shot of painkiller.

When it came my turn in the operating room, I was given a spinal block instead of a general anesthetic, and the surgery began. I propped my head up and watched as they worked on my leg, but soon decided to just lay back and wait until it was over. Just a month or so earlier I'd been here on assignment, photographing the surgeons in this very operating room as they worked on other wounded Marines. Little did I know then that they'd soon be working on me.

I'm not sure how long the surgery lasted, but when the doctors finished I was taken back to a bed in the ward. At that time, one of the doctors asked if I wanted my parents to be notified that I'd been wounded and was in the hospital. I told him no, and said I would write to them. I didn't want to worry them unnecessarily, as my injuries were not life-threatening. I wrote to my father on November 1, 1967, explaining what had happened.

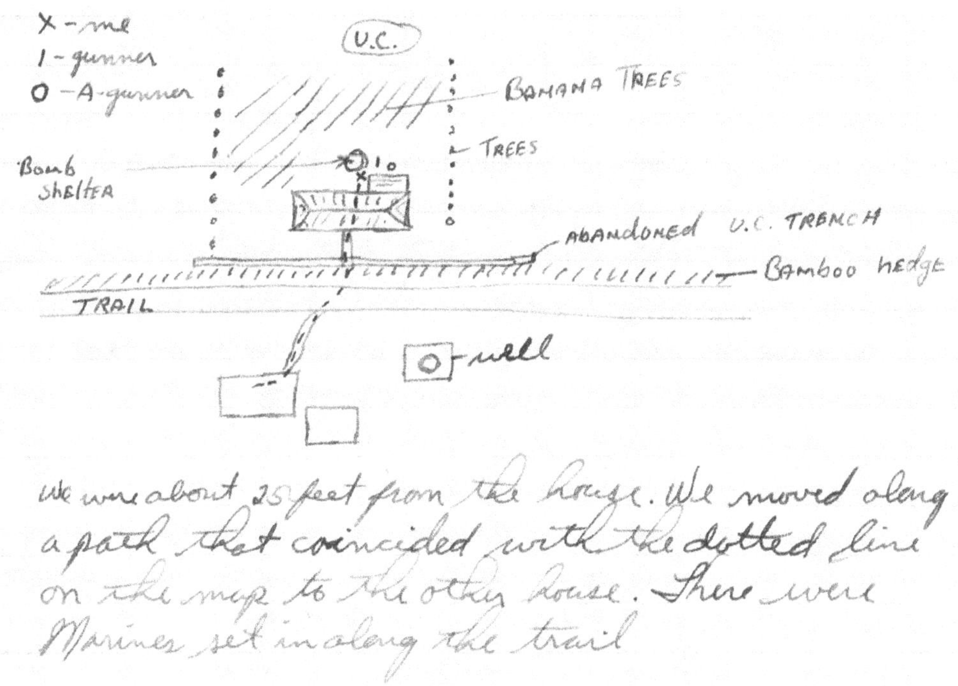


A sketch of the area where the author was wounded; from a November 1, 1967, letter to his father while hospitalized at the US naval hospital on Guam. PHOTO BY L/CPL. DENNIS FISHER

The next morning several senior officers and my CO, Captain Christmas, came in with a USO entertainer. Each of us was presented with a Purple Heart medal, and some were informed they would soon be medevacked out of Vietnam for further treatment. Mary Grover, a Hollywood actress traveling with a USO show, came over and talked to me for a while and posed for some photos. I was sure I had seen her on TV, but couldn't place her.

After they left, one of the orderlies told me they would be taking me down to the airport at

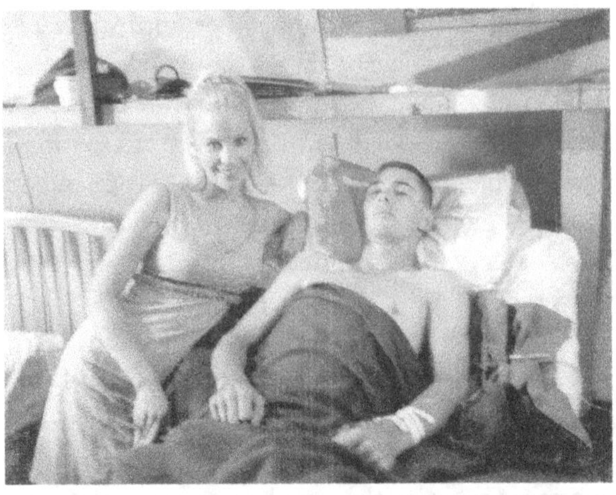

Hollywood actress Mary Grover visited wounded Marines at the naval hospital in Da Nang as part of a USO tour. She is seen here posing with L/Cpl. Dennis Fisher for a Polaroid photo on October 1, 1967. AUTHOR'S COLLECTION

Da Nang in the next day or two where I would be loaded on a C-141 medevac plane bound for Clark Air Force Base in the Philippines. I don't remember the exact timing for all this, but in a few days I was transported to the airport and was on my way to Clark AFB. I believe, but am not totally sure, that the hospital at Clark AFB served as an evaluation site for the wounded coming out of Vietnam. After the medical staff completed their evaluation, the wounded were then transferred to hospitals around the Pacific that specialized in various types of trauma. I remained there overnight, and the following day I was placed on another medevac plane bound for the naval hospital on Guam, where I arrived at 2210 hours on October 6, 1967. It was here that I would spend the next couple of months in Patient Ward A-3, healing and recovering my strength.

I was weighed as part of the check-in process, and much to my surprise, my weight had dropped from 195 to 165 pounds during the nine months I had been in Vietnam. Lots of exercise and living mostly on C-rations seemed like the primary cause. I don't think I had an ounce of fat on me when I arrived at the hospital. Other than my wounds, I was in pretty good shape. During the previous nine months I'd had a bout with dysentery and had a wisdom tooth removed at the field dental facility, but that was the extent of any medical complaints.

For the first week I was closely watched and examined daily. A Penrose drain protruded from the surgery site to prevent a buildup of fluids, and I was confined to bed, receiving Demerol shots every four hours for pain. Finally getting a chance to closely examine the wounds on my thigh and knee, I noted that one five- or six-inch incision connected the two wounds. The incision had then been sutured shut with stainless-steel wire. I had no feeling on the top of my leg between the knee and hip, which I attributed to some sort of nerve damage. But all in all, I considered myself pretty lucky. The wound on my foot was small and healing well.

All I could do now was try to enjoy some downtime. The nurse encouraged me to get out of bed as soon as possible and walk around our ward as best I could. The corpsmen and nurses were great and did all they could to make us comfortable and get us back in shape. One of the nurses told me that after I had healed up enough, I would be scheduled for physical therapy to regain the range of motion in my leg.

In the meantime, I was getting to know some of the other Marines who were there with me. We would kill time by playing cards, chess, or just talking about home. One thing I didn't do was photographically document my stay in hospital. All my personal and professional cameras were back in Vietnam, so I didn't have the wherewithal to record my time there.

The hospital also had a movie theater, and once I was able to get around, it provided some entertainment and a way to spend an afternoon. I became acquainted with a civilian patient named Tom Foye from Arlington, Virginia. Tom was with the Peace Corps in the Truk district and was in the hospital for observation. He had some great stories of his life in the South Pacific, which stood in stark contrast to what the rest of us on that ward had been experiencing. His tales of a tropical island and beautiful Micronesian women had us all ready to jump ship and head back with him.

Nearing the end of my time in the hospital, on November 19, Tom and I got liberty from the hospital and went into the interior of the island to the site of a tank battle from World War II, about 2,500 meters south of Nimitz Hill. We found three US tanks and three very shot-up Amtracs, but no Japanese equipment. These rusting hulks were ghostly reminders of the fighting that went on back in July and August 1944 that left nearly 1,800 Americans and over 18,000 Japanese dead. Little did Tom or I know at the time that a Japanese holdout from that battle was still roaming the island, and would not be captured until 1972.

As time went on and my leg was healing up, I went on liberty from the hospital more often. One day two young ladies came to the ward to visit with us. They were air force dependents of men who were stationed at Anderson AFB, located about fifteen miles away, at the north end of the island. Margaret Bock, one of these ladies, came to visit me several times and asked if I would like to go with her to Cocos Island. This was a small island off the southern tip of Guam that had been set up with recreational facilities for the servicemen stationed there. The navy ran a ferry service to and from the island, so on November 18, the day before Tom and I took our little excursion to the battlefield, Margaret and I were off for a day at the beach.

It was kind of surreal. Just six weeks before I had been out in the bush in the middle of a firefight, and now I was relaxing with a pretty young lady on a tropical island. We had a very nice day, and for just a little while I was able to forget about Vietnam. After returning to Vietnam we corresponded for a while, but the thing I remember most was her kindness at a time when I sorely needed it.

Shortly after our trip to Cocos Island, an air force officer came into our ward and asked if anyone would like to come up to Anderson AFB for a barbecue. I think Margaret must have told them about our situation, and their offer was quickly taken up by about a dozen of us who were well enough to leave the hospital. A bus arrived at the appointed hour the next day and we were off to visit the base. This was a B-52 base at the time, and they were flying Operation Arc Light bombing missions for us in Vietnam. While the grills were warming up, they took us out to the flight line for a close-up look at the B-52s. I had never seen one on the ground, especially one loaded with ordnance and ready to leave on a mission. They could carry 64,000 pounds of bombs both internally and on wing struts. That's a lot of 500- and 750-pound bombs.

After a tour of the flight line they took us to a room where they had laid out a number of aerial bomb damage assessment photos. Now it was our turn to point out land features and key elements in the photos and give them our assessment of the effectiveness of their missions.

But enough talk. We could smell the steaks cooking and were ready to sit down and enjoy some great food and a few beers. The air force outdid themselves in hosting this little soiree, and everyone had a wonderful time. The party finally came to an end in the late afternoon, and the bus arrived to return us to the hospital. We all skipped dinner that evening.

Promotion to corporal came while I was hospitalized. A naval officer came on the ward one day and said that he was there to present my promotion warrant and a letter from my CO, Captain George R. "Ron" Christmas. I never thought I would receive a promotion warrant while in pajamas. It took some of the dignity out of the proceedings, but did add a little to my bottom line and put me officially in the ranks of noncommissioned officers (NCOs).

I mention Captain Christmas because he was one of the best COs I had in Vietnam. He was later transferred to Hotel 2/5 and led his men during the thick of the fighting in Hue during the Tet Offensive. He was severely wounded during the battle and would receive the Purple Heart and the Navy Cross for heroism. The Navy Cross is one step below the

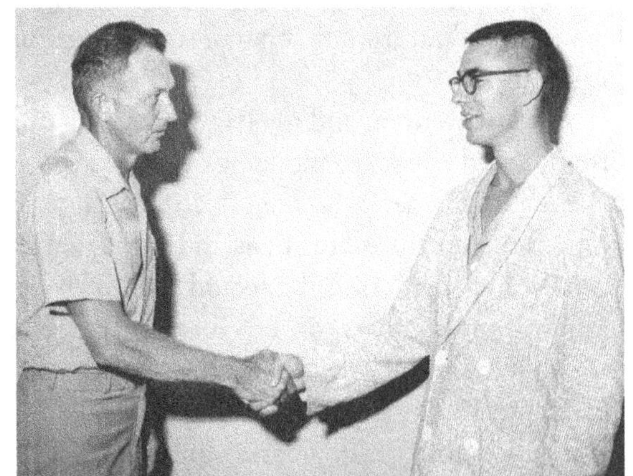

L/Cpl. Dennis Fisher is seen in this Polaroid photo being promoted to corporal while recovering from shrapnel wounds in the US naval hospital on Guam. AUTHOR'S COLLECTION

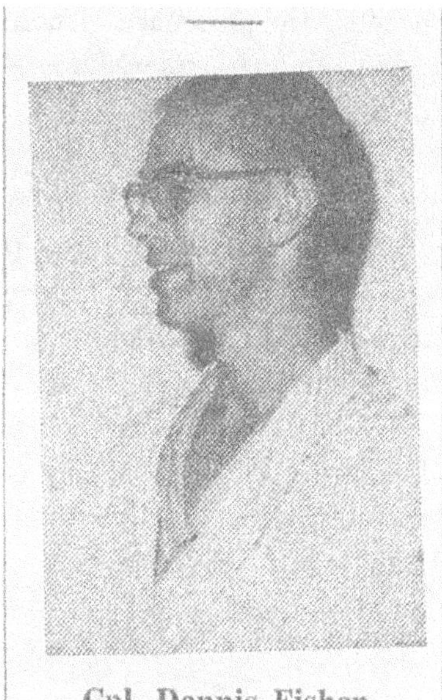

**Cpl. Dennis Fisher**

★ ★ ★

GUAM, Mariana Islands—Marine Corporal Dennis I. Fisher, son of Mr. and Mrs. Paul N Fisher of 309 W. Main St., Ligonier, was recently promoted to his present rank during ceremonies at the U.S. Naval Hospital in Guam.

Corporal Fisher was wounded last September while photographing combat operations near Da Nang, Vietnam. Following initial treatment at the U.S. Naval Hospital, Da Nang, he was air-evacuated to the U.S. Naval Hospital in Guam.

A newspaper clipping from the *Ligonier Echo*, L/Cpl. Dennis Fisher's hometown newspaper, reporting on his promotion and hospitalization. AUTHOR'S COLLECTION

Medal of Honor, and the highest award given by the US Navy/US Marine Corps. He survived and went on to attain the rank of lieutenant general (three stars).

Things were moving faster now, and a few days later, on November 22, nearly two months after being wounded, I was declared fit for duty, discharged from the hospital, and transferred to a casual transit company with the Marines on the naval base in Agana, Guam. I said good-bye to all the corpsmen and nurses and thanked them for taking care of me during my recovery. My expectation was that I would never see any of them again, and that was true, except for a corpsman named Ward. (More on that later.) Transportation arrived in a few minutes, and after a short ride to the base, I was checking in with Casual Company. Shortly thereafter I received orders back to Vietnam via Okinawa.

I arrived at Camp Butler on Okinawa on December 4. It was the stopping point for Marines going to or coming back from Vietnam. In the case of Marines like me who had been medevacked and were returning to Nam, it was also the point where we were reunited with all our personal effects. When a Marine was wounded and medevacked out of the country, a senior NCO would inventory and pack his personal belonging and ship them off to Okinawa, where they remained until he was either returned to duty in Vietnam or shipped to a hospital stateside.

My things had been stored in a footlocker and sea bag at my hooch in Da Nang when I was wounded. I went over to the warehouse where they were now stowed and looked through the contents to see if everything was there. I was very disappointed to see that all of my personal camera equipment was missing. Actually, I was a lot more than disappointed— I was pissed, and anxious to get back to my unit and find out who'd walked off with my equipment. On top of that, I saw some of my negatives protruding from a crack in the footlocker. Sadly, an unknown number of them had fallen out and were lost.

I retrieved my sea bag with all the essential things I needed. The personal effects in the footlocker needed a little repacking, and then I had the whole thing bound with metal bands to hold it together for the trip back to Vietnam. Now it was time to get ready for my flight.

Several buses arrived to take us to the airfield: one for junior enlisted men, and one for NCOs. As a new corporal, I proudly boarded the NCO bus. Sitting there lost in thought as others took their seats, I heard a loud booming voice call out "Well, if it isn't Private Fisher on my NCO bus." I knew that voice well. It was my senior drill instructor from boot camp, Staff Sergeant Richardson, who was on his way to Vietnam. I was surprised that he remembered me.

I flashed my corporal's stripes and jokingly told him I expected a little more respect out of him now. We had a nice chat on the way to airfield as I fielded his questions about what to expect in Vietnam. After a short wait in the terminal, we boarded the plane, and my return to Vietnam began.

# Chapter 6

# Back to Duty

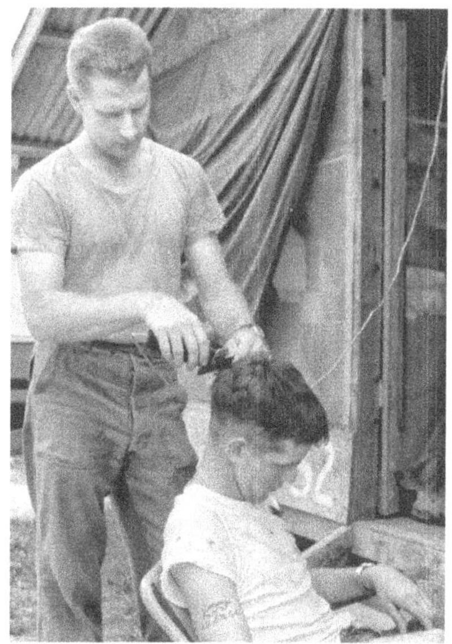

Cpl. Bill Page (left) gives Sgt. Jim Colton (right) a haircut outside their hooch at Headquarters Battalion, Service Company, at Da Nang, where both served as combat photographers with the 1st Marine Division. PHOTO BY CPL. DENNIS FISHER

An uneventful flight from Okinawa placed me back in Vietnam on December 7, and after hitching a ride for the short drive to the Photo Lab at 1st Division, I checked into my unit. The drive took me around the airfield, through Dog Patch, past the Freedom Hill PX, and into the Division Headquarters area, the same route I had taken a year ago when I first arrived in Vietnam. Everything was familiar and little had changed in my two-month absence.

Walking toward our hooches to drop off my gear, I was enthusiastically greeted by Corporal Bill Page. Before I even had a chance to ask, he said that too much stuff seemed to disappear on Okinawa, so they had kept my camera gear locked up in the lab until I returned. Thanking him, we headed over to the lab to see who was there and get caught up on the things that had been happening during my absence. Most notable was the appearance of many new faces around the lab, as well as some that were missing. The good news was that no one had been killed.

My stay here was destined to be a short one. The first thing I did after checking in was to submit a leave request.

I had previously extended my tour in Vietnam for six months in order to secure the transfer to the Combat Photo Section. Another bennie that came with the extension was thirty days of free leave anywhere I chose to go. Well, I wanted to go home for Christmas, and in no time I had orders in hand for

Pennsylvania. I immediately began the process of checking out. This should have been rather pro forma, since I had just checked in a few days earlier. The checkout with most sections went smoothly, as each was initialed off—until it came to my weapon.

All the equipment you are issued is listed on a five-by-seven "Memorandum Receipt for Individual/Garrison Equipment" card. When you were issued or turned in equipment, Supply pulled your card from their file, annotated the quantity of each item, and you initialed the entry. According to their records I still had my .45 pistol. I told the Supply clerk that I didn't need one in the hospital. He told me that I was checked out with the pistol and he wasn't going to sign off on my checklist until I turned it in.

The last place I had seen it was at Charlie Med when I got off the medevac and tossed it in a Conex box with the rest of my gear, two months ago. Off I went to Charlie Med to see what I could find, and sure enough, there in the box, lying in a pool of monsoon rain for the past several months, was my pistol. It was heavily rusted and adhering to the inside of the leather holster. I finally managed to extract it from the holster, remove the magazine, and eject the round from the chamber.

Back to the armory I went, where I told the clerk I had found the pistol and laid it on the counter. I had even rubbed off enough of the rust so he could read the serial number, but that wasn't enough. He wanted the whole pistol cleaned and ready to be reissued. This seemed like a pointless exercise, due to its deteriorated condition. I could see that I was getting nowhere with this guy. His behavior was typical of the way some rear echelon office pogues, who never saw a day of combat, would treat the men who came in from the field. In civilian life we would call them bean counters, but in the Marines, they were office pogues, or REMFs. To make a long story even longer, I told Warrant Officer Huntley what had happened. He went over to the armory and spoke with the unit commander, and soon, my checkout list was finally complete.

The day before my departure I was notified to report to the transit facility at Da Nang. I had my sea bag with clothes and a uniform plus a ditty bag with my orders, cameras, and personal items I would need for the trip. I hitched a ride with some army soldiers who dropped me off at the Freedom Hill PX on the way to airfield. They were heading out the Hill 37 and couldn't take me all the way to the transit facility.

I grabbed my gear out of the jeep, waved as they drove off, and decided to stop for a hamburger before seeking another ride to the airfield. As I was walking to the PX I heard a clanking sound coming from my ditty bag. I opened it up and found two bottles of Johnnie Walker Red Label Scotch. What the hell was going on here? It suddenly dawned on me that I had grabbed a ditty bag (these were sold in the PX and all looked the same) that belonged to one of the army guys. My orders, cameras, and other personal items were now on their way out to Hill 37, and if I wanted to get on the plane back to the States, retrieving them in pretty short order was a priority.

Hill 37 was the base I was operating out of when I was wounded, and finding the location was no problem. Getting there and back before my flight the next day was another matter. Asking around the PX quickly produced an offer for a ride to the transit facility at the airfield where I could check in and drop off my sea bag. The clerk checked me off on the manifest but said he needed a copy of my orders to actually let me board the plane. If it had just been the orders, I could have gone back to the Photo Lab and gotten another copy, but the cameras were another matter.

Once checked in, it was time to start looking for a ride to Hill 37. This was out in Indian country, and I didn't have a weapon, flak jacket, or helmet. Tracking down those soldiers to return their scotch and retrieve my cameras and orders was now my primary mission.

There wasn't much traffic on the road, and I was offered a ride by some Vietnamese who were driving an Esso gasoline tanker truck. Making it about halfway to Hill 37, they turned off in another direction. Motioning them to stop, in my best Vietnamese I said "Dung lai." The big truck rolled to a stop and I got out.

By now it was starting to get dark, and I was on a road that was frequently the site of ambushes and mine incidents. It was a lonely and scary feeling standing along the road with the light rapidly fading. When all hope seemed to have faded, a Mighty Mite appeared. I stepped out in the middle of the roadway to make sure the driver saw me in the dim light. It was a couple Marines returning to Hill 37, and they were rather perplexed to see me out on the road so close to nighttime, with no weapon. I explained the situation and they said they knew where the army had set up a comm site on the hill, and they dropped me off there. I was able to quickly locate the men who'd been wondering who had run off with their scotch, and we effected an exchange of ditty bags. Inquiring about a flight back to Da Nang, they said, "You're out of luck for today—the last admin run's been here and gone, but you should be able to get out in the morning."

My flight the next day was in the afternoon, so I had a reasonably good chance of making it. There was nothing to do now but wait, so I decided to see if I could locate any of the Marines from Lima 3/7 that I'd been with when wounded. I didn't find anyone, but a corporal was nice enough to point out a cot for the night. After a run to the chow hall, I crashed and quickly fell off to sleep. It had been an exciting day.

Early the next morning found me waiting at the LZ for any helicopters that might arrive. Before long a Huey landed and dropped off several men. A quick chat with the crew chief confirmed they were on their way to An Hoa, but he said they would be heading back to Da Nang after that stop. He motioned me on board and off we went. I made it back to the transit facility with three hours to spare. Thus began my trip back home for thirty days' leave and a return to the real world for a little while.

On December 15, I was on TWA Flight 94, leaving Los Angeles for the cross-country flight home. We landed at about 1700 hours, the sun already below the horizon, the winter landscape of western Pennsylvania bathed in a warm afterglow of light.

It was good to be home.

# Chapter 7

# Home for the Holidays

MY MOM AND DAD WERE AT THE AIRPORT IN PITTSBURGH TO GREET ME, AND IT SURE was good to see them again. There were lots of hugs, and I could see the relief in their eyes that I was home. During the hour-long ride home to Ligonier they filled me in on all the latest town news, and I brought them up to date on my recent hospitalization. When we arrived home, all my brothers and sisters were there to greet me with a lot of questions about my experiences in Vietnam. The house was already decorated for Christmas and the joy of that season was definitely in the air. With jet lag washing over me, I crashed early that night, back in my own bed and a world away from Vietnam.

The cold and snow of a Pennsylvania winter contrasted significantly with the tropical climate I had become accustomed to. Although I settled into the routine of being back with my family, things had changed for me. It's hard to put into words, but I was not the same person that had excitedly headed off to boot camp a year and a half ago. The war had left its mark, and I could never get back the innocence of the high school boy that went off to college in 1965. In its place was a maturity born of war, hardship, and suffering, recorded on the film in my camera and etched forever on my mind. Physically I was home, but mentally I was still in Nam. Immersing myself in holiday activities helped keep my mind off the war, and I spent the month catching up with my family and visiting with high school friends who were home from college.

I had been itching for a new motorcycle during my time in Vietnam, and in early January my dad and I headed over to Greensburg to the local Triumph dealer, where I bought a brand-new shiny red 1968 Triumph Bonneville. After a few instructions on the controls and starting procedures, I rode it home in a snowstorm. She was a beauty, and although this wasn't exactly ideal riding weather, I did get a few days to ride it around town before putting her away in the basement to await my return.

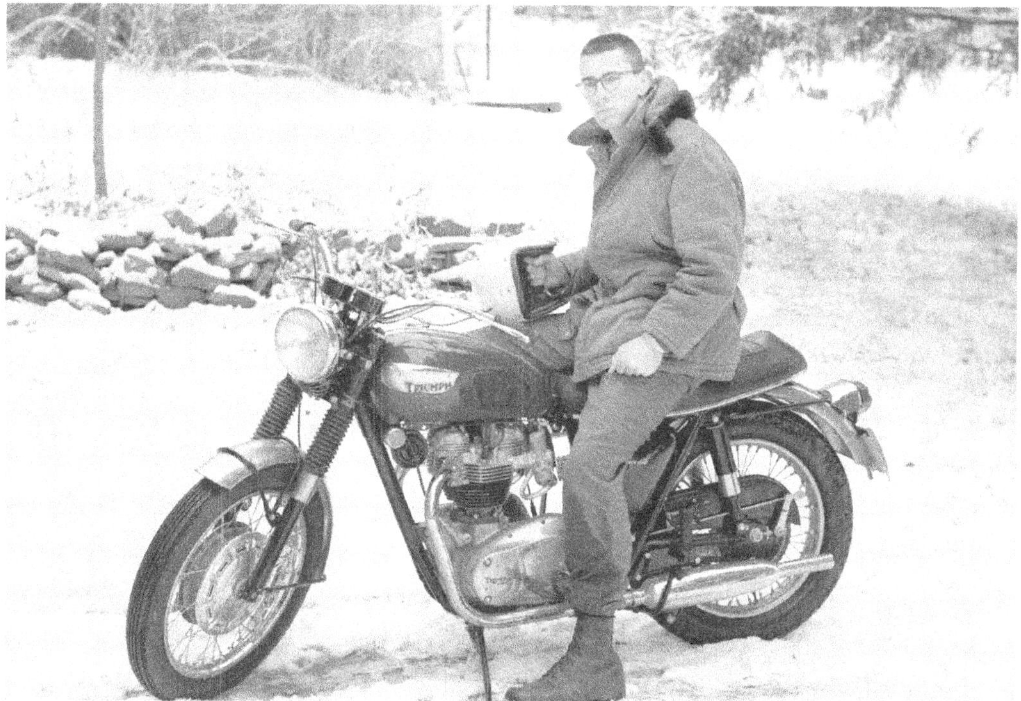

Cpl. Dennis Fisher shows off his new 1968 Triumph Bonneville while home on leave in Ligonier, Pennsylvania, in January 1968, after being hospitalized for shrapnel wounds. PHOTO BY PAUL FISHER/ AUTHOR'S COLLECTION

I really don't recall a lot of other details from this trip and don't have a journal of that time to refresh my memory. I remember the Christmas Eve church service at the Pioneer Presbyterian Church, where my church family welcomed me back with hugs and handshakes. On returning home after the service, my mom prepared homemade cinnamon rolls and hot chocolate for the family. I remember walking around the Diamond and admiring the Christmas decorations. Visiting my friends Charlie Stahl and Jake Grimm at Fort Ligonier brought back memories from two years ago when I was there, working for Jake, who led the archaeological investigation at the fort, and Charlie was the groundskeeper. Jake was busy with Christmas preparations but asked me to come back after the holidays to look at the latest artifacts they had unearthed at the fort.

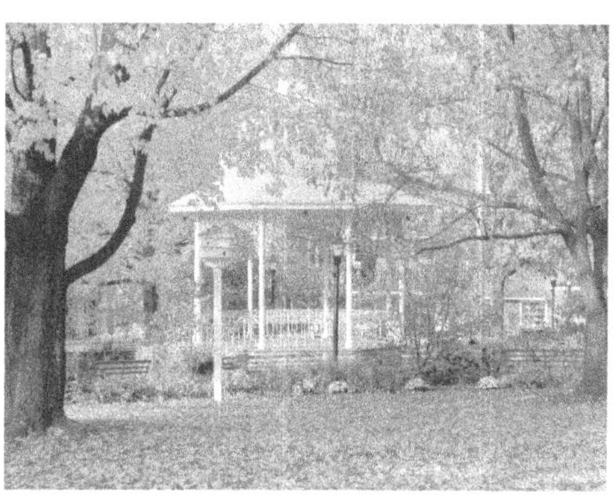

The bandstand on the Diamond town center at Ligonier, Pennsylvania, in the fall. PHOTO BY CPL. DENNIS FISHER

Charlie was a Korean War Marine veteran, and he opened up to me about his experiences in Korea. Considering me a fellow combat veteran, he felt it was okay to share what he'd gone through, as he knew I would understand. I went up the street to Butch's house (Sergeant Lucien Moscinski) to see if he might be home for the holidays, but if I remember right, his mom said he was at his base in California. I'd lost track of him after I transferred to Photo, and I believe his tour was about up by then, and he probably rotated back to the States.

My brother and I were walking around town one evening when we happened upon a group of Christmas carolers from the Methodist church singing "Silent Night." I reflected back on my previous Christmas, which was spent on the *Gaffey* at Okinawa. I began pondering how many of the five thousand Marines who had sailed with me were now dead or wounded. The true purpose of the Christmas holiday seemed to be crowded out of my mind by thoughts of Vietnam.

The weather had moderated a little, and I took the opportunity to visit more friends. On my return Harriette, my sister, was waiting for me with a telegram in her hand. This was back in the days before the Internet and e-mail. Telegrams were the official method of communication, and this one was directing me to report to Travis AFB in California for transit to Vietnam on January 17, my twenty-first birthday. While I'd known my return to Vietnam was imminent, as it had all been spelled out in my orders, now it was real. It was time to head back to the war.

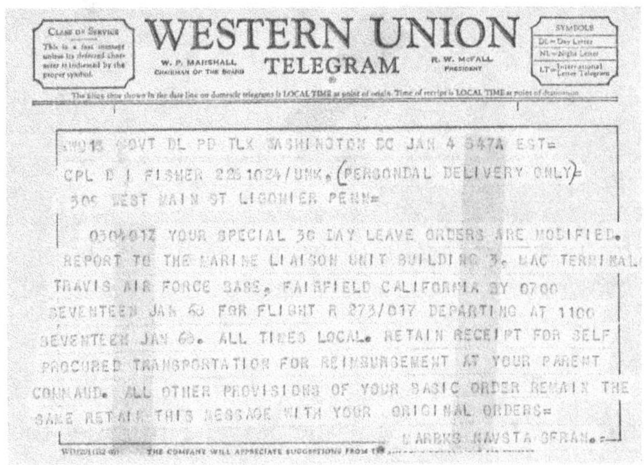

A telegram directing Cpl. Fisher to report to Travis AFB for transit to Vietnam. AUTHOR'S COLLECTION

My parents drove me to the Pittsburgh airport, and amid more hugs and tears, it was time to depart once again. On January 16, my flight lifted off into the blackness of a cold winter night as I began my journey west to California. A short drive from San Francisco brought me to Travis AFB the following morning, and within a few hours I was winging my way back across the Pacific.

Sitting in the comfort of a big jet airliner, thoughts of my leave at home and how quickly it had gone by were rapidly giving way to those of my return to Vietnam, upon which I would still have seven more months to go. Seven months doesn't seem like a long time, but over there it seemed like a lifetime. A lot could happen in seven months, or for that matter, in seven minutes. It would turn out that 1968 would see the most intense combat of the war, and in a few weeks I would be right in the middle of it.

# Chapter 8

# Foxtrot 2/7

I arrived at the Da Nang airfield via Okinawa and stepped out into the hot, humid air under a light rain. This was a big change from the Pennsylvania winter I'd just left. I grabbed my bag and hitched a ride over to the Photo Lab at 1st Division Headquarters. It was like coming home amid the warm greetings and familiar faces. I was back, and ready to get to work.

The next few days were spent checking in and getting equipment issued. Tet was coming up, and the Vietnamese, both sides, had previously declared a truce during the Lunar New Year holiday so soldiers could take some leave and see their families. It was very much like our Christmas holiday in that respect. Usually things were pretty slow this time of year, and as major combat operations slowed, so did our photo work. My expectations were that I would have a month, from the middle of January to the middle of February, to get reacclimated and get back in the routine of covering the war. I hadn't been on an operation since I was wounded at the end of September, three and half months ago.

Shortly after my return we had a barbecue out behind the lab, and with nearly everyone in from the field, it was a fun get-together. Having been in the hospital for two months and then home on leave for another, I'd missed the arrival of a new influx of photographers. There were a number of new faces in the crowd, almost making me feel like the new guy. Fortunately there were still

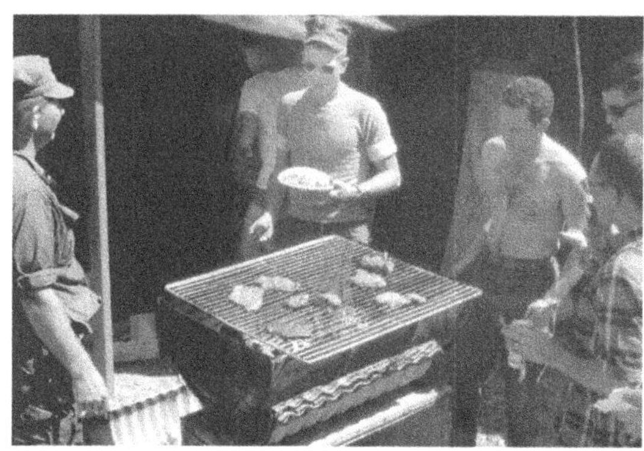

SSgt. Mo Upton prepares steaks for the Combat Photo Section of the 1st Marine Division during some downtime just prior to the Tet Offensive in January 1968 in Da Nang. PHOTO BY CPL. DENNIS FISHER

enough of the "old-timers" to make me feel at home. The food was great, and we all had a chance to relax for the day.

The barbecue was a great welcome home, and I looked forward to a relaxing reintegration into the role of combat photographer. But all thoughts of slowly getting back into the swing of things came to crashing halt when the NVA launched a series of nationwide attacks throughout South Vietnam in the early-morning hours of January 30, 1968. Within a couple weeks of arriving back in country, the Tet Offensive burst upon the scene, and some of the worst fighting of the war began, with an intensity that hadn't previously occurred in Vietnam. Just sixty miles north of us, Hue was being overrun, and the MACV Compound in that city was under siege. Corporal John Pennington and Sergeant Bill Dickman, and maybe a few others whom I've forgotten, were sent up to cover that action there.

Part of that assault was a rocket attack on the Da Nang airfield and as quick as I could grab my cameras, I was on a CH-46 with Corporal J. J. Crites, en route to Foxtrot 2/7, where we joined up with 1st Platoon. They were hot on the trail of the retreating VC who had launched the attack, and we soon caught up with them—or at least, their rear security.

We were traveling through thick undergrowth in single file, and the twisty, winding nature of the trail limited visibility. As our point man rounded a bend he came face-to-face with a VC. The encounter ended quickly in a short exchange of gunfire. I heard the shooting and made my way to his position and began taking photos.

The VC was lying lifeless on his back as the lieutenant and one of the sergeants went through his belongings. The pursuit of the rest of the VC more or less ended there, as the grunts stopped to check the body for documents or anything that Intel could use. Crites, who was fairly religious as I recall, asked if we were going to bury the dead VC. The grunts overhead this and a look of bemusement spread across their faces. One jokingly offered to lend Crites his e-tool. Although Crites was new, and this may have been the first dead VC he had seen, the sight

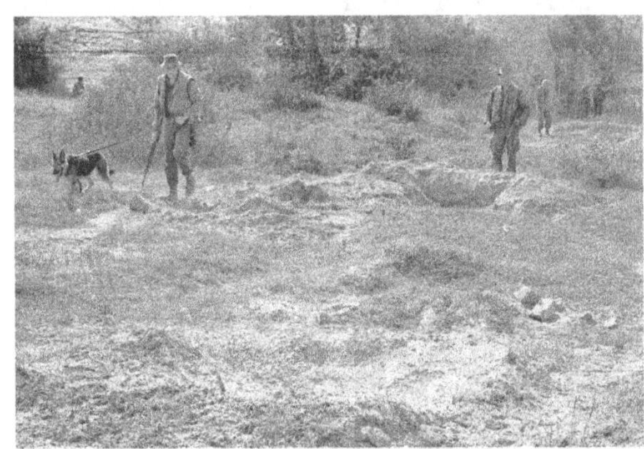

Marines sweep through a rocket launch site following an attack on the Da Nang airfield in February 1968. PHOTO BY CPL. DENNIS FISHER

of the dead and wounded would become common during the upcoming year.

The patrol continued until late in the afternoon without any further contact, so Corporal Crites and I returned to base.

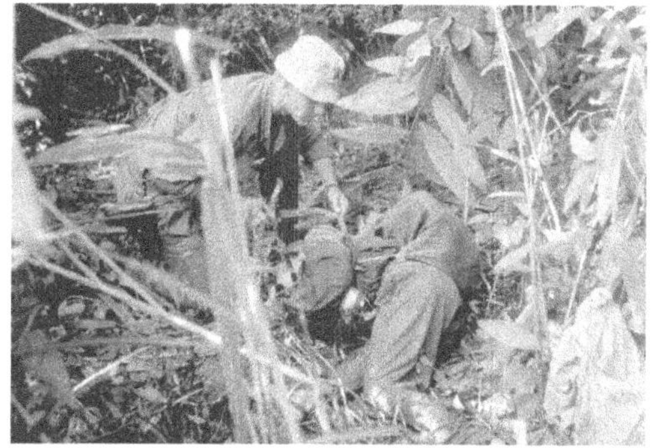

A Viet Cong killed by Marines from Foxtrot 2/7 following a rocket attack on the Da Nang airfield in February 1968. PHOTO BY CPL. DENNIS FISHER

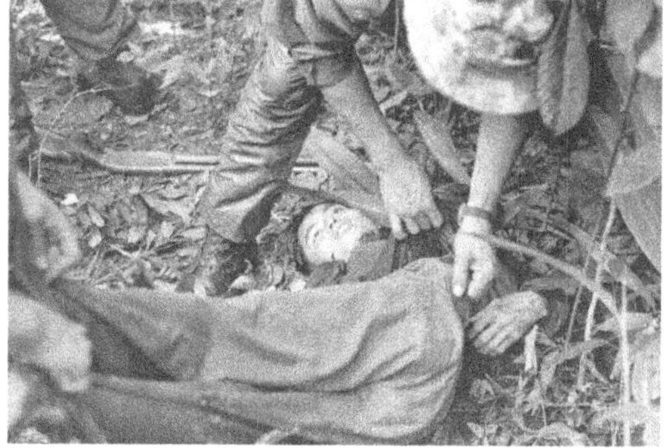

Marines from Foxtrot 2/7 search the body of a dead Viet Cong for documents or anything that would be of value to intelligence analysts following a rocket attack on the Da Nang airfield in February 1968. PHOTO BY CPL. DENNIS FISHER

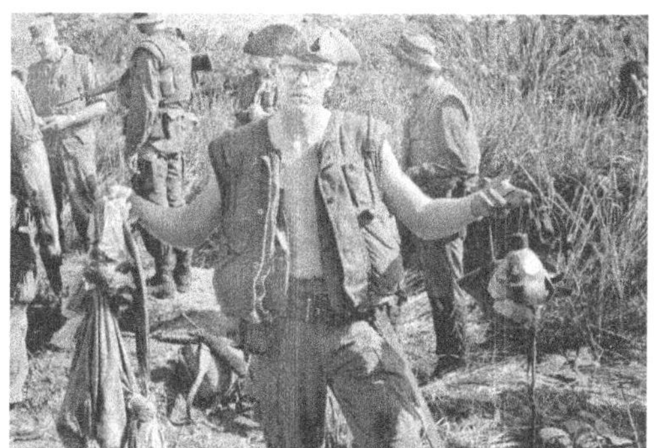

A Marine from Foxtrot 2/7 displays the pack and canteen removed from the Viet Cong killed following a rocket attack on Da Nang in February 1968. PHOTO BY CPL. DENNIS FISHER

The 3rd Marine Division had their headquarters at Phu Bai, just eight miles south of Hue, along with their Division Photo Lab. They were providing the bulk of the photo coverage for the operations between there and the DMZ. Try as I might to get sent up there, Top Brown reminded me that the 3rd Division had that area covered. For the next couple of weeks, I was covering three- to four-day infantry sweeps and reconnaissance in force patrols with the 7th Marines, but no big named operations. Not much contact.

Top Brown finally relented and told me that around the middle of February, I would be transferred up to Phu Bai, along with some of the combat correspondents from ISO, to join Task Force X-Ray. Our unit was too shorthanded to let me go just then. He also informed me that he had sent a letter to CMC (Commandant of the Marine Corps) requesting that my primary MOS be changed from 0311 infantry rifleman to 4631 still photographer. I was really stoked to hear that, as it confirmed in my mind they had confidence in my abilities as a photographer. He also let me know that my rotation date to return to the States had been set for August 16. That was half a year away, and with all that was going on, it seemed like a really long time. A lot could—and did—happen in the ensuing six months.

# CHAPTER 9

# Operation Rock

## *Dai Loc*

BY THE BEGINNING OF MARCH, 1968, COMBAT OPERATIONS WERE PICKING UP AROUND Da Nang. My transfer north to Task Force X-Ray at Phu Bai had been put on hold. Instead, I was sent back out to the 7th Marines to cover Operation Rock, a search-and-destroy mission, with Lima 3/7. The op was scheduled to run from March 6 through 10 in the area between Dai Loc and An Hoa. This was the same unit I was with when wounded the previous September.

March 5 found me in the back of a deuce and a half with some other Marines, headed along Route 14 out to Hill 37 at Dai Loc, where I would join them. Checking in with Captain Shaver, the Lima Company CO, I told him I was with Division Photo and had been sent out to cover his unit on the op. He welcomed me and said he would let the platoon commanders know I would be traveling with them. He proceeded to give me a quick overview of Operation Rock and pointed me in the direction of 1st Platoon.

I asked around for 1st Squad, the "Dirty Dozen" I'd been with the previous September. Finding them nearby, I met the squad leader, Corporal Arnold Kirk. The op was due to kick off the following morning, March 6, and I wanted a chance to talk with the men and find out more about their part in the op. In the roughly six months since I had been with them, only two men remained from the original squad. Most had completed their tours and gone stateside, and a few were recovering from wounds. The turnover in the infantry units was high, and this was a prime example.

Operation Rock was a battalion-size operation that included Hotel, India, and Lima companies from 3/7, plus elements of the army's 5th Armored Cavalry. Kirk told me it was being conducted in the Foster area. I hadn't heard about Operation Foster and asked him about it. He told me it happened last November, while I was in the hospital, after the VC had attacked the district headquarters and several nearby refugee camps. They had killed a number of civilians and destroyed over five hundred homes, leaving many families

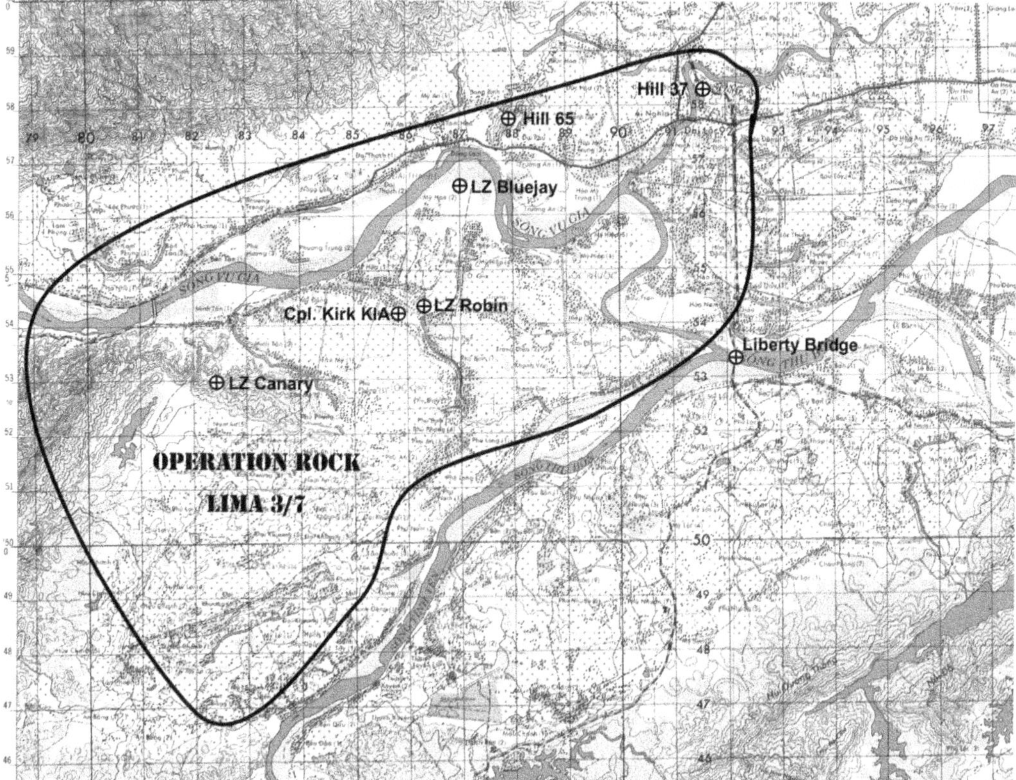


The Operation Rock area was the site of Operation Arizona in 1967 and, more recently, Operation Foster.

homeless. There hadn't been a lot of fighting recently, but they did find and destroy many tunnels and bunkers, as well as capturing enough rice to feed an army, fifty or sixty tons from what he heard later.

Once he'd described the area we were going to, I recognized it as what we'd called Arizona territory after an even earlier operation that was in progress when I'd joined the Combat Photo Section in June of the previous year. After our brief chat, I headed down to the chow hall to grab a bite to eat and get ready for the op.

We boarded CH-46s at Hill 37 around 1000 hours the next morning and were flown to LZ Bluejay in the operational area. I began taking photographs even though there wasn't too much going on yet. Everyone was in good spirits as we crossed some rice paddies and moved into a village. We began encountering local villagers and tried to move them to the rear in case fighting should erupt. Many of them had been relocated to refugee camps but for various reasons had moved back. The interpreters became suspicious of a few young men and they were detained, but other than that, the op was starting off rather quiet.

That didn't last long.

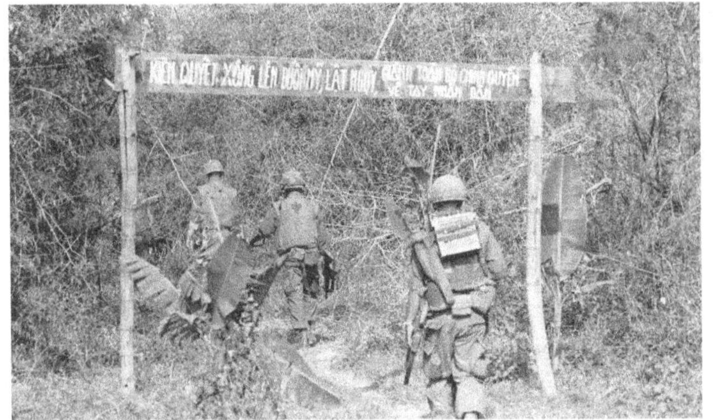

Marines enter a village under a Viet Cong sign during Operation Rock on March 6, 1968. The sign was meant for the local Vietnamese, and translated, reads, "Resolutely rush forward to defeat the Americans, overthrow the puppet regime, and win the entire government back to the people." PHOTO BY CPL. DENNIS FISHER

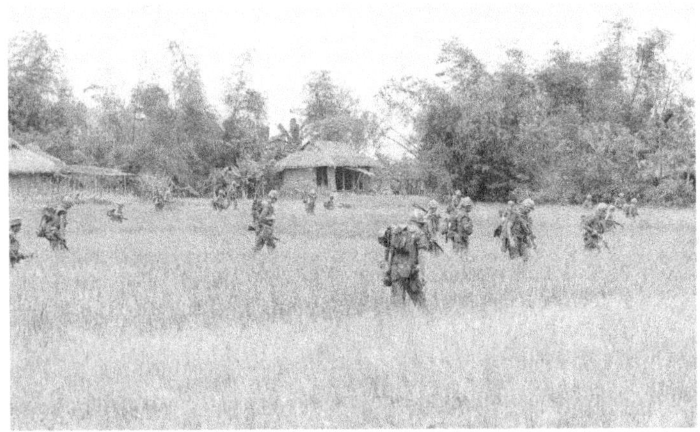

Marines from Lima Company 3/7 sweep through a village near Dai Loc in search of a Viet Cong base camp during Operation Rock on March 6, 1968. PHOTO BY CPL. DENNIS FISHER

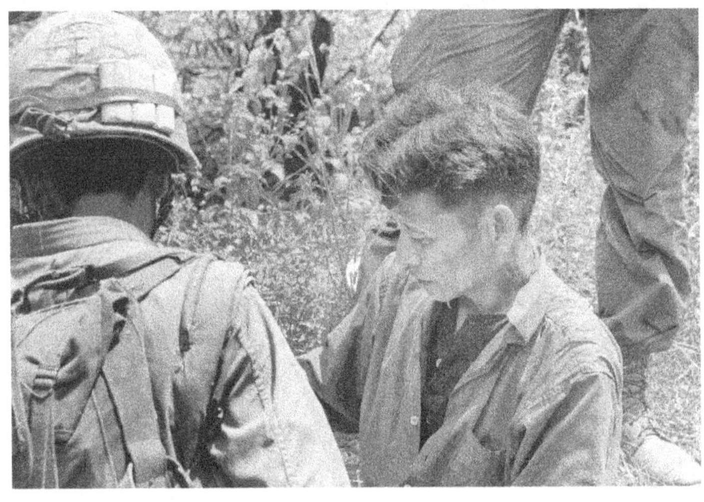

A Marine from Lima 3/7 checks the identification of a Vietnamese man during Operation Rock near Dai Loc on March 6, 1968. PHOTO BY CPL. DENNIS FISHER

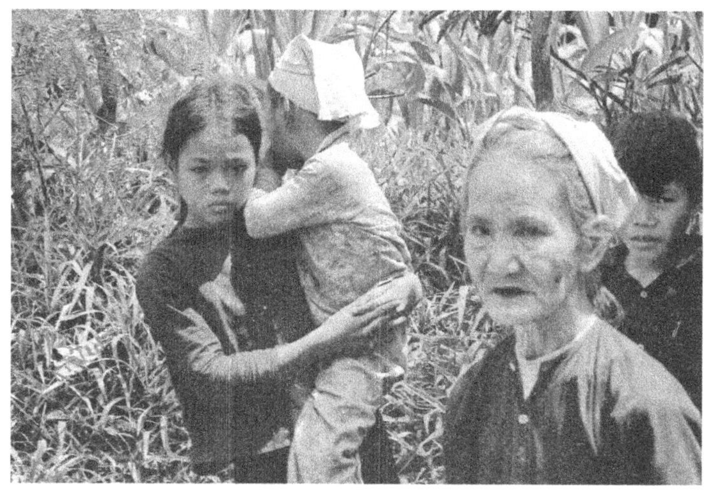

Vietnamese refugees being moved to safety during Operation Rock near Dai Loc on March 6, 1968.
PHOTO BY CPL. DENNIS FISHER

We heard that India Company had been in contact and lost one man KIA. By early afternoon we were in contact and receiving incoming small arms fire, mostly sniper fire, and had one man wounded. Artillery support and air strikes began pounding the enemy positions and chased them out of the area. After that, things quieted down again, but we knew the enemy was close by.

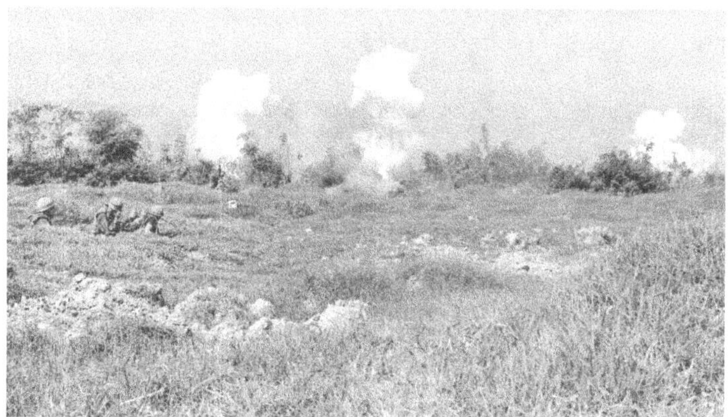

Marines from Lima 3/7 take cover as air strikes soften up enemy positions in a tree line during Operation Rock on March 6, 1968, near Dai Loc. PHOTO BY CPL. DENNIS FISHER

I ran into Corporal R. J. "Del" Del Vecchio, a friend and fellow combat photographer from my unit, who was also covering the op. We chatted for a while and filled each other in on the activities we had witnessed thus far. But we didn't have long to talk, as the grunts were beginning to move toward their next objective. So I bid him farewell with a promise to meet up back at the lab after the op concluded. As I started to leave, he took a couple of photos of me and gave a thumbs-up.

We swept toward the enemy's location and eventually arrived in the area that had been hit with the artillery and air strikes. It was now getting late in the day, so we settled in for the night and established a night defensive perimeter. The chances of being mortared during the night were pretty good, so everyone was ordered to dig in. Several tanks had joined us in the afternoon and they stayed with us that night, providing some serious firepower should the need arise.

As soon as it started to get dark we began receiving incoming small arms fire and heavy mortar rounds. I stopped counting at twenty, but I think we were hit with at least twice that number. This continued until almost midnight, leaving one man dead and four others wounded. Once the mortars stopped I half expected that a night attack was coming, but that didn't materialize, and things were more or less quiet until morning. None of us got much sleep.

The morning of the second day, March 7, dawned hazy, and after the events of the night before, everyone was on high alert. We realized

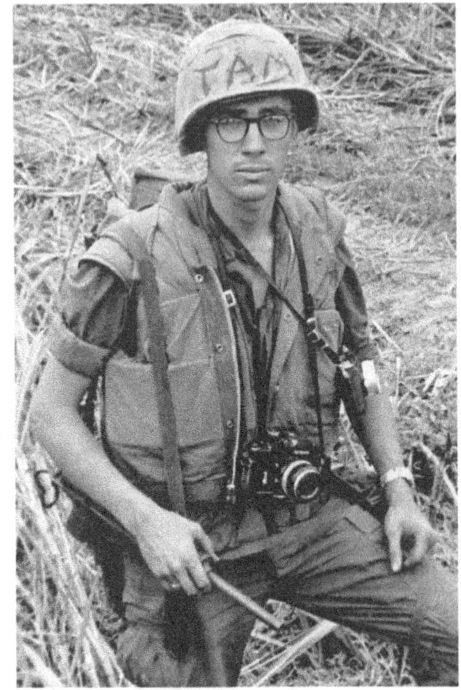

Cpl. Dennis Fisher during a lull in the fighting as he provided photo coverage of Lima 3/7 during Operation Rock on March 6, 1968. PHOTO BY CPL. R. J. DEL VECCHIO/ AUTHOR'S COLLECTION

the enemy knew where we were. The tanks fired up their engines and departed early. Finishing up a cold C-ration breakfast, I went looking for Corporal Kirk to find out what was planned for the day. Everyone had saddled up and was ready to move out when he came back from speaking with the platoon commander. Kirk passed on information about our first objective to the squad, along with what was planned for the platoon that day.

The men had begun moving toward that objective when the enemy opened up on us, and all hell broke loose. Caught by surprise, automatic weapons fired from a bamboo hedge line about thirty to fifty yards away on the other side of a dry rice paddy broke the calm of the morning. We were caught in the open, and men were diving for any cover they could find. Those who couldn't find any hit the deck and played dead in hopes that the enemy would concentrate on someone else.

Without hesitation, I took a running jump into a nearby bomb crater and landed near Corporal Curiel, one of the 60mm mortar crew members. Instinctively checking my camera settings, I began taking photos of the action around me. The Marines behind us shot over our heads at the enemy, who continued to return fire back at them. Several incoming mortar rounds landed among the men caught out in the open, wounding ten of them. The sound of the M60s, M16s, and M79s rose to a loud crescendo as our fire superiority soon gained the upper hand. The enemy pulled out, leaving their rear security to cover the retreat.

As I peered out of the bomb crater I saw John Bachelor, our grenadier, firing his blooper at the Viet Cong's position. Suddenly he ran from cover, grabbed one of the wounded men, and dragged him off the field and into the bomb crater. It was Corporal Kirk. John was calling for a corpsman as he approached us, and one arrived quickly.

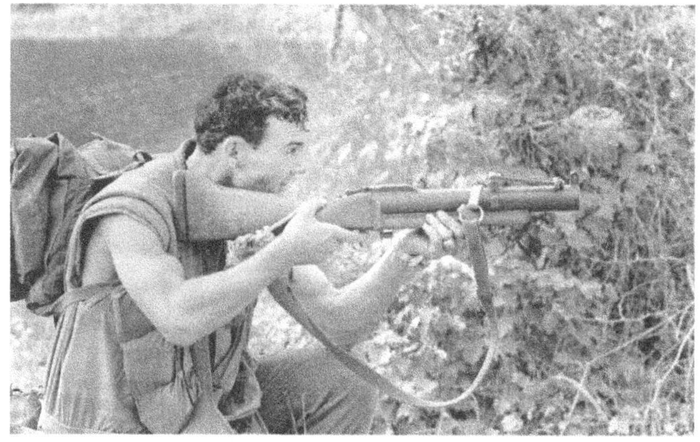

Corporal John Bachelor, with Lima 3/7, firing on Viet Cong position with his blooper (M79 grenade launcher) during an Operation Rock firefight on the morning of March 7, 1968, near Dai Loc. PHOTO BY CPL. DENNIS FISHER

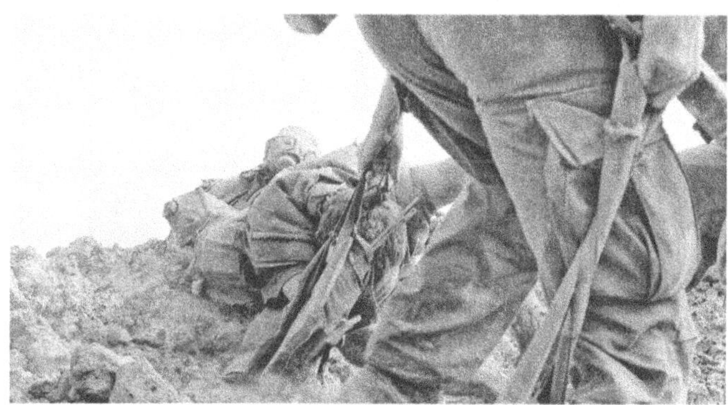

Corporal John Bachelor drags wounded Marine Cpl. Arnold Kirk out of the line of fire during an Operation Rock firefight on the morning of March 7, 1968, near Dai Loc. Both Marines were with Lima Company 3/7. PHOTO BY CPL. DENNIS FISHER

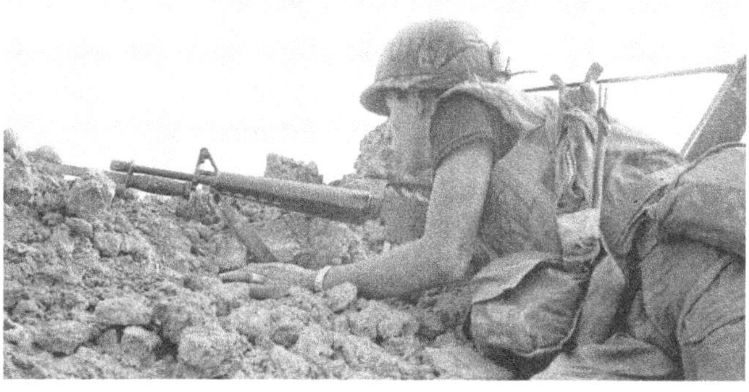

Cpl. Curiel, a mortarman with Lima 3/7, preparing to leave the cover of a bomb crater in a firefight during Operation Rock, March 7, 1968. PHOTO BY CPL. DENNIS FISHER

In fact, the corpsman was right behind him, and quickly decided that the steep walls of the crater and torn-up earth was no place to try and work on Kirk. The shooting had pretty much stopped by now, so all four of us—the corpsman, the grenadier, the mortarman, and the photographer—grabbed Kirk by the limbs and took him to level ground. We couldn't see any wounds and wondered what was wrong. After stripping off his 782 gear (helmet, flak jacket, weapon, etc.), the source of his wounds became apparent when his cartridge belt was removed. This tight-fitting web belt had been acting like a pressure dressing on the bullet wounds he had received right through it.

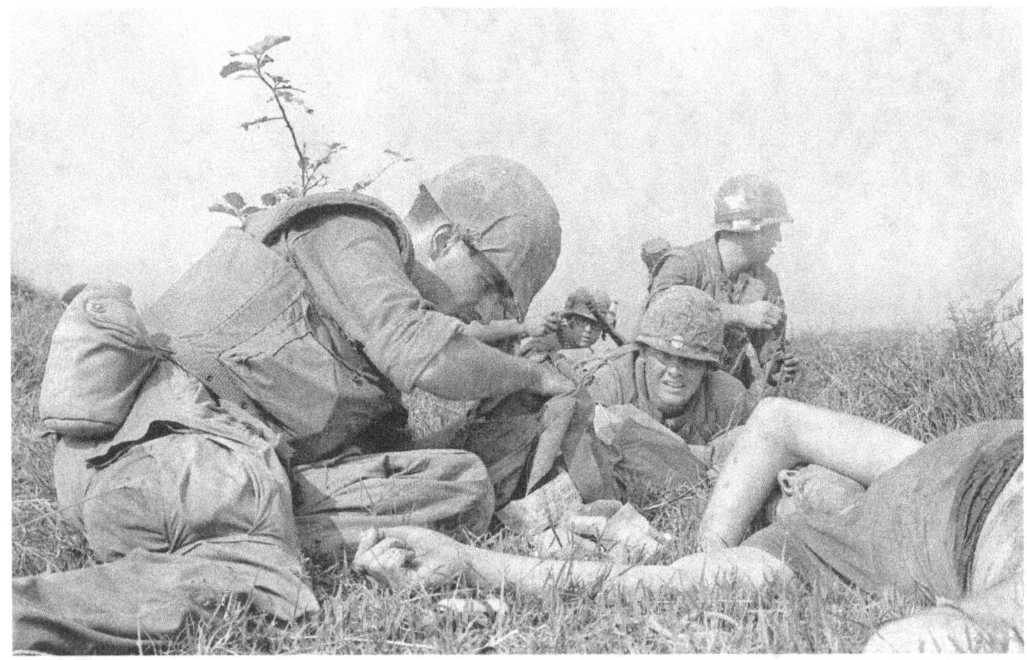

A corpsman treating Marine Cpl. Arnold Kirk from Lima 3/7, who was wounded in an ambush during Operation Rock on the morning of March 7, 1968, near Dai Loc. PHOTO BY CPL. DENNIS FISHER

Corporal Curiel left to join up with the rest of the 60mm mortar team and began firing on the enemy. John left to pursue the Viet Cong, and I stayed for a few minutes to help the corpsman while awaiting a medevac chopper for all the wounded. The platoon commander directed an M60 machine-gun team and some grunts to protect us and set up security for the landing zone in preparation for the arrival of the medevac.

At this point it looked like we were losing Kirk. His veins had collapsed, and the corpsman was having a hard time starting an IV. He asked me to start mouth-to-mouth resuscitation, taking over once the IV was in place. I held the IV bag.

Kirk seemed to be going into shock. His breathing became irregular, and things did not look good. The corpsmen were not supplied with adrenaline, so there wasn't much else

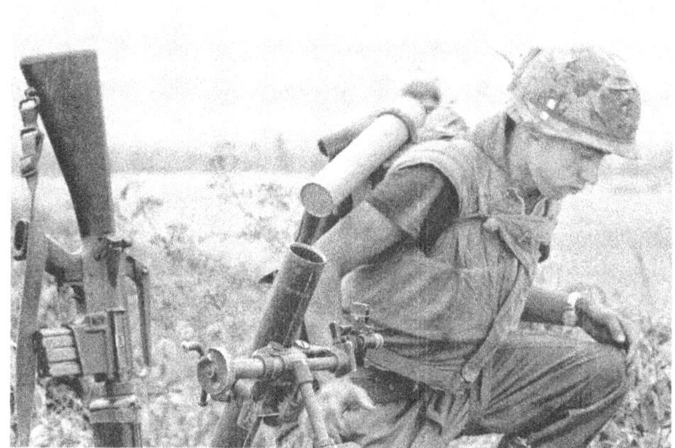

Cpl. Curiel, a 60mm mortarman with Lima 3/7, fires on the enemy during a firefight, Operation Rock, March 7, 1968, near Dai Loc. PHOTO BY CPL. DENNIS FISHER

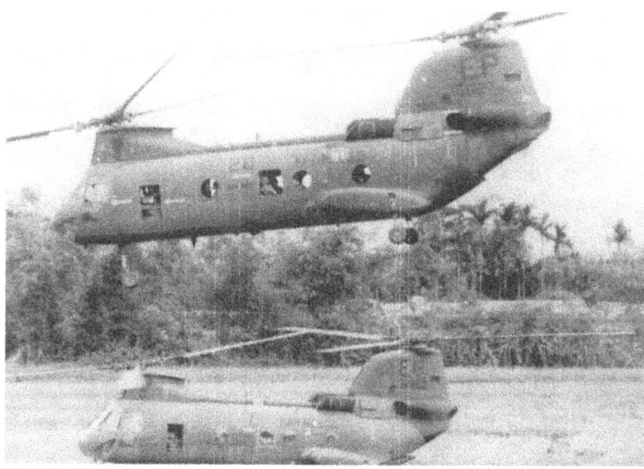

A CH-46 Sea Knight helicopter provides medevac for wounded Marines from Lima 3/7 following a morning ambush and firefight on March 7, 1968, during Operation Rock, near Dai Loc. PHOTO BY CPL. DENNIS FISHER

that could be done other than getting him medevacked back to the hospital. Soon more help arrived, and I left to rejoin the unit as they pursued the retreating VC. The rest of the wounded were being attended to by another corpsman and moved toward the LZ as they awaited the medevac.

At this point I moved to the 60mm mortar team's position and resumed taking photos of the battle. As best I recall, seven of the ten who were wounded were medevacked and the other three were patched up and continued on the op. I only spent a day with Corporal Kirk, but I was very comfortable with his leadership abilities, and quite frankly, the 7th Marines were about as tough an outfit as I had ever photographed.

This day did not turn out very well for Lima 3/7, and the commander decided around 1800 hours to load us on helicopters and take the unit to Hill 65 at An Hoa. With two dead and fourteen wounded out of just that one company, we were pulled out of the field and held in reserve for the night. At the time, I didn't realize what was going on and stayed with the platoon as they boarded the choppers. The night was uneventful, but I was left pondering the events of the day as I tried to get some sleep. The ambush was a close call, and left me wondering if I would make it to the end of my tour.

Bright and early the next morning we were back on the helicopters, returning to the op, where the company was positioned as a blocking force. One platoon was sent out with Hotel and India companies to conduct search-and-destroy operations, and I went with them. The following days were spent sweeping through the area, destroying tunnels, bunkers, and enemy supplies. Shortly after noon on March 10, Lima Company came across eight freshly dug graves that contained the bodies of VC killed during the fighting. About the same time, we got word over the radio that the op was being ended. In the midafternoon, I joined up with 1st Platoon and we were helicoptered out. The rest of the company, along with the CP group, continued to another location on Amtracs.

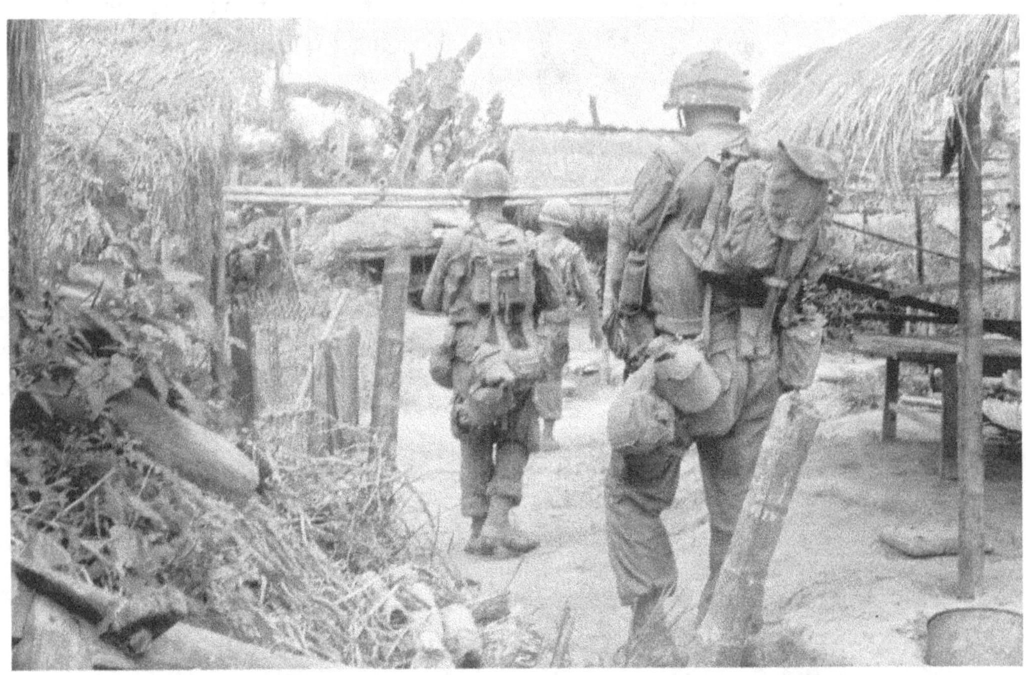

Marines from Lima 3/7 sweep through an enemy base camp during Operation Rock on March 8, 1968, near Dai Loc. PHOTO BY CPL. DENNIS FISHER

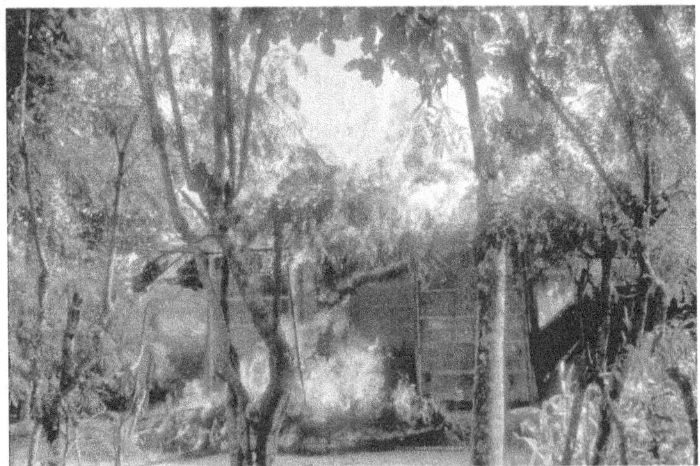

Marines from Lima 3/7 destroy an enemy base camp discovered during Operation Rock on March 8, 1968, near Dai Loc. PHOTO BY CPL. DENNIS FISHER

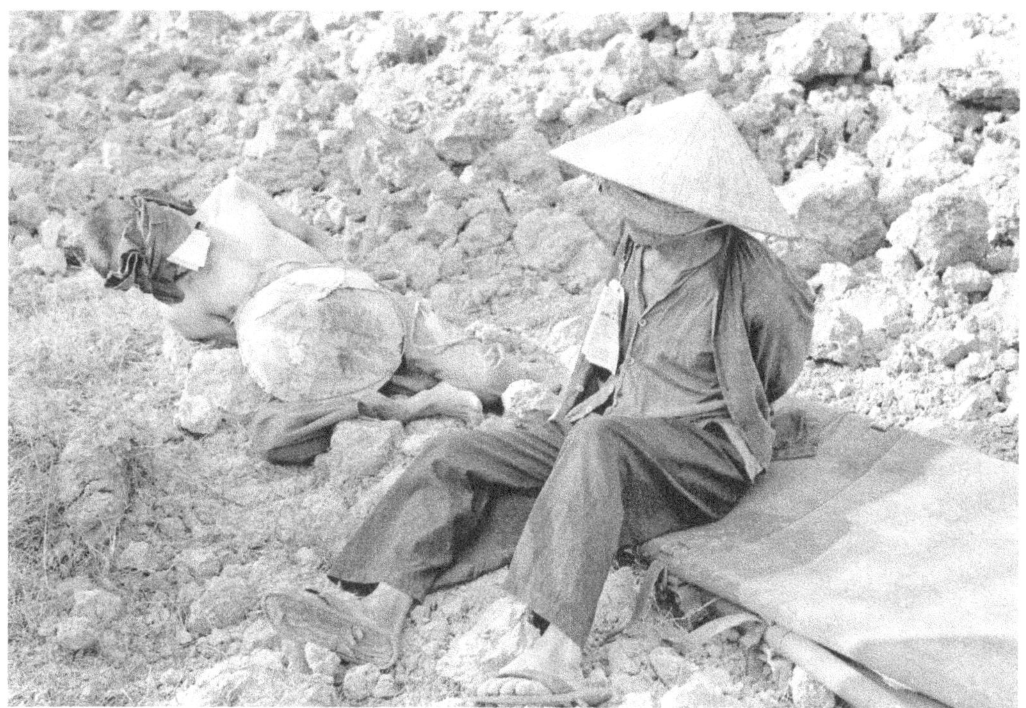

Captured Viet Cong await transportation to the rear for interrogation during Operation Rock on March 8, 1968, near Dai Loc. PHOTO BY CPL. DENNIS FISHER

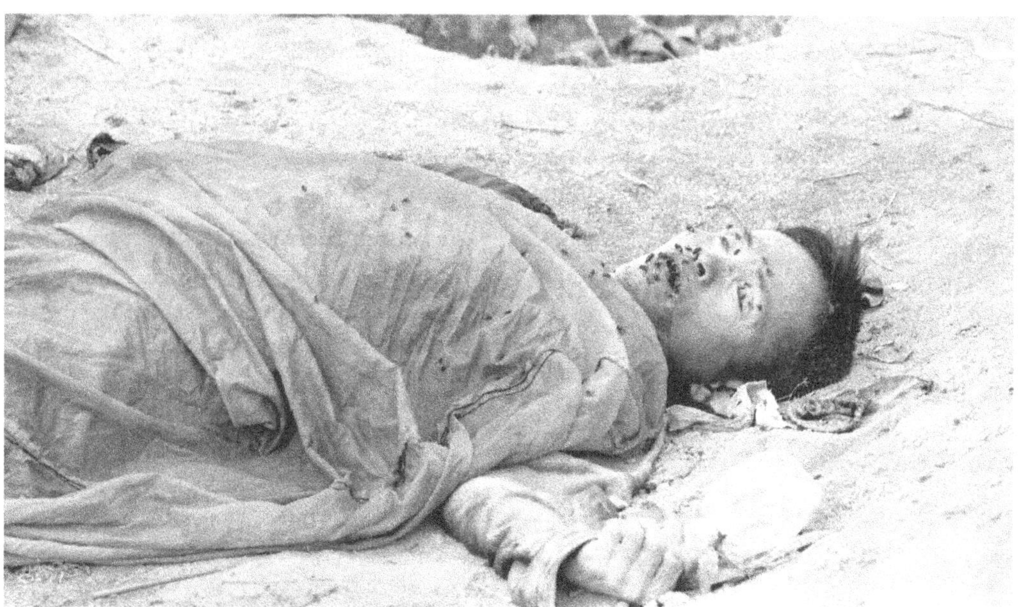

Marines encounter the enemy dead left behind by retreating Viet Cong during Operation Rock on March 8, 1968, near Dai Loc. PHOTO BY CPL. DENNIS FISHER

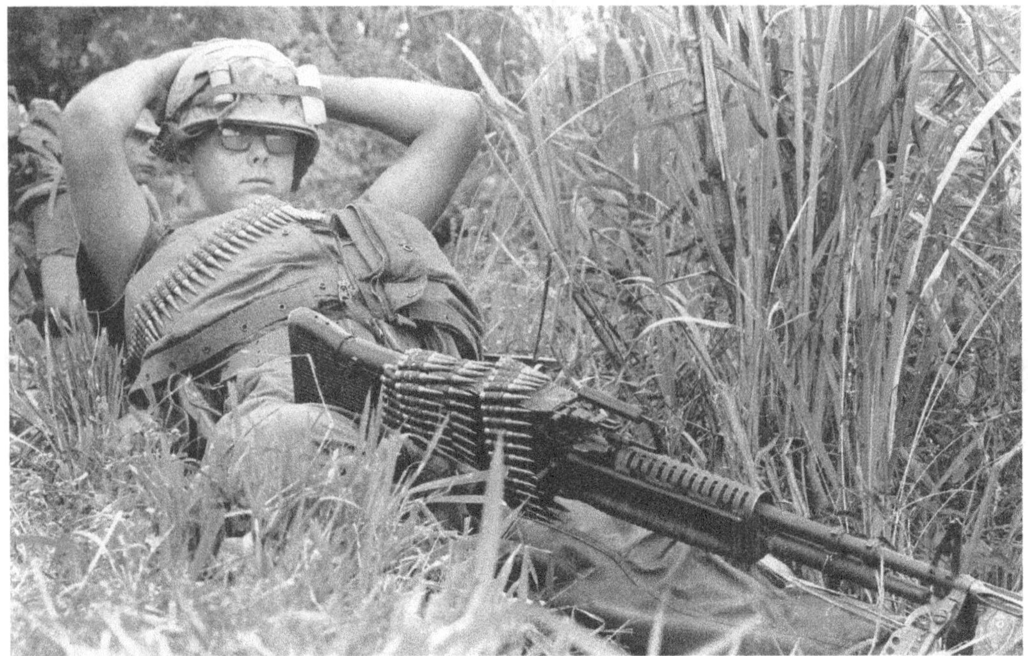

An unidentified Marine M60 machine gunner from Lima 3/7 takes a break during Operation Rock near Dai Loc. PHOTO BY CPL. DENNIS FISHER

The toll of an operation is reduced to numbers for the after-action reports: killed, wounded, captured, detained, equipment captured or destroyed, supplies captured or destroyed. Somehow, the numbers fail to capture the human experience of what happened. The photographs help put a face to some of the numbers, but nothing can record the thoughts and feelings of the men who were there.

The numbers for Operation Rock were three men KIA and twenty-seven wounded. The enemy lost thirty-five killed and thirty-three captured or detained. When out in the field, you're really only aware of what is going on right around you or what you may hear in radio traffic. It wasn't until all the companies submitted their after-action reports that the full scope of the operation was known to the lower echelons. The officers and command staff knew what was going on in real time, but the rest of us had to wait until later to find out.

This was not a big operation as search-and-destroy missions go, unless you were one of those killed or wounded, but it was typical of those being conducted in the "rocket belt" around Da Nang during Tet.

# Chapter 10

# Task Force X-Ray

## *Phu Bai*

Sitting in the back of a CH-46 on my way back from Operation Rock, I was replaying the events of the past few days in my mind. Being back in the field again and seeing how easy it was to get wounded or killed was not lost on me. The ambush left me a little shaken; there was no comparison between what I'd just experienced and the ambush training we'd had back in the States. In training there is no expectation of dying, but when the real thing happens and the bullets are flying, you know your life could come to a screeching halt. It was a really close call that would be a portent of combat operations to come.

I arrived back at the Photo Lab late in the day on March 10, stopping by the office to let Gunny Kruger know I was back. He told me that as soon as I finished processing my film and filling all the print requirements, I should get packed up. I was finally being detached to work with Task Force X-Ray up at Phu Bai. There were several ISO guys heading up there too, and I found that the photographers would be working out of their office. *Hallelujah*, I thought. *It was about time.* The fighting in Hue city was over, but the remaining NVA and VC had moved out into the surrounding countryside and dug in. It would take some serious fighting to drive them out, and I was going to be there to photograph it. But first, it was time for a shower, some hot chow, and a chance to write a letter to my mom and dad.

The next few days were spent in the lab, processing and printing the film from Operation Rock. Amid the smell of stop bath and hypo, with my Dektol-stained fingers I cranked out all the prints from the op. But it didn't end there; the prints needed to be captioned, stamped, and distributed. As soon as I was done, I packed up my gear and headed for the airfield at Da Nang.

Photographers were provided with repeat travel orders, so I simply showed up, presented my orders, and asked to be manifested on the next flight to Phu Bai. As luck would have it, they were in the process of loading a C-130 with replacements that was headed up there. This was a cargo plane, and we were seated in rows on the floor, shoulder to shoulder, facing the rear of the aircraft for the short seventy-mile flight. Gus Hasford, one of the ISO troops, called out to me. I saw him, already seated further back in the aircraft. It was hard to talk over the sound of the engines, but I told him I would join up with him when we landed. I unslung my pack and weapon and placed them on my lap as I took my place on the floor.

I couldn't see outside once the ramp closed, but I could hear the engines spooling up, and the aircraft began to move. The flight went by quickly, and we were back on the ground in fifteen minutes or so. As soon as I got off the plane I started looking for Hasford among the throng of grunts that were deplaning, and soon spotted him. He told me he had contacted Lieutenant LaPage at the ISO office before we'd left and he was sending someone over to pick us up.

Our ride soon arrived and we were deposited at the ISO hooch across from the 3rd Division Headquarters. All the hooches, whether for office use, workspace, or living quarters, were built of the same sixteen-by-thirty-two-foot design of plywood and two-by-fours, with screen sides and a corrugated-steel roof. Gus and I were assigned to one of the nearby hooches that had been partitioned off in the middle. The other half served as a supply storage area.

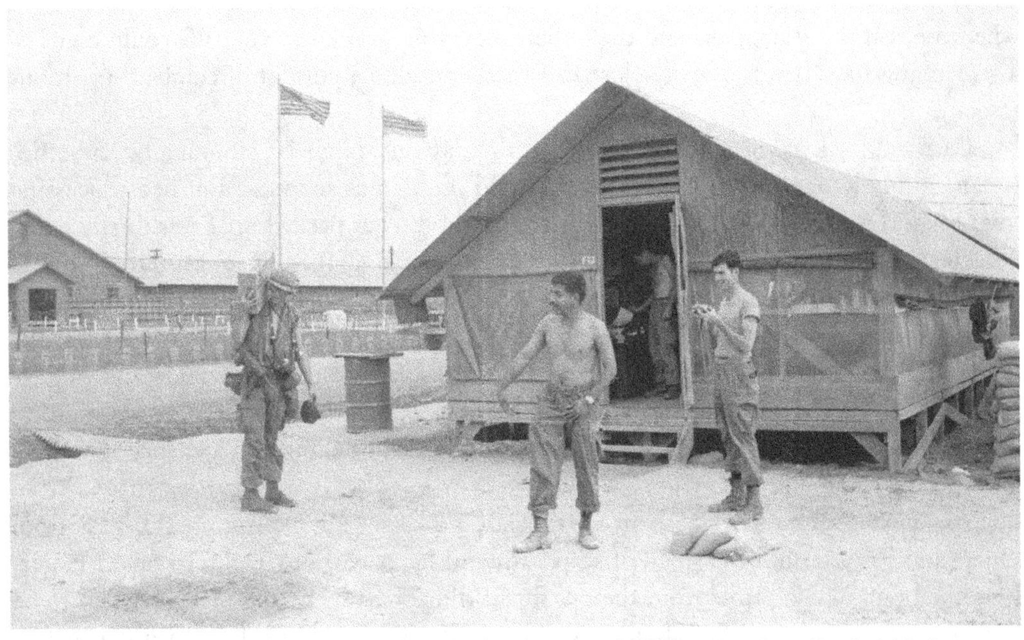

The Information Services Office is seen here in the summer of 1968 across from the 3rd Marine Division Headquarter. Pictured in the photo (from left to right): Cpl. Dennis Fisher, Sgt. Dave Martinez, and Cpl. Tom Donlon. Cpl. Fisher was the subject of some good-natured ribbing as he prepared to leave for an operation with the 5th Marines. PHOTO BY CPL. EARL GERHEIM/AUTHOR'S COLLECTION

Gus was a bit eccentric—more about him later. Suffice to say, we dropped our gear and went back to the ISO office to see what was going on in this area. I also needed to find out where the 3rd Division Photo Lab was located so I could introduce myself and find out about using their facilities to process and print my film.

On March 15, shortly after I arrived, I was directed to meet up with Lieutenant Maurice Green, the 2nd Platoon commander with Delta 1/5. This was the same unit I'd been with on Operation Cochise last August, down at Que Son, but I didn't recognize any of the faces. Many of the units had been shuffled around during Tet, and the 5th Marines were now strung out along a fifty-mile stretch of the coast between Hai Van Pass, just north of Da Nang, and Phu Bai.

The platoon was preparing to move out on a tank and infantry sweep along Route 545, south of Phu Bai, and I was sent to photograph it. The sweep was uneventful, with no enemy contact; other than a few shots of Staff Sergeant Tomlinson—the M48 tank commander of the "Eve of Destruction," behind his Ma Deuce on the turret—there wasn't much of interest to photograph.

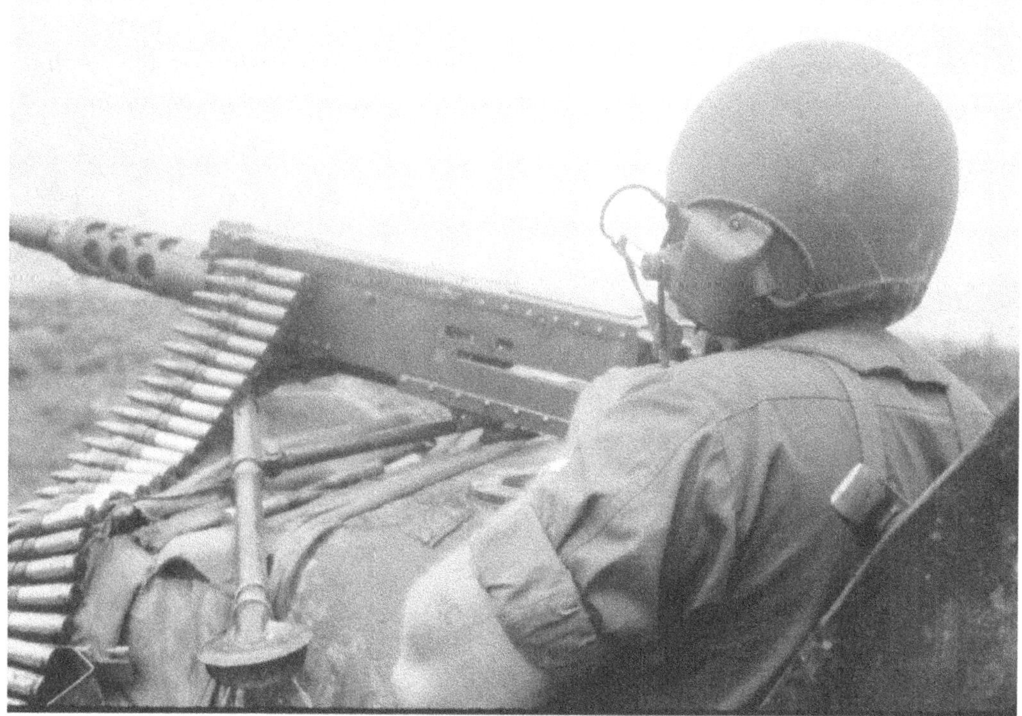

Marine tank commander SSgt. Tomlinson with Alpha Company, 1st Tank Battalion, mans his .50 caliber M2 Browning machine gun atop the turret of the "Eve of Destruction" M48 Patton tank during a tank/infantry road sweep with Delta 1/5, south of Phu Bai. PHOTO BY CPL. DENNIS FISHER

Back at Phu Bai, the next week or so was spent settling into my new unit and making friends with the 3rd Division Photo Lab guys. Discussing how dangerous it was for photographers was one of the big topics. During the war the Marines would ultimately lose twelve photographers. Of those, one died of illness, and another in a commercial plane crash returning from R&R. Out of the remaining ten who were KIA, seven would die in combat in 1968, making it the deadliest year of the war for Marine combat photographers.

At the time I was assigned to Task Force X-Ray, we had only lost one photographer in 1968. The 3rd Division photographers were still talking about losing Corporal Bill Perkins the previous October. He was shooting mopic (motion picture) on Operation Medina with Charlie 1/1 when he was killed. He threw himself on a grenade to save the lives of the men he was photographing, and would later be awarded the Medal of Honor—the only combat photographer ever to be so honored. I guess it was best that we didn't know what lay ahead in the months to come.

I had finally made it up to Phu Bai and was anxious to get out on one of the named operations in the area. There was a lot going on, and all the enemy that had been driven out of Hue had repositioned themselves out in the surrounding countryside, where they continued to be a problem. Operation Ford had kicked off on March 14, to confront a VC main force battalion that was operating in that area, but I arrived too late to participate in that one. The op was conducted in a coastal area just east of Hue, which would continue to be a source of aggravation for the Marines. More operations would soon follow.

# CHAPTER 11

# Operation Houston

## *Nui Bach Ma*

On March 24 I headed south to Nui Bach Ma to join up with Foxtrot 2/5 for Operation Houston. They had just returned from the fighting in Hue and now occupied a jungle outpost located on a mountaintop above Hai Van Pass, just north of Da Nang. This area was occupied by the French back when they were fighting in Vietnam during the Indochina War. I believe Bach Ma was a resort for them, as there were a number of chalets, a swimming pool, and other amenities dispersed around the mountain's summit. They were all overgrown and had fallen into disrepair, but it was evident it had been a nice place at one time. I also suspect that the 4,100-foot altitude provided a more comfortable climate during the heat of summer.

My ride to their location was aboard a twin-rotor CH-46 Sea Knight helicopter. This was a resupply run, and there was a pallet of cargo slung underneath, plus some passengers inside. I had flown many times on CH-46s, known as one of the workhorses for transporting troops and supplies. Riding in one was an exercise in sensory overload, with rotor noise and the high-pitched whine of the turbines. Add to that the smell of jet fuel that permeated the air and occasional bursts of machine-gun fire, and you have some idea of what it was like. All the windows had been removed, and between the rush of air and the whine of the turbines, it was just about impossible to talk to anyone. The crew members had headsets and mics for

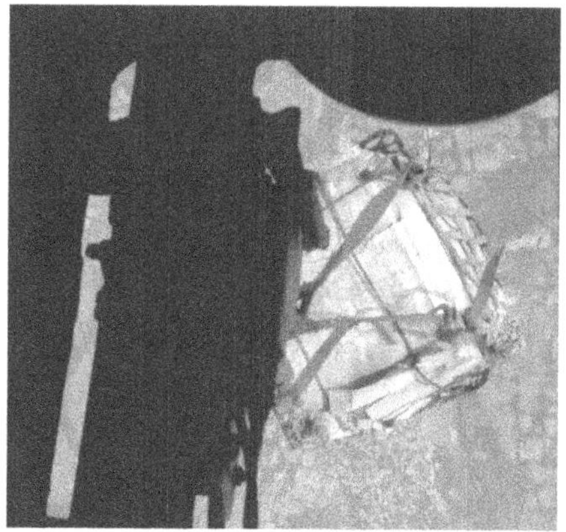

External cargo slung underneath resupply helicopter en route to Nui Bach Ma during Operation Houston in March 1968. PHOTO BY CPL. DENNIS FISHER

communications, but nothing was provided for the passengers, so we just settled in on the nylon seats along the side of the cargo area and enjoyed the rush of cool air.

The two door gunners were constantly on alert, watching for muzzle flashes from anyone shooting at us. They wore flight helmets with sun visors, Nomex flight suits, and gloves—all of which made them look pretty formidable when positioned behind their machine guns. Our particular chopper had two M2 .50 caliber machine guns mounted just aft of the pilots on either side. They were fed from one-hundred-round ammo cans mounted on the side next to the gun's feed ramp. Despite the protection these weapons provided, one of my biggest concerns in Nam was getting shot down or crashing during takeoff or landing. The H-34 that crashed in front of me during Operation Cochise the previous year hadn't done anything to ease that fear. It was just something you had to live with; it was certainly safer than traveling to a location by truck with the risk of being ambushed or hitting a mine.

The flight on this day was without incident, and once the external cargo was released, the chopper moved over to the LZ and we were dropped off. Marines who got off with me said it was only a short walk to the CP, and I followed them up to their headquarters. Along the way we passed a large concrete monument erected by French engineers, marking the summit of Nui Bach Ma.

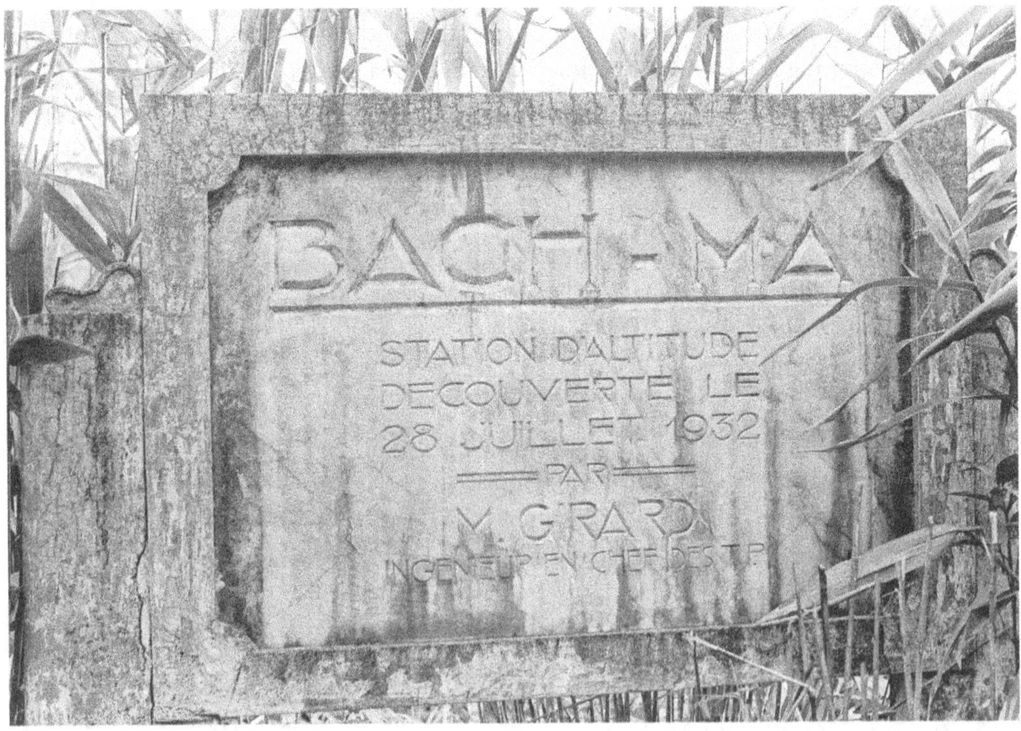


Survey monument placed atop Nui Bach Ma by French engineers during their occupation of Vietnam. PHOTO BY CPL. DENNIS FISHER

The air was definitely cooler up there, a welcome change from the hot and humid conditions down at sea level. We wended our way among the old chalets until we arrived at the CP, which had been established in one of the vacant buildings. A typical Marine Corps red sign with yellow stenciled letters greeted us with "Welcome to the 5th Marines CP Group." I introduced myself to a Marine in the CP and he directed me to the Fox Company CO, Captain Downs. He briefed me on their plan for this op and told me I could travel with any platoon I liked, but to let the platoon sergeant know so he could include rations for me.

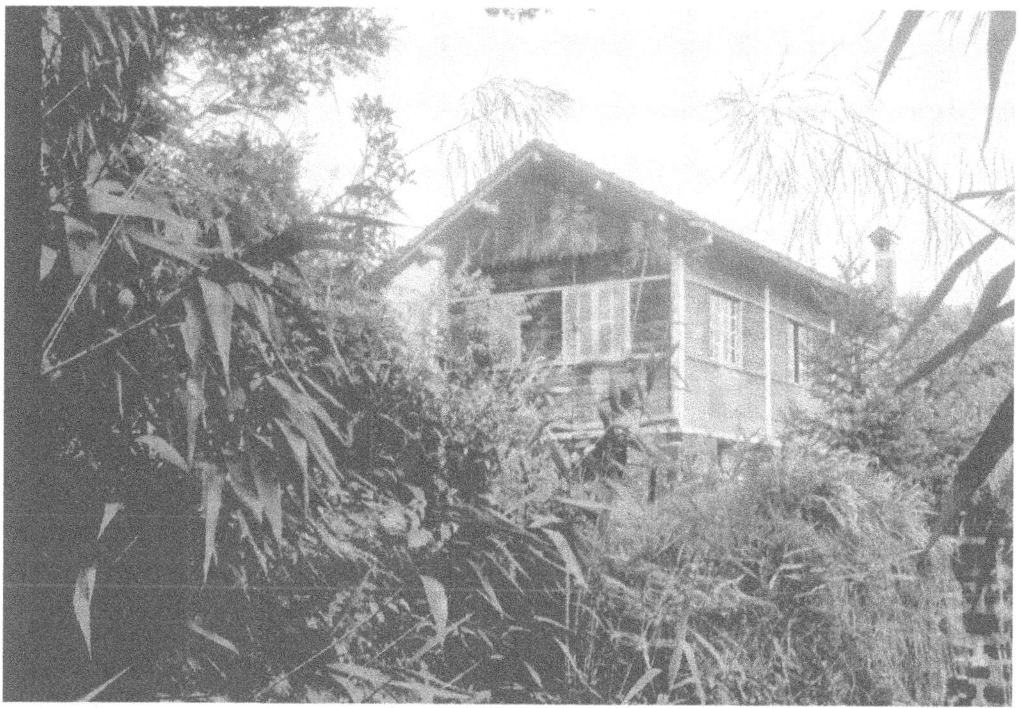

A chalet on Nui Bach Ma built by the French during the Indochina War. PHOTO BY CPL. DENNIS FISHER

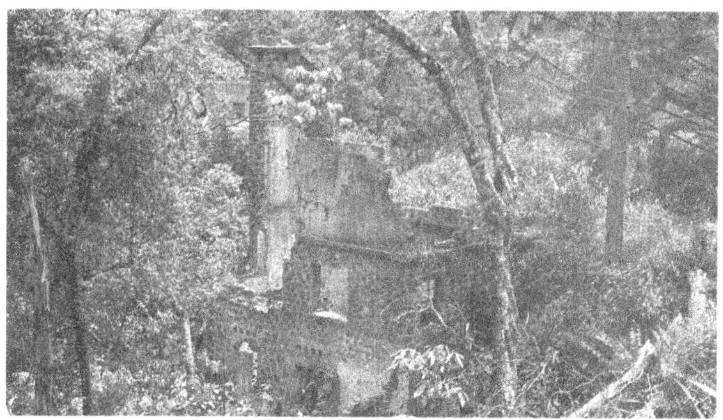

Crumbling ruins on Nui Bach Ma from the French colonial period—a testament to the previous owner's presence atop the mountain. PHOTO BY CPL. DENNIS FISHER

Operation Houston was an ongoing op and had been in progress for some time before I arrived. For the men of 2/5, this duty was a welcome relief from what they had endured in Hue. They would go out for five to ten days patrolling the area, by their very presence denying it to the enemy. This was nothing like the house-to-house street fighting in the battle for Hue City, a battle that ranked right up there with the bloodiest fights the Marines were involved in during the Vietnam War.

It was now late afternoon and we weren't leaving until the following morning, so I took the opportunity to look around the place. While checking out an old stone monastery building, I encountered a Marine who was standing guard. He began telling me about the fighting in Hue they had been engaged in, commenting that they had lost sixty-five men killed and over four hundred wounded during the previous month. He was glad to be out of that place and back in the bush.

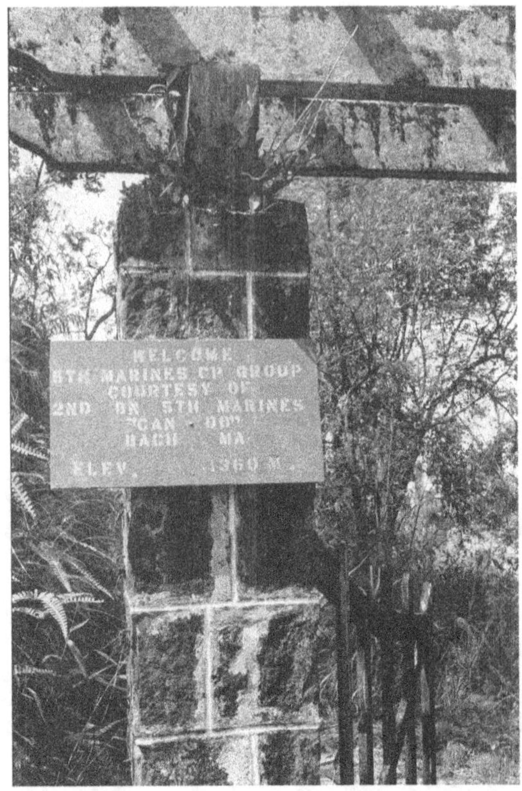

A sign greets visitors to 2nd Battalion, 5th Marine Regiment, located on Nui Bach Ma. PHOTO BY CPL. DENNIS FISHER

As we spoke, I spotted an approaching CH-53 with a cargo net full of C-rations slung underneath, and headed for the LZ to get some photos. As I made my way over there I began to reflect on what the 5th Marines had gone through in Hue. Hearing his account of the fighting up there and the number of casualties they'd suffered was heartbreaking. So many young men lost; but for the grace of God, and my transfer to Photo, I would have been right there with them.

The downwash from the rotors was tremendous and could knock you over if it caught you off balance. The LZ was carved out of the side of a hill and wasn't large enough to accommodate a helicopter of this size, which was the biggest we had. He hovered off to the side and dropped the net full of rations and then sort of half landed and half hovered as the crew passed the remaining supplies out of the window.

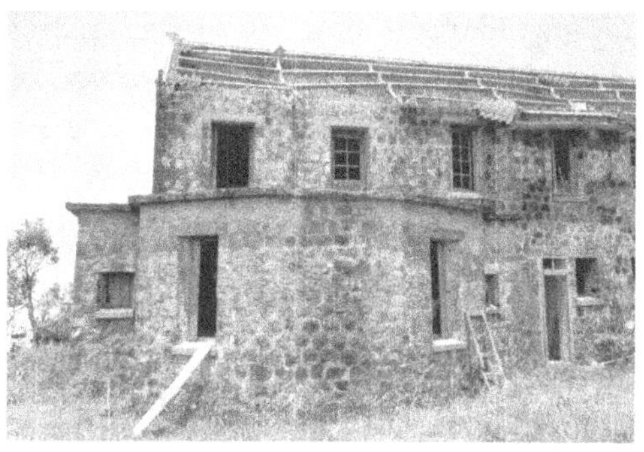

An old monastery building on Nui Bach Ma near the 2nd Battalion, 5th Marine Regiment command post. PHOTO BY CPL. DENNIS FISHER

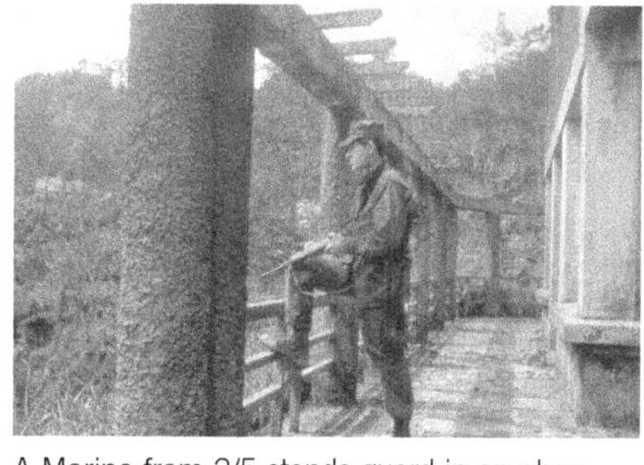

A Marine from 2/5 stands guard in an abandoned monastery building on Nui Bach Ma in March 1968. PHOTO BY CPL. DENNIS FISHER

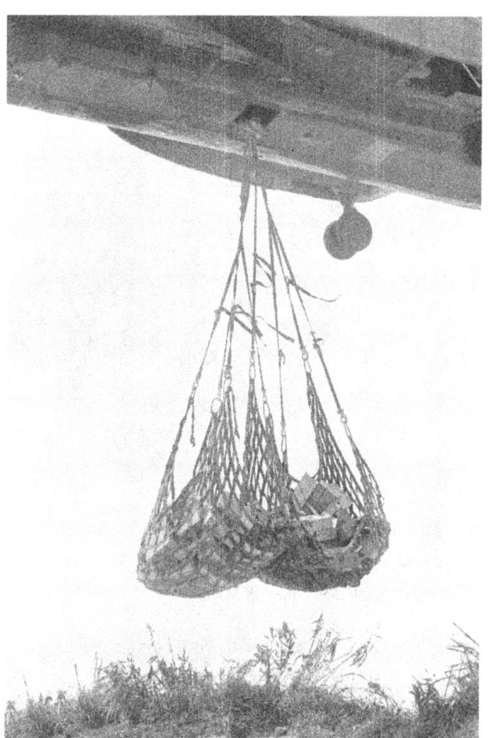

Resupply of rations arriving via helicopter at 2nd Battalion, 5th Marine Regiment command post on Nui Bach Ma in support of Operation Houston in March 1968. PHOTO BY CPL. DENNIS FISHER

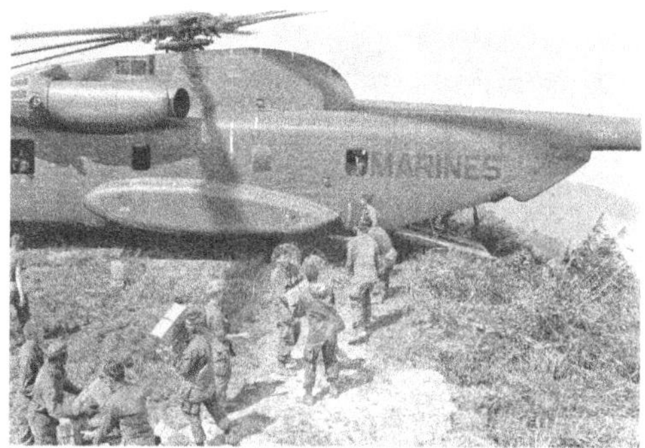

Once the CH-53 drops its external load of rations, additional cases are passed out the window to waiting Marines from Fox Company 2/5 in preparation for Operation Houston on Nui Bach Ma in March 1968. PHOTO BY CPL. DENNIS FISHER

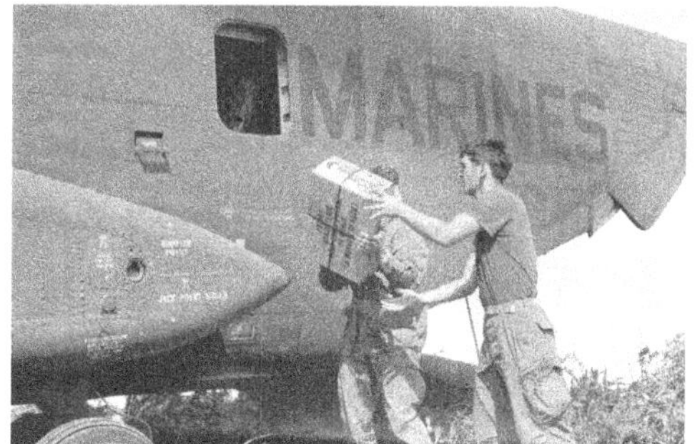

Rations being offloaded from a CH-53 in support of Operation Houston on Nui Bach Ma by Marines from Fox Company 2/5 in March 1968. PHOTO BY CPL. DENNIS FISHER/COURTESY OF NARA STILL PICTURE BRANCH

The next morning, we moved out on the operation, more of a company-in-force patrol than a big operation. A few sniper rounds quickly got our attention on the afternoon of the second day. It sounded like an M1 carbine, but I couldn't be sure. Everyone opened up in the direction of the gunfire emanating from a nearby tree line, but very quickly the call of "Cease fire" was heard, and the shooting stopped. A sweep was conducted through the area but didn't reveal anything. Nothing much was encountered over the next day, but the following day we did come across an abandoned rocket launch site and the skeletal remains of a recently killed VC left on the field by his comrades. All the vegetation surrounding the skeleton was also dead, killed off by the products of decomposition.

Finding human remains was not uncommon; you could smell them long before finding them. The smell of human decomposition is very strong and distinct. I'm not sure how to describe it other than to say that once you've experienced it, you won't forget it.

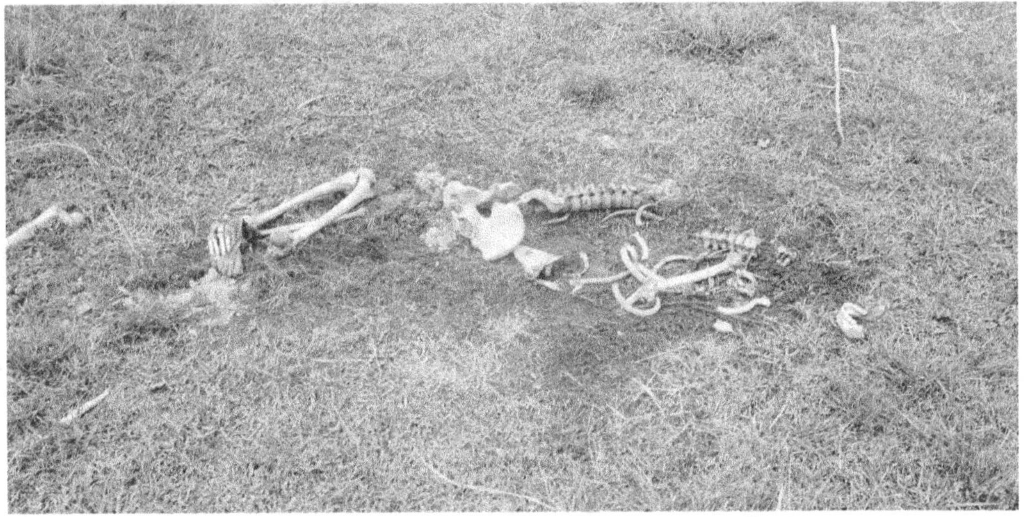

The skeletal remains of Viet Cong left behind by the enemy from a previous engagement, discovered by elements of Fox Company 2/5 near a rocket launch site during Operation Houston, March 1968. PHOTO BY CPL. DENNIS FISHER

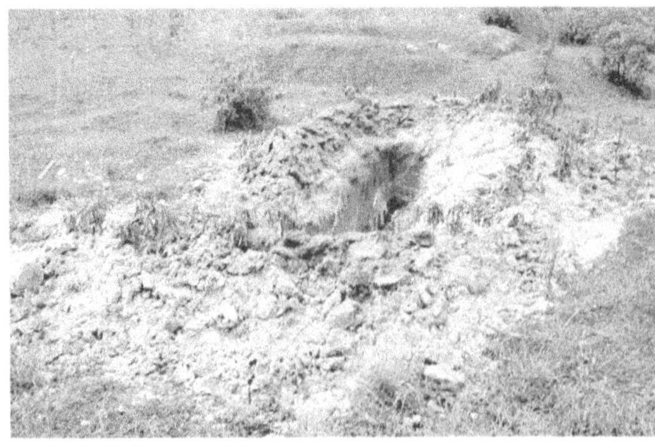

Viet Cong fighting position discovered by Fox Company 2/5 near a rocket launch site in the vicinity of Nui Bach Ma during Operation Houston in March 1968. PHOTO BY CPL. DENNIS FISHER

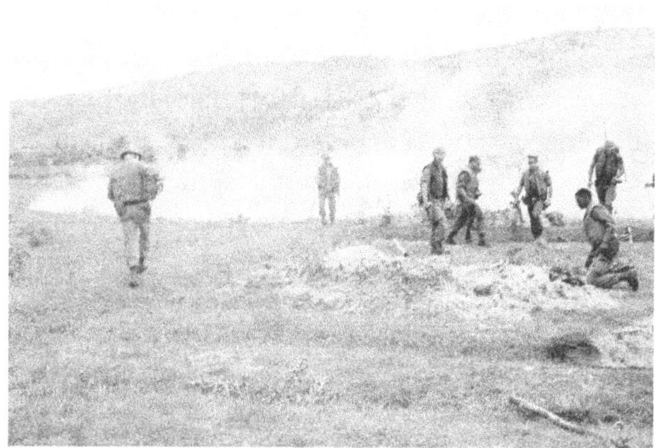

Radioman from Fox Company 2/5 pops a yellow smoke to mark the landing zone for an approaching resupply helicopter during Operation Houston in March 1968, near Nui Bach Ma. PHOTO BY CPL. DENNIS FISHER

The third day out we were resupplied with ammo and rations. The radioman popped a yellow smoke to mark the LZ, and the 46 spiraled in for a landing. Everyone pitched in to unload the chopper, and he quickly took off. Among all the military supplies was a big red nylon bag containing mail for the unit and a box full of goodies addressed "To Any Marine," which was divvied out among everyone present.

Included in the box were some letters from sorority girls at Elmira College in New York who had assembled the treats and sent them to Vietnam. I picked up one of the letters and decided to write to her. Her name was Nancy Van Mater and she was from Piscataway, New Jersey. We started a correspondence that would continue through the rest of my tour in Vietnam, and for some time after I was back in civilian life. In light of my flagging correspondence from Tammy, her letters were just the morale boost I needed. They were funny and sort of crazy, and the envelopes were decorated with bold graphics that she enhanced. We really hit it off, and I was looking forward to meeting her on my return to the States. Ultimately that would never happen, not for lack of trying; I never had the chance to meet her and tell her in person how those letters brought some welcome light into the darkness that was Vietnam.

During that resupply I was introduced to long-range patrol rations (LRPs), or lurps, as they were called. Being decidedly different from the C-rations we normally received, they were freeze-dried meals packaged in a tough plastic bag. The only preparation required was to heat up some water in your canteen cup, pour it in the bag, shake it up, wait a few minutes, and it was ready to eat. It was a welcome change to our menu out in the field, but that was the first and only time I ever had them. The MREs (meals ready-to-eat) of today replaced both the MCI (meal, combat, individual; or "C-rations") and the LRPs in the early 1980s.

We returned to the base camp after only eight days in the field and I caught a ride on a resupply chopper back to Phu Bai. My chance at a big named operation had been a bust. I headed back under a cloud of disappointment, though the short flight to Phu Bai didn't give me much time to think about it. Instead, my thoughts turned toward hot chow, a shower, and some sack time.

First stop was at my hooch to drop off all my war gear/cameras and then head over to the chow hall, which must have been designed by the same architect that conceived of our hooches. What distinguished this one was the number of shrapnel holes in the walls and concrete floor. These were the result of previous rocket and mortar attacks on the base.

Moving up to the serving line I was greeted with the aroma of liver and onions, my least favorite meal in the world. Going hungry or pulling some C-rations out of my pack back at the hooch seemed like a better idea, but I settled for a canteen cup full of chocolate milk and a dessert from the mess hall.

A good shower and a change of clothing soon had me feeling much better. I went over to the ISO hooch to see who was there and what was going on. Lieutenant LaPage said he was glad to have me back, as he needed me to join up with 1/5 the following day for another tank and infantry sweep. So much for a couple days' rest.

Back at the hooch I busied myself cleaning my cameras and assembling what little film I had exposed during Operation Houston for processing. As day turned to night, it was time to sack out and get a little rest for the next day's assignment, with Lieutenant Green. However, my hopes of a good night's sleep were quickly dashed as the 105mm artillery battery in our compound began firing harassment and interdiction rounds (H&Is) on and off through the night. I was used to this, but on this night I just couldn't get to sleep for more than a half-hour at a time.

The month of March was basically shot, and moving into April I was hearing about heavy fighting going on all over I Corps. Amid the clacking of typewriter keys in the ISO hooch as correspondents worked on their stories, Corporal Earl Gerheim, Corporal Gus Hasford, and I were pondering when we were going to get out on one of the big ops. So far the units I had been assigned to cover were not caught up in any big battles.

That was about to change.

CHAPTER 12

# Operation No Name II

## *Hue*

I returned to Phu Bai on April 2 after leaving Operation Houston. Before having a chance to process my film, I was sent down to join Lieutenant Maurice Green and Delta 1/5 on another tank and infantry sweep along Route 545, south of Phu Bai. This was a narrow, single-lane paved road that was heavily overgrown with elephant grass

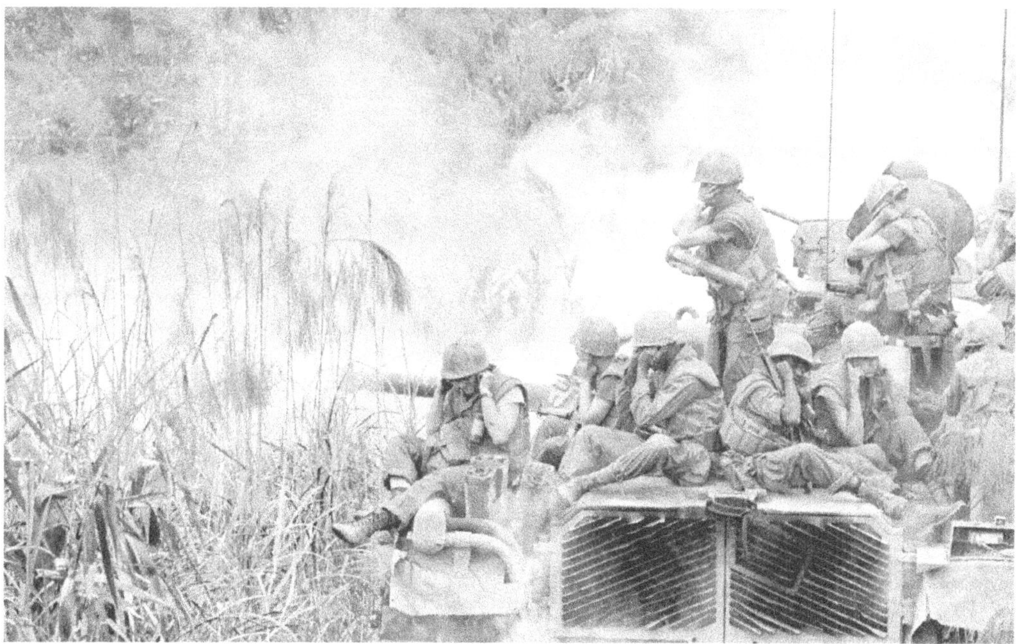

Marines from Delta 1/5 cover their ears as the M48 from 1st Tank Battalion opens fire on the enemy during a tank and infantry sweep south of Phu Bai in April 1968. PHOTO BY CPL. DENNIS FISHER/COURTESY OF NARA STILL PICTURE BRANCH

91

in many places, limiting visibility and making it a good place for an ambush or booby traps. Green and his 2nd Platoon, along with tanks from Alpha Company 1st Tank Battalion, were the only units involved in the sweep.

We were transported by trucks down Route 1 and met up with the tanks near the intersection with Route 545. The weather was hot for April, and many of the men were wearing only T-shirts and soft covers while leaving their flak jackets and helmets behind. It wasn't just the men; Lieutenant Green was dressed in the same fashion. In my helmet and flak jacket, I was feeling a little overdressed.

The sweep began uneventfully, but soon gave way to sporadic sniper fire. One of the tanks opened up with its 90mm main gun and quickly put an end to that. The photo I took of the tank firing with a number of Marines riding on it has been widely distributed in both print media (books, magazines, and newspapers) and in more recent times, online. This was my first photo to appear in a stateside publication, *Leatherneck* magazine, and I was feeling gratified that my photos were finding a larger audience. This would be the second of three tank and infantry sweeps I would go on with Delta 1/5. It only lasted for the day, and I was back in Phu Bai by early evening.

When not out in the field we were kept busy photographing events on and around our base at Phu Bai. The day following the tank sweep I was assigned to cover the dedication of Camp Bruno Hockmuth. Major General Hockmuth was the 3rd Marine Division commander who had died in a helicopter crash near Hue the previous November. The base was named in his honor, and Lieutenant Generals Krulak and Cushman were there to preside over the ceremony, along with Lieutenant General Lam of Vietnam and Lieutenant

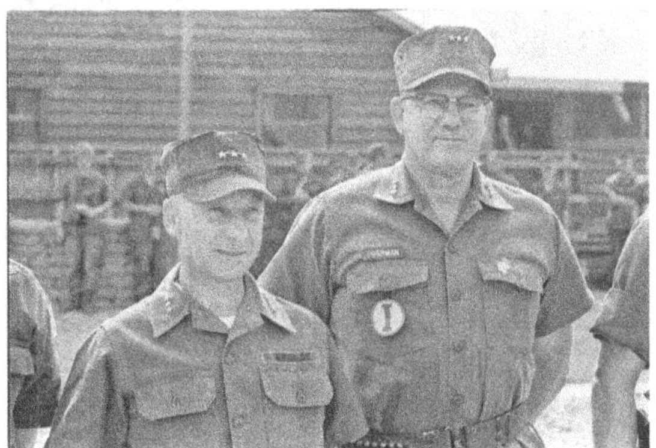

Lt. Gen. Victor H. Krulak and Lt. Gen. R. E. Cushman preside over the dedication of Camp Bruno Hockmuth at Phu Bai in April 1968. PHOTO BY CPL. DENNIS FISHER

General Rossow of the US Army. Events like this—promotion ceremonies, awards and decorations ceremonies, and MEDCAPs—made up the bulk of our non-combat photography.

Even though the fighting in nearby Hue had ended in March, the NVA and VC who survived didn't just quit and go home. They moved out into the countryside and dug in for a fight. The 27th Marines had run an op called No Name I in the area east of Hue beginning on April 6, to try and clear out NVA from the 804th Main Force Battalion. This enemy unit had been a constant source of aggravation for the Marines, who were constantly subjected to mortar attacks on their compound and sniping at their patrols.

These No Name operations were smaller affairs as combat operations go, comprising just a few companies, and were not considered large enough to merit a proper name, such as Cochise or Allen Brook. Those named operations always involved multiple battalions and lots of supporting arms. However, these small unit actions comprised much of the fighting in Vietnam and were every bit as deadly as the larger operations.

Good Friday and Easter were coming up, so I asked the lieutenant if Earl Gerheim and I could cover the religious services for the chaplain. Earl was a combat correspondent and we often worked together. The lieutenant gave me that "Nice try, Fisher, but we have a war to cover here" look. Instead, he directed us to join up with the 27th Marines on Good Friday, April 12, and cover Operation No Name II. Normally we would have joined up with them the day before the op kicked off, but this late notification precluded that, as the unit was already on the move.

Trying to make up for lost time, Earl and I quickly pulled our gear together and got ready to leave. The weather had been rainy, normal for that time of year, so I pulled on rain pants over my utilities just in case we got caught in the rain. I threw some C-rations in my pack, grabbed my camera gear, a couple of canteens, grease gun, helmet, and flak jacket, and went down to the airfield with Earl, looking for a ride.

Getting a helicopter out to their location in the field proved fruitless due to bad weather and heavy ground fire. Unable to get to them by air, we opted for plan B, catching a ride in a supply truck to their command post at the La Son School east of Hue the next morning. There were few people to speak with at the command post, as most of them were in the field, including the battalion commander and the COs from Alpha, Bravo, and Delta companies. While discussing possible ways to reach their location, we overheard radio traffic from Alpha Company indicating that they and Delta Company were in need of ammo resupply.

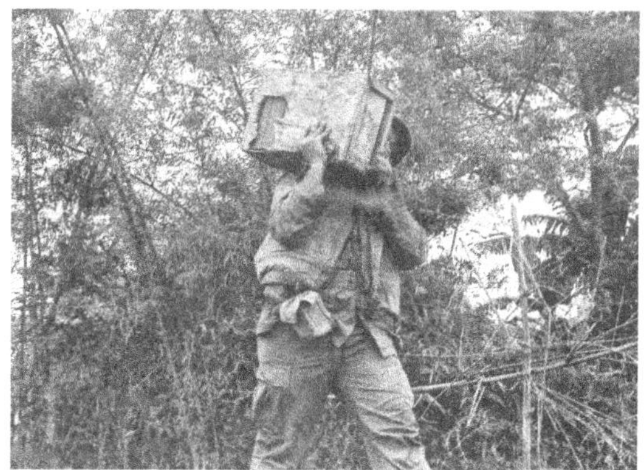

A Marine from Delta 1/27 carries a resupply of ammunition to his company, engaged in a bitter firefight during Operation No Name II in April 1968. PHOTO BY CPL. DENNIS FISHER

One of the Marines mentioned that a truck was being loaded with ammo and replacements, and that this would be our best way to reach the fighting. So we climbed aboard a deuce and a half that was loaded with cases of M60, M16, M79, and 60mm mortar ammo, along with a number of replacements, and headed east down Route 522 for about a mile and a half. We had no escort and were a little nervous riding in a truck full of ammo. Mines and ambushes were a concern in this area, which only added to the uneasiness. The road didn't lead directly to the Marines' position, but the driver was able to get us within a half-mile or so.

As soon as the truck pulled to a stop, everyone quickly dismounted, pitched in to unload the truck, and picked up a case of ammo to carry to the fighting. There was one case of 60mm mortar rounds left, so Earl and I grabbed the rope handles on either end of the box and took off, following the grunts. These wooden cases held ten rounds and weighed fifty-five pounds, so with all your other gear, it was too much for one guy to carry.

We were about a thousand yards from the fighting at this point, which was still going on hot and heavy. The sound of automatic weapons fire and mortars in the distance indicated our direction of travel. The group kept moving down dirt trails along bamboo hedge lines toward the sound of the firing. As we got closer, the enemy spotted our approach and began shooting at us. A few rounds could be heard snapping overhead, but most were falling short, into the rice paddies. That was a real motivator to pick up the pace. Earl commented that there wouldn't be much of us to send home to Mama if a lucky shot hit the case of mortar shells. I guess I should have been scared, but frankly, since most of my attention was focused on my footing on the trail and keeping up with the grunts, I wasn't overly concerned.

The sound of the shooting was getting pretty close as we approached

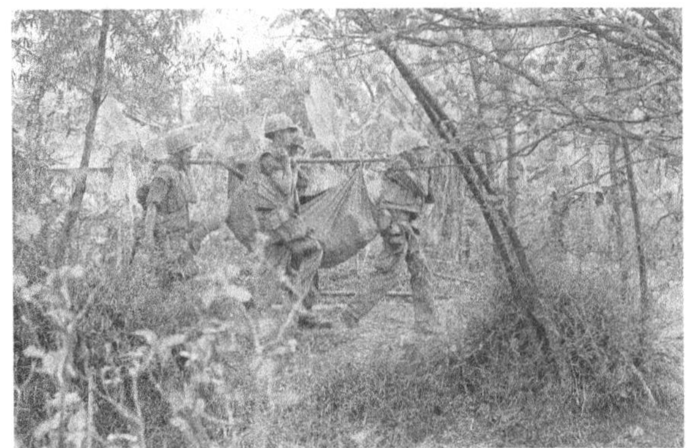

Marines from Alpha Company 1/27 remove one of their dead following a heavy firefight on April 13, 1968, during Operation No Name II. PHOTO BY CPL. DENNIS FISHER

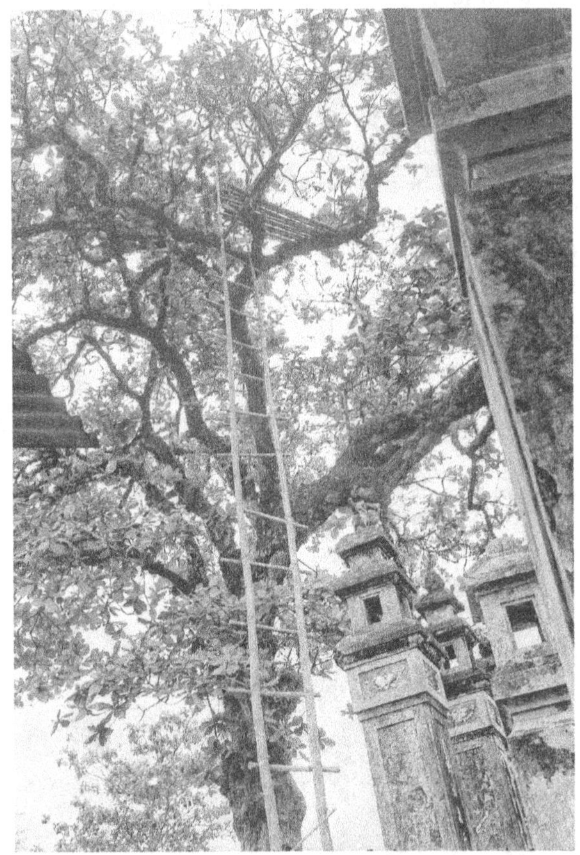

A sniper/lookout platform abandoned by the enemy as Marines from Delta 1/27 approached during Operation No Name II, east of Hue, in April 1968. PHOTO BY CPL. DENNIS FISHER

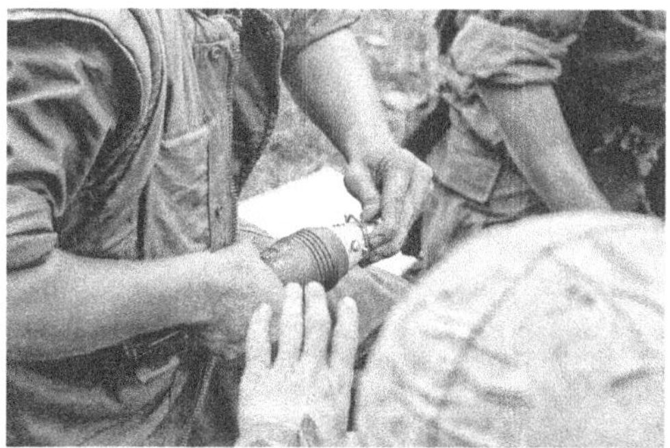

A 60mm mortar crew with Delta 1/27 preparing a high-explosive round for firing in support of nearby Alpha 1/27 during Operation No Name II, east of Hue, April 1968. PHOTO BY CPL. DENNIS FISHER

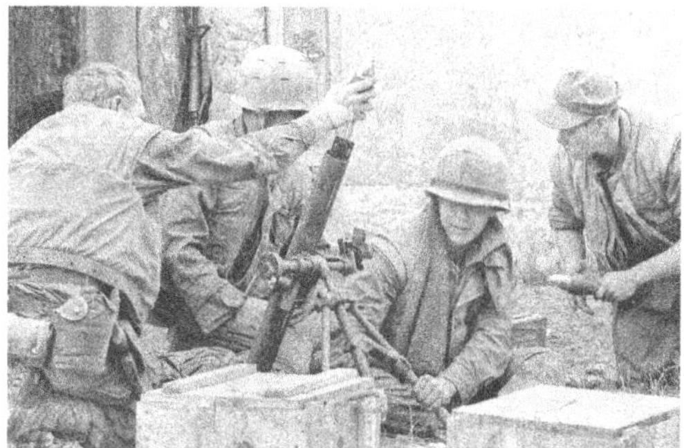

A 60mm mortar crew with Delta 1/27 firing a high-explosive round at an entrenched enemy in support of Alpha 1/27 during Operation No Name II, east of Hue, April 1968. PHOTO BY CPL. DENNIS FISHER

a small canal and followed a well-worn path to our left. Across the canal I could see Marines from Alpha Company bringing out one of their dead, and I paused to take a few photos. This was just of one of many casualties they had suffered the day before, and on that morning.

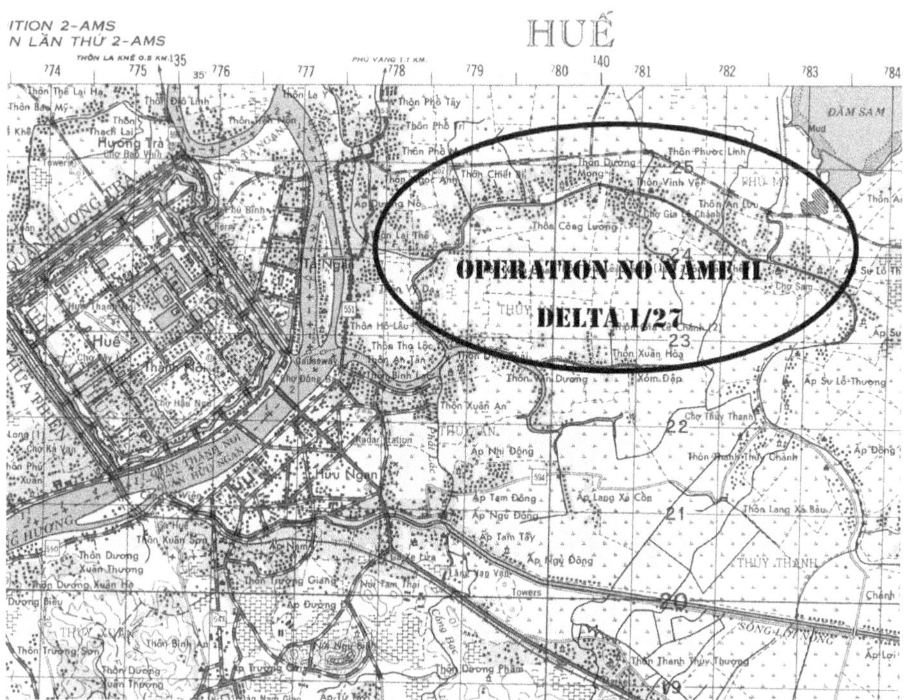


A map of the operational area and movement of 1/27 Marines during Operation No Name II in April 1968.

Continuing on, we came to a pagoda with a courtyard fronted by a four- or five-foot masonry wall. It faced the canal that was serving as Delta Company's defensive position when we arrived. The company was further spread out along the canal, with some of the men occupying abandoned enemy trenches. Overhead was an abandoned enemy sniper nest in a tree, testament to their preparation and watchfulness.

Earl and I dropped off the case of shells with the mortar crew and I started taking photos of them in action. The enemy was less than one hundred yards away on the other side of the canal. They were so close that mortar shells were being fired without any powder increments. The powder increments look like tea bags and are nestled between the fins. The range of the mortar is basically controlled by the elevation angle of the barrel and the number of powder increments.

The general plan of the operation was to sweep east along the canal with Delta Company on the north side and Alpha Company on the south (see map). Bravo Company had been driven a mile or so farther east in trucks and inserted to act as a blocking force.

When we arrived, Alpha Company on the south side of the canal was heavily engaged in fighting, and Delta Company was firing across the canal into the enemy's flank, with everything at their disposal. I was shooting some photos of Corporal Ed Mahseet, the Delta Company commander's radioman, who was laying down a base of fire with his M16. Ed was a Comanche Indian about five-foot-eight, sturdily built, with facial features and skin color that left no doubt about his ethnicity. He was affectionately known to his fellow Marines as Little Chief, which distinguished him from Big Chief, who served in

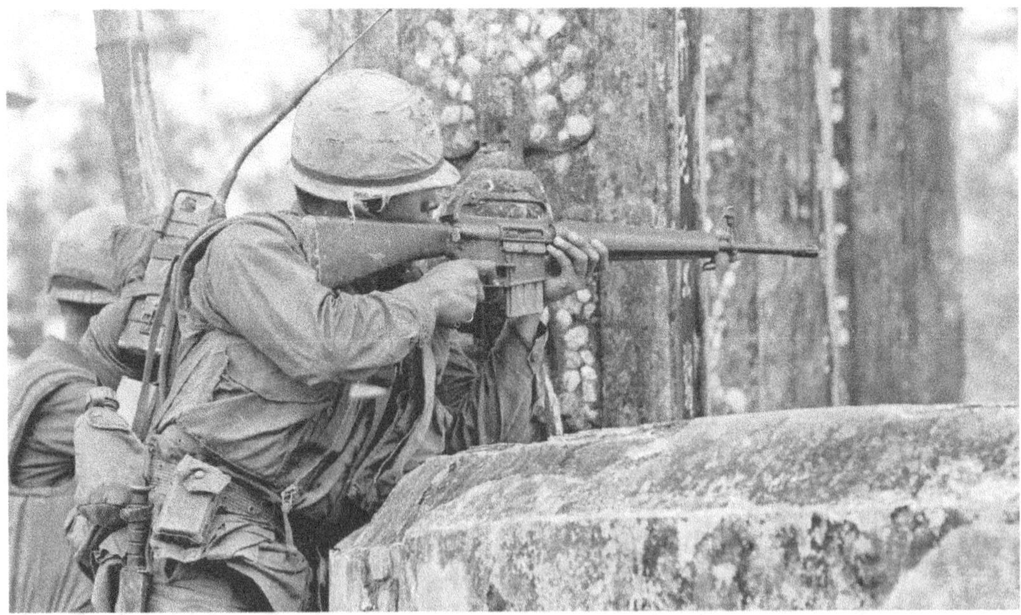

Cpl. Edmond Mahseet, the Delta Company commander's RTO, engaging the enemy with his M16 during a firefight, Operation No Name II, east of Hue, April 1968. PHOTO BY CPL. DENNIS FISHER

another company. He was anything but little, and well respected by everyone for distinguishing himself in hand-to-hand combat with the enemy using only his KA-BAR knife in an earlier night attack. He was one tough Marine.

Finishing up with Ed, I was trying to stay low and find some other subjects. My attention was drawn to the top of a pagoda where Private First Class Geoffrey Rowson was perched. He'd climbed up the sloping tile roof with his M60 machine gun and was pouring fire into the enemy across the canal. A stream of spent shell casings rattled down the slope of the roof and poured off onto the ground as I began taking photos of him in action. I was concerned that his exposed position would make him a target for NVA snipers in the area. He continued engaging the enemy for a few more minutes, knowing full well the danger he was in until Captain Kahler told him to get down off the roof. Geoffrey, along with his assistant gunner, would be killed in action a few months later in an intense firefight during Operation Allen Brook, south of Da Nang.

I moved back toward the wall for cover as the tempo of the firing from both Delta and Alpha companies increased. I began to wonder if the NVA were going to try and assault our position. You could see movement behind the bamboo hedge line across the canal, and it began to look more and more like that was their plan.

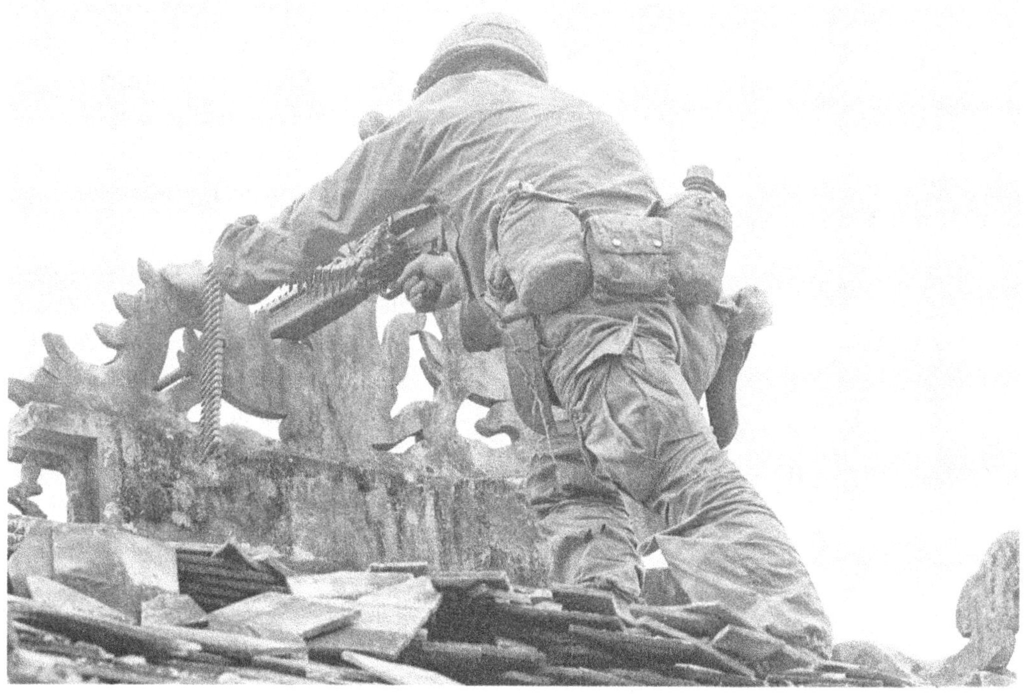

PFC Geoffrey Rowson with Delta 1/27 lays down suppressing fire on enemy positions during Operation No Name II, east of Hue, April 1968. PHOTO BY CPL. DENNIS FISHER/COURTESY OF NARA STILL PICTURE BRANCH

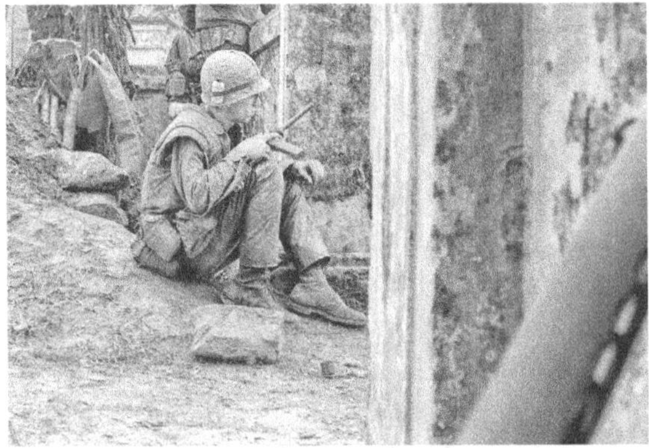

Cpl. Dennis Fisher during lull in fighting, Operation No Name II, east of Hue, April 1968. PHOTO BY CPL. EARL GERHEIM/AUTHOR'S COLLECTION

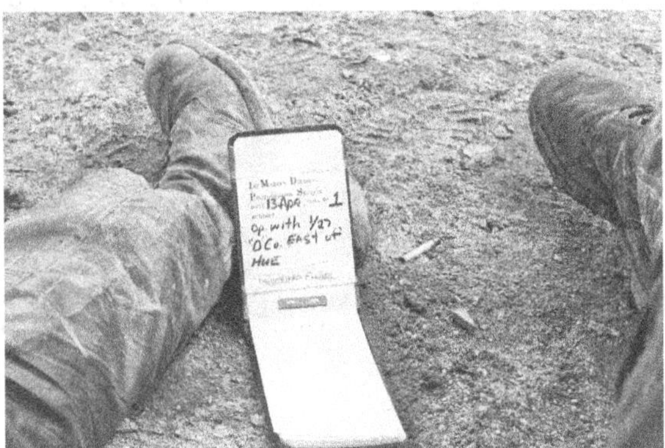

A 1st Marine Division combat photographer field slate for a 35mm film camera, Operation No Name II, east of Hue, April 1968. PHOTO BY CPL. DENNIS FISHER

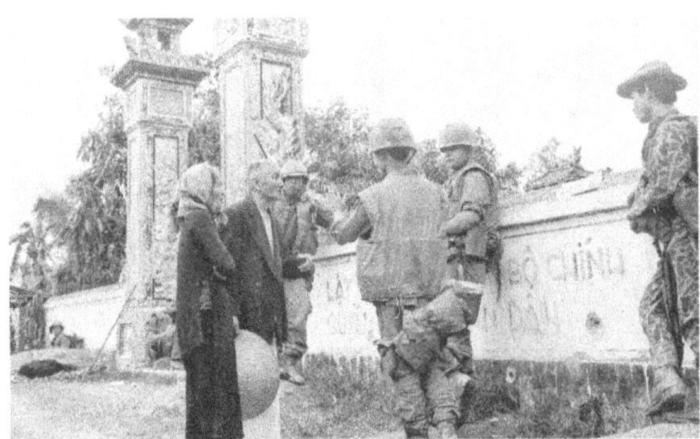

Interpreter, Cpl. Edmond Mahseet, and Capt. Kahler, CO of Delta 1/27, question local villagers about VC movements during Operation No Name II, east of Hue, April 1968. PHOTO BY CPL. DENNIS FISHER

My old infantry instincts kicked in. I put down my camera and opened fire with my grease gun at two NVA who were making a rush for the hedge line on the other side of the canal, adjacent to a small bridge. I wasn't the only one to see them, and at least half a dozen guys opened up with their M16s. Their fate was unknown, and no one was going to cross the bridge to find out. (Alpha Company would later sweep the area, but I never heard what, if anything, they found.)

As I replaced the empty magazine with a full one, the firing began to slack off. It appeared this was a rearguard action by the NVA to cover their withdrawal, and we weren't going to be overrun after all. I relaxed for a few minutes and took in the smell of burnt gunpowder hanging in the air. Out of the corner of my eye, I saw Earl taking a photo of me. I felt a little guilty being caught with a weapon in my hands instead of a camera, but I wasn't taking any chances after being wounded the previous year, having adopted a better-safe-than-sorry attitude when it came to self-preservation.

I took advantage of the moment to shoot a slate for this roll of film. Everything had been happening so quickly that I'd neglected to shoot one at the beginning of the roll. Slates are used to identify your film among all the other rolls as they are processed and dried in the lab.

Captain Patrick Kahler, the Delta Company CO, passed the word for everyone to get ready to move out. A few civilians appeared as we prepared, and our interpreter engaged them in conversation. One was a French doctor who had married a Vietnamese during the French occupation and remained in the country after the war. Even though he was fluent in Vietnamese he would only speak French, and since we didn't have anyone conversant in that language, we had to depend on his wife for what little intel she could provide. I think he wanted to make sure we didn't mistake him for Vietnamese, or more specifically, a VC.

Speaking of the VC, Delta Company had a Kit Carson scout named Nguyen Hien who had surrendered to the Americans and taken advantage of our Chieu Hoi program to become a scout for our side. These ex-VC were screened and trained under the program and assigned to Marine units. Their knowledge of VC tactics and operations was a big help. The ones that had proven themselves capable and trustworthy were issued weapons. Nguyen is shown in the photo reloading his M16 magazine during a lull in the fighting. His possession of such a weapon was a testament to his field performance and trustworthiness.

In addition to the Kit Carson scout, we had some PFs (popular forces) along with us. They were from a local militia group and not very well trained. Although they couldn't really be counted on in a pitched battle, they knew the locals and who

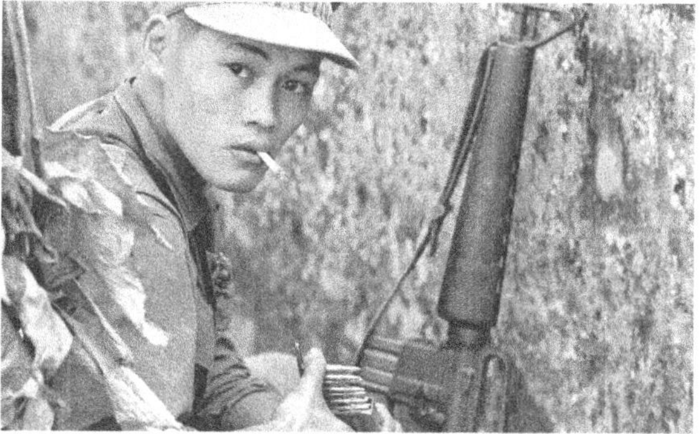

Kit Carson Scout Nguyen Hien reloads the magazine for his M16 following a firefight with enemy forces during Operation No Name II, east of Hue, April 1968. PHOTO BY CPL. DENNIS FISHER

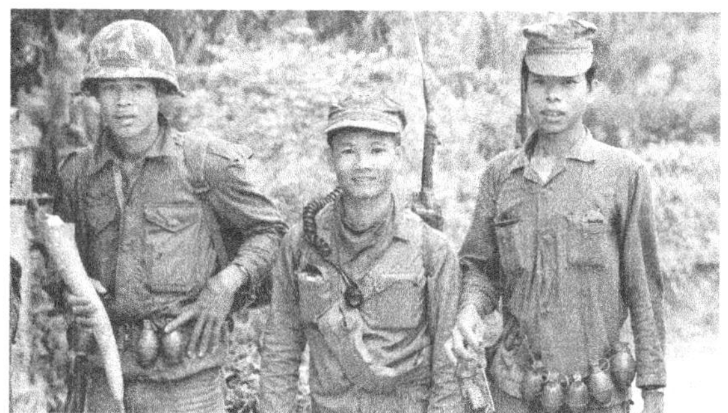

Local militia (popular forces) awaiting instructions as Marines from Delta 1/27 prepare to move out on day two of Operation No Name II, east of Hue, in April 1968. PHOTO BY CPL. DENNIS FISHER

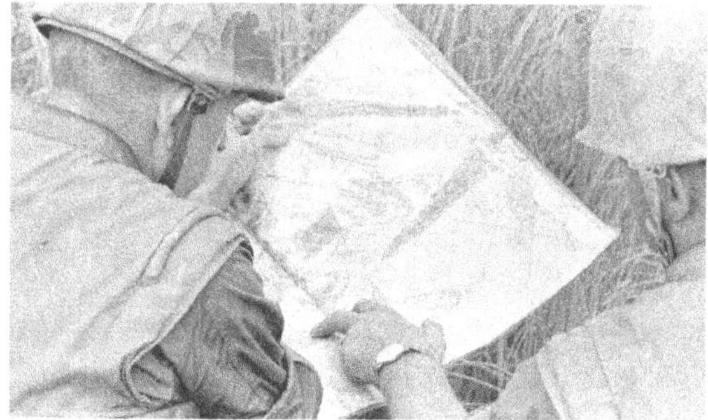

Lt. Col. Greenwood (left), CO of 1/27, and Delta 1/27 CO, Capt. Kahler (right), discuss plans to relieve Bravo during heavy fighting on Operation No Name II, east of Hue, April 1968. PHOTO BY CPL. DENNIS FISHER/COURTESY OF NARA STILL PICTURE BRANCH

the VC sympathizers were. We were supposed to have ARVN support too, but they were pulled off the op at the last minute to support another mission, and Bravo Company took over their responsibilities, as I recall.

While all of this was going on, we heard that Bravo Company, the blocking force, had walked into an ambush and had taken many casualties. One platoon was surrounded and their commander, Lieutenant Kettner, had been killed, with many others wounded. Captain Kahler had a hurried meeting with Lieutenant Colonel Greenwood, the battalion commander, on the best plan of action, and then impressed on everyone the urgency of relieving Bravo Company.

Thus, both Delta and Alpha companies began moving toward their position. However, Delta Company was encountering numerous mines and booby traps, and Alpha came under heavy automatic weapons fire. They called in artillery, and Delta was forced to proceed cautiously, with frequent firefights erupting as we got closer to Bravo. The heavy overcast had prevented any type of aerial support or medical evacuation of the wounded. This whole op had turned into a major engagement, and casualties were mounting quickly. Finally, around 1100 hours, we met up with Bravo Company and their CO, Captain Allen. He had been wounded by artillery and was visibly relieved to

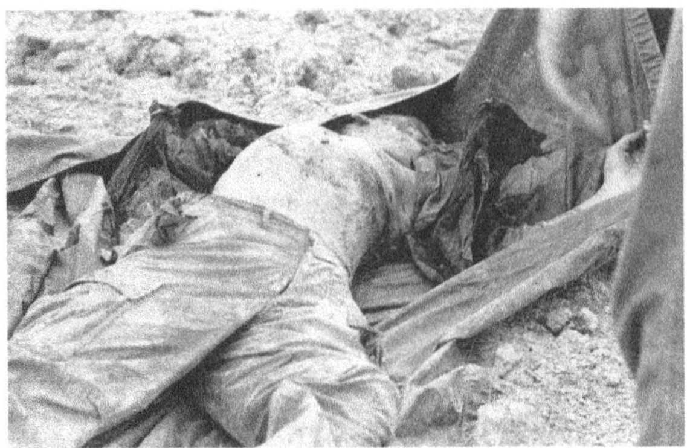

Marines prepare to remove the remains of one of their dead, an unidentified Marine from Bravo 1/27, killed in action during heavy fighting on April 13, 1968, during Operation No Name II, several miles east of Hue. PHOTO BY CPL. DENNIS FISHER

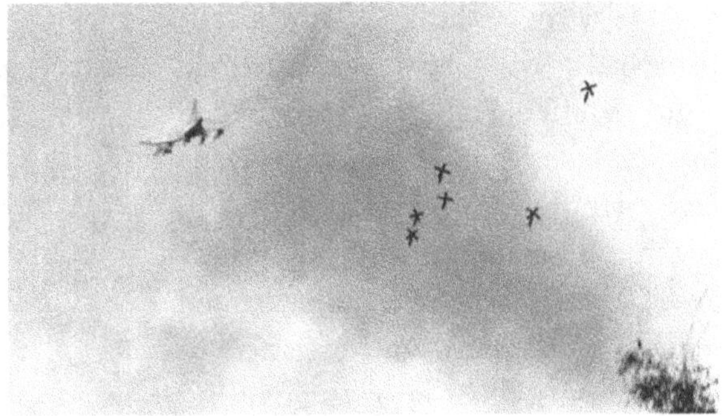

F-4 Phantoms provide close air support during Operation No Name II, dropping 250-pound "snake-eye" high-drag bombs "danger close" to Marine positions east of Hue in April 1968. PHOTO BY CPL. DENNIS FISHER

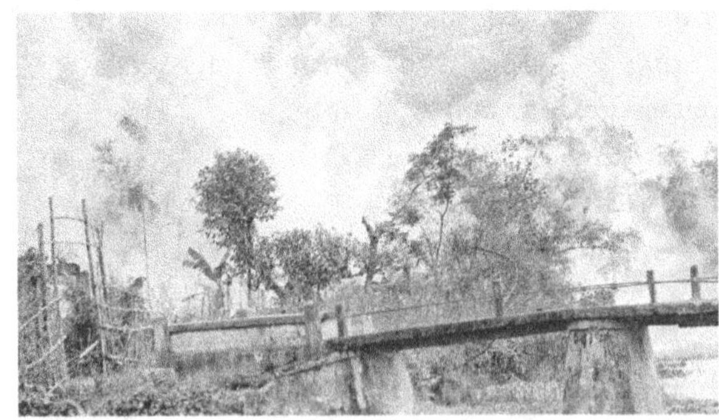

An airstrike on enemy positions in support of Alpha 1/27 during Operation No Name II, east of Hue, in April 1968. PHOTO BY CPL. DENNIS FISHER

see us. The enemy had been dug in with trenches and bunkers, as well as having overlapping fields of fire for their automatic weapons. They were well prepared, and it showed in the number of casualties suffered by the Marines.

Charlie Company had been dispatched from their base to render assistance and to set up an LZ to evacuate the wounded and dead once the weather broke, which it finally did in the afternoon. This also permitted fixed-wing fighter planes to come to our aid with close air support using bombs and rockets. F-4s and F-8s came swooping in with 250-pound bombs and rockets, which took the fight out of the NVA/VC. They seemed to melt away into the surrounding countryside. The rest of the afternoon was spent removing the wounded and dead from the battlefield. The toll was higher than I'd ever seen in two days of fighting: twenty-eight men KIA, and many more wounded.

Once the dead and wounded were evacuated, the word was passed to set in for the night and a night defensive perimeter was established. It had been a long, sad day for 1/27, and the usual banter among the men was rather subdued as they chowed down on C-rats and prepared for guard duty. This was the worst one-day loss of Marines I had witnessed during my time in Vietnam thus far, and coming as it did on Easter weekend, I couldn't help but imagine what it would be like for all the families back in the States. For the parents, wives, brothers, and sisters, it would forever brand the Easter weekend as an unimaginable tragedy. Unfortunately for the families back home, unlike Christ, these Marines would not rise from the dead.

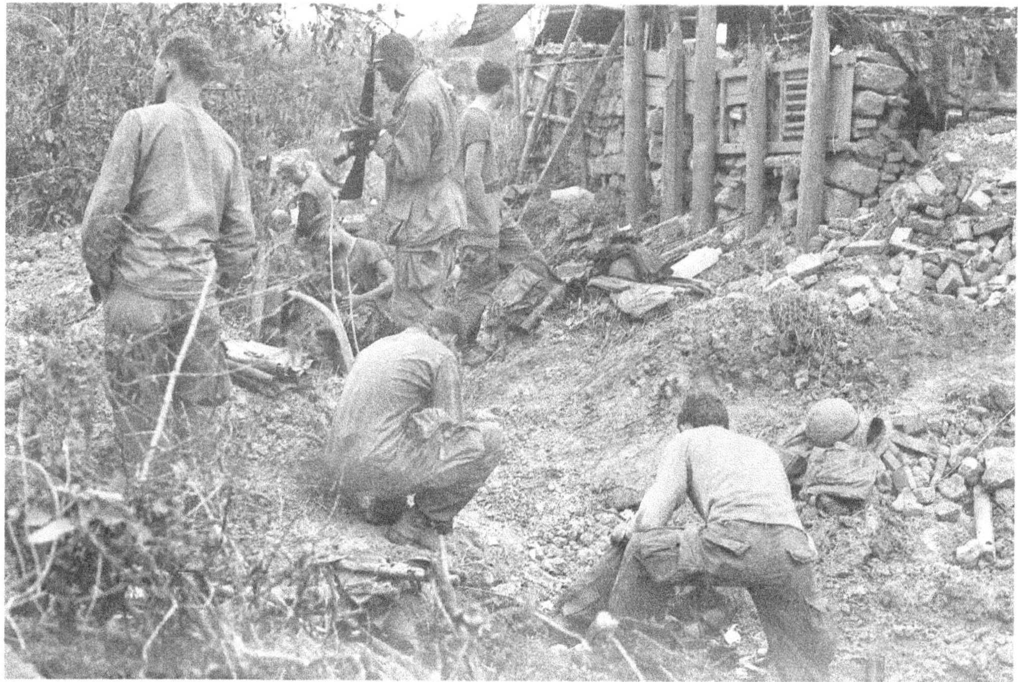

Marines from Delta 1/27 dig in for the night following heavy fighting during day two of Operation No Name II, east of Hue, April 1968. PHOTO BY CPL. DENNIS FISHER

Earl was busy gathering details and information for his story about the battle. For me, the light was quickly fading and no longer adequate for photography, so I found a place to dig in for the night and waited for him to return. I took advantage of the last bit of daylight to clean my camera and lenses so everything would be ready to go in the morning.

When Earl got back we discussed the day's events and broke out our rations for a quick meal. He gathered from discussions he'd heard between the battalion and company commanders that the enemy had pulled back to an area they controlled, closer to the ocean, and that a larger force of Marines would be needed to engage them.

It had been a long day, and I hoped it would be a quiet night as I rolled up in my poncho and tried to get comfortable in the position I had prepared for the night. Digging in for the night—or, more correctly, "preparing your night defensive position"—was essential to protecting yourself from a mortar attack or from an enemy night assault. We always tried to take advantage of natural terrain features to avoid as much digging as possible. In this instance I dug a hole about two and a half feet wide, twelve inches deep, and six feet long, piling up the excavated earth around the edge to make it a little higher. My helmet, pack, and other equipment would be piled around the edge near my head for added protection. A small hip hole finished off my position, for a little added comfort. I attached a poncho liner to my poncho for warmth and took a towel out of my pack to serve as a pillow. It was important to know where you'd placed everything because unexpected events might occur during the night that would require you to pack up and move to another position. No flashlight or illumination of any sort could be used, as it would make you an instant target. Knowing where you placed all your equipment was essential.

Even on a quiet night in the field, there was no chance of getting a real night's sleep. Your senses were on heightened alert, and every time someone got up to relieve themselves or men moved around as the guard was changed, you woke up. Not knowing whether or not the NVA or VC would attempt a counterattack, everyone was ordered to be extra vigilant, although no one needed to be reminded after what had happened during the day.

The night was quiet and uneventful except for Rebel, our German shepherd scout dog, whose frequent barking was giving away our position. His alerts were normally a good thing, but he didn't distinguish between

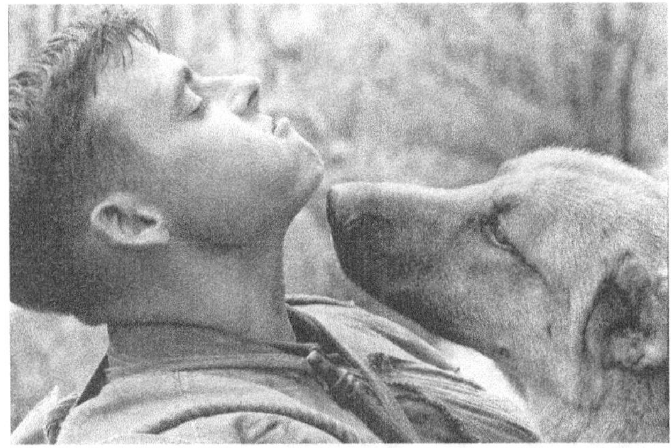

Cpl. Roy Jergins and his scout dog Rebel, supporting Delta 1/27 during Operation No Name II, east of Hue, April 1968. PHOTO BY CPL. DENNIS FISHER/COURTESY OF NARA STILL PICTURE BRANCH

the locals and the VC or NVA. Captain Kahler directed the dog's handler, Corporal Roy Jergins, to quiet him down or to take him and move to a remote section of our perimeter. Roy couldn't get him to quiet down; Rebel would start barking whenever he caught a whiff of Vietnamese. So Roy finally gathered up his gear and, with Rebel in tow, moved somewhere else.

It was too dark for me to see where he went, but I didn't hear Rebel any more that night. The scout dogs were a valuable asset, and their keen senses saved many Marine lives. The dog teams were actually part of the Military Police, and would be attached to infantry units during combat operations. When not in the field, they were used to help guard other facilities.

The op continued for another day with little contact, and ended on a sad note. One of the Huey gunships that was supporting the op radioed that he was low on fuel and was going to have to head back to base. He also said that he still had a number of rockets (2.75-inch folding-fin rockets), and that if we had any suspected enemy positions, to mark them with smoke and he would shoot them up before he left.

So our 60mm mortar crew fired a Willie Pete (white phosphorus) round into an area where we had taken some sniper fire. The gunship opened fire, but one of the rockets had a bent or damaged fin, and instead of flying straight and true, it corkscrewed and smashed into the Marines, seriously wounding one. A ten-inch-long piece of shrapnel had penetrated his flak jacket and was buried deep into his chest. The pilot saw what happened and immediately set down and picked him up for an impromptu medevac. I thought for sure he was a goner, but when I stopped by the hospital at Phu Bai a couple days later to check on him, he was doing fine, all things considered.

So ended No Name II—but it would not be the end of fighting there. This had been a bad place ever since the NVA were driven out of Hue. Earl and Sergeant Dale Dye, both combat correspondents, had been on Operation Ford the

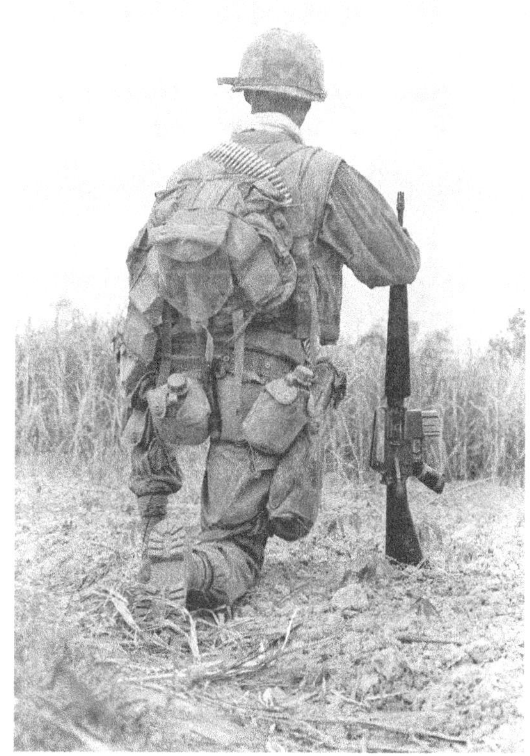

A Marine from Delta 1/27 prepares to move out at the completion of Operation No Name II near Hue in April 1968. PHOTO BY CPL. DENNIS FISHER

previous month, covering Echo 2/3 in this same area. The Marines would be back with a multi-battalion force and all the supporting arms in the area on Operation Baxter Garden a little over a week later. I didn't know it then, but I would be back, too.

As a postscript to this account, I should mention that when Lieutenant LaPage told Earl and me that we would be going out with the 27th Marines, we'd looked at each other a bit dumbstruck, thinking we were being punished for some unknown reason. The 27th Marines were new in the country, having been diverted to Vietnam while en route to a training exercise in the Philippines from their base in Hawaii. This was a result of the Tet Offensive, and the need for more Marines to quickly shore up the operations there. The scuttlebutt was that they were an untried and inexperienced unit, and going out with them could be downright dangerous.

While that was mostly true, I would say that they were well disciplined, and led by experienced officers and NCOs. They fought hard, and in my limited experience with them, I observed they were always on the offensive; I never saw them give up any ground. They were moved around southern I Corps where needed, and spent most of their time around Da Nang and Hue, participating in a number of major operations like Baxter Garden and Allen Brook, as well as a series of No Name ops such as the one I joined them on. I participated in both Baxter Garden and Allen Brook, but was traveling with other units and didn't have an opportunity to photograph them in action again. The word spread quickly among the various units during combat operations, and we heard what was happening with other units on the op. In the case of Allen Brook, 1/27 was in the thick of some of the worst fighting and took many more casualties.

In the end I had great respect for them, especially considering the fact they were pulled out of a comfortable billet at Kaneohe Bay in Hawaii and dropped into some of the fiercest fighting of the war. Two excellent accounts of their tour of duty in Vietnam were presented in *To the Sound of the Guns: 1st Battalion, 27th Marines from Hawaii to Vietnam 1966–1968* by Grady T. Birdsong and *Young Blood: A History of the 1st Battalion, 27th Marines* by Gary Jarvis, PhD. Both books were written by members of the 27th Marines who served with them in Vietnam.

# CHAPTER 13

# Operation Baxter Garden

## *East of Hue*

BACK IN PHU BAI ONCE AGAIN, I PROCESSED MY FILM AND COMPLETED ALL THE ATTEN-dant paperwork necessary to caption and number the negatives and get them sent off to HQMC, along with some prints for Earl's story. Talk around the ISO hooch was that after the 27th Marines got their noses bloodied during No Name II, there was a new operation in the works called Baxter Garden, to go back into that area with overwhelming force and clean the place out once and for all.

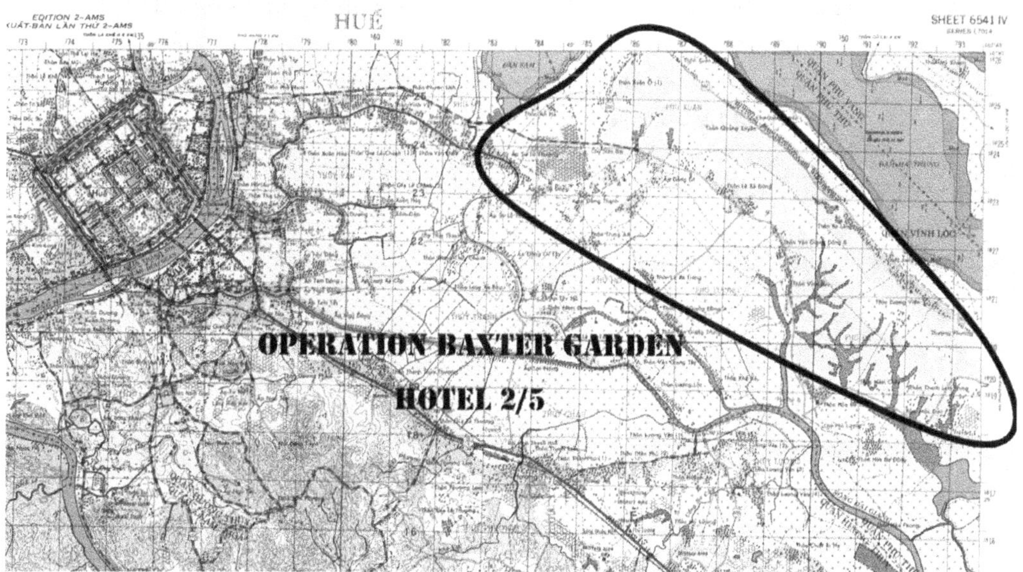


A map showing the location where Operation Baxter Garden was conducted in April 1968.

The No Name ops run in that area were not the only attempts to do this. Operation Ford, mentioned earlier, which ran from March 14 through 20, was conducted in the same area against the same 804th NVA Battalion. Combat correspondents Corporal Earl Gerheim and Sergeant Dale Dye were dispatched from ISO to cover that op with Echo 2/3. Both were wounded, with Dale distinguishing himself during the heaviest part of the fighting, providing critical first-aid treatment to wounded Marines and taking over for the assistant gunner on an M60 machine-gun team who was wounded. He was doing all this while wounded himself. His heroism under fire did not go unnoticed, and he was awarded the Bronze Star with a combat V for his actions that day. I recently spoke with Earl, who provided the following narrative:

> *The late afternoon and night before, we had been in a big fight with the NVA on Operation Ford. We were with Echo 2/3 and our blocking force, Charlie 1/1, was slammed into by the NVA. Echo Company got on line and assaulted five hundred meters across open sand to relieve our blocking force. Dale got hit in the arm and my right pants side was ripped after I got hit twice with grenade fragments. Dale A-gunned for Corporal Darrel Beebe, and they fired 2,600 rounds into the enemy positions.*

With the benefit of their experience in mind, plus what I had just encountered on Operation No Name II, I began preparing for what was shaping up to be a pretty big operation. Perhaps the biggest takeaway was the sheer number of Marines who had been wounded by mines and booby traps. Coupled with the knowledge that the enemy was well emplaced in prepared positions, this operation could end up being a slugfest.

Lieutenant LaPage let us know that Operation Baxter Garden was going to be kicking off on April 19, and in addition to the photographers and correspondents from Task Force X-Ray, there would be others coming up from Division to travel with the various battalions involved. On the photo side I personally ran into Lance Corporal Pete Wilber, a combat mopic photographer, and PFC Ed "Sully" Sullivan, who was shooting stills. Both were friends from the Division Photo Lab in Da Nang. There may have been others, but those were the ones I met on the op. We walked along together for a while on the afternoon of April 20, but soon split up, and I didn't see them again on that mission.

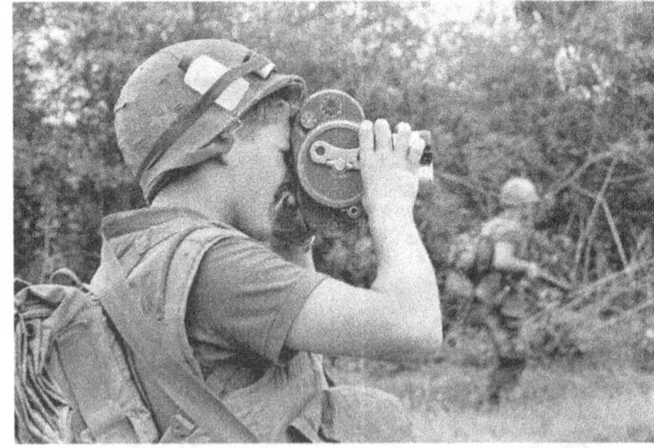

L/Cpl. Peter Wilber, a mopic photographer with the 1st Marine Division, captures Marines from Hotel 2/5 on film during Operation Baxter Garden along the coast, east of Hue, April 1968. PHOTO BY CPL. DENNIS FISHER

I was assigned to Hotel 2/5 for this operation, and from the start it was clear the Marines were tired of messing around with these guys—they meant to "kick ass and take names." The official purpose of the op was a rice denial mission. It included not only Echo and Hotel companies from 2/5, but also Bravo from 1/5 and Charlie and Delta from 1/27. I had just been with Delta 1/27 on No Name II and Hotel 2/5 on Houston, so I was seeing some familiar faces.

In addition to the infantry units there was a platoon of tanks from the 1st Tank Battalion, as well as Amtracs and Ontos antitank vehicles from other units in the area. We had artillery support, with 105mm and 8-inch howitzers, 4.2-inch and 81mm mortars, 106mm recoilless rifles mounted on mules (the mechanized variety, not animals), plus fixed-wing fighter planes and helicopter gunship support from above. Two battalions of ARVNs also participated in the op. Although this seemed like an overwhelming force to me, we would be pursuing the same 802nd NVA main force battalion (MFB) that 1/27 was up against during No Name II. There were also an unknown number of VC and possible elements of the 804th NVA MFB.

The terrain we would be facing was rather benign. It was a flat coastal area covered with rice paddies. Small villages lined the trails and roads, and the population here was known to be sympathetic to the communists. The eastern part of the operational area was on the coast and consisted of sandy back beach terrain and some woods. The whole area was interspersed with bamboo hedge lines and small trees. And, as the Marines found out on Operations Ford and No Name II, the place was heavily booby-trapped and mined.

We were flown out by helicopter on the morning of April 19, but heavy ground fire forced the chopper I was in to turn back. I was finally able to get out the next day on a resupply chopper that dropped me off with a bunch of supplies around lunchtime. I followed Marines from Bravo 1/5, who were taking some of the supplies back to their unit, with the hope of meeting up with Hotel 2/5 somewhere along the way.

Finding 2/5 was put on the back burner for the time being as I arrived in the aftermath of a serious firefight and began taking photos. I soon found myself at the location of the battalion aid station that had been established in the field, manned by a medical officer, a chief petty officer, and three corpsmen.

As I came up the trail, I saw the carnage the firefight had wrought on this unit. Just ahead, four dead Marines were lined up on stretchers, their faces covered, lying there in full battle gear and flak jackets as a corpsman filled out casualty tags. The color had not yet drained from their bodies and they looked like they were sleeping. Another dead Marine was being brought in on a stretcher, with more arriving at regular intervals. Wounded Marines began arriving too. The medical personnel were patching up the wounded while another corpsman continued tagging the dead. We had corpsmen assigned to all the infantry units who rendered initial treatment and, depending on the severity of the injuries, would either patch the men up and return them to duty, prepare them to be medevacked, or on this operation, render first aid and send them to the aid station. There they would receive further treatment before being evacuated.

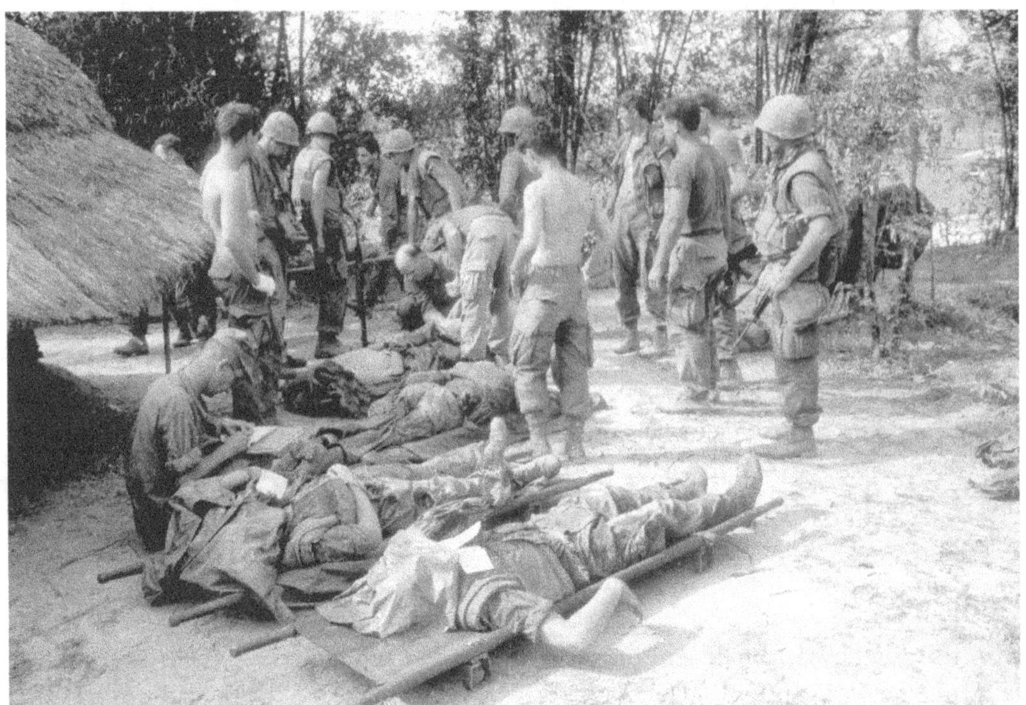

Marines KIA from Bravo 1/5 are tagged and prepared for evacuation by medical personnel at the battalion aid station during Operation Baxter Garden along the coast, east of Hue, April 1968. PHOTO BY CPL. DENNIS FISHER

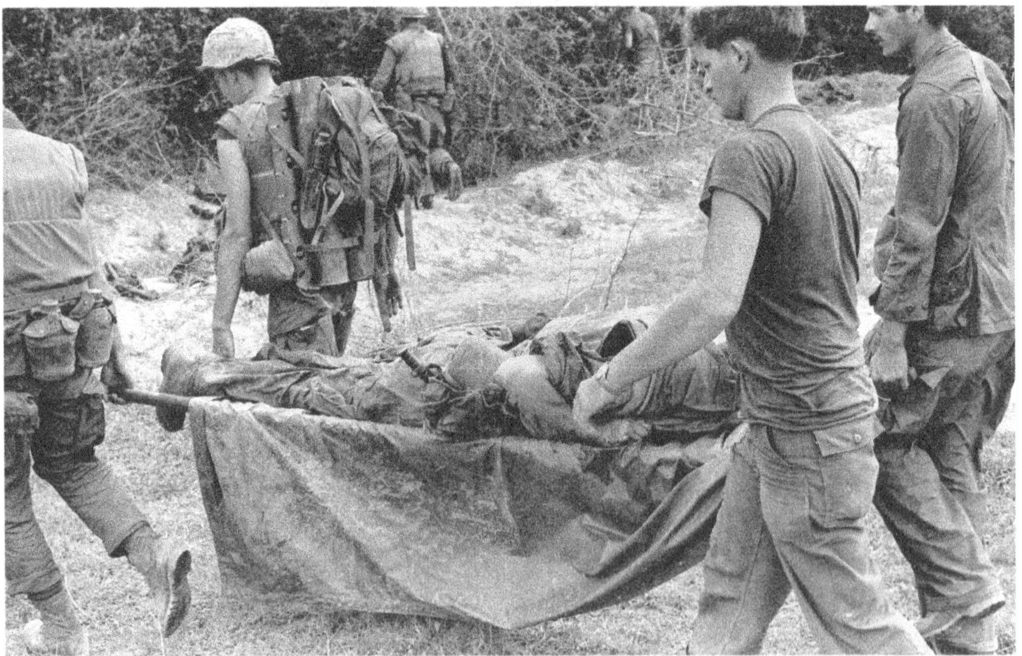

Wounded Marines from Bravo 1/5 being moved to a battalion aid station for treatment and medevac during Operation Baxter Garden, east of Hue, April 1968. PHOTO BY CPL. DENNIS FISHER

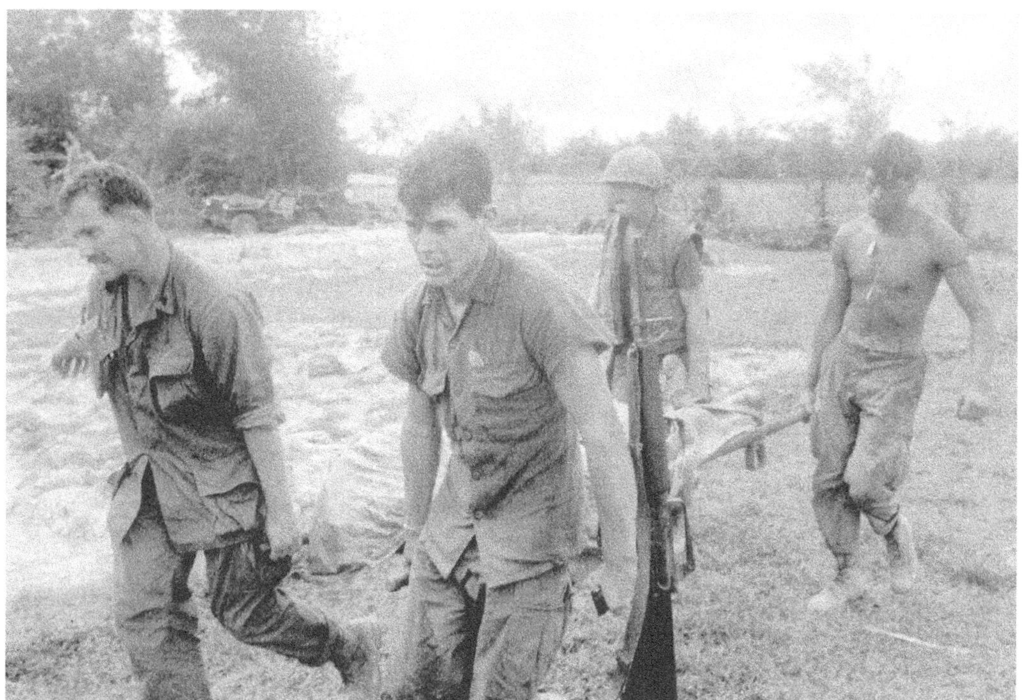

A Marine from Bravo 1/5 KIA during Operation Baxter Garden is removed from the field by fellow Marines during fighting east of Hue in April 1968. PHOTO BY CPL. DENNIS FISHER

Having an aid station out in the field was a big help in stabilizing the severely wounded and getting them back to the hospital for treatment. Calling it an aid station may be a bit of an overstatement. It was a patch of ground outside a thatched Vietnamese home in the shade of some trees where the medical team set up their treatment area.

I continued taking photos as some of our Marines bombarded the enemy with 81mm mortars, a 106mm recoilless rifle, 105mm artillery, air strikes, and helicopter gunships, along with calling in another platoon to help them out. My attention was drawn to a nearby 106 crew that had spotted the enemy in a tree line ahead of us and quickly brought their gun to bear on the position. Several HE rounds from the 106 cleared them out, and we continued. This may have been the same group that ambushed the men I photographed being brought in to the aid station.

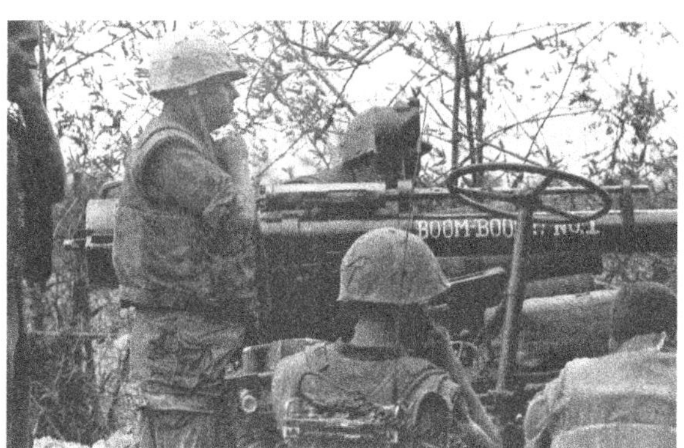



A 106mm recoilless rifle crew preparing to fire on an enemy position in support of Bravo 1/5, east of Hue, during Operation Baxter Garden, April 1968. PHOTO BY CPL. DENNIS FISHER

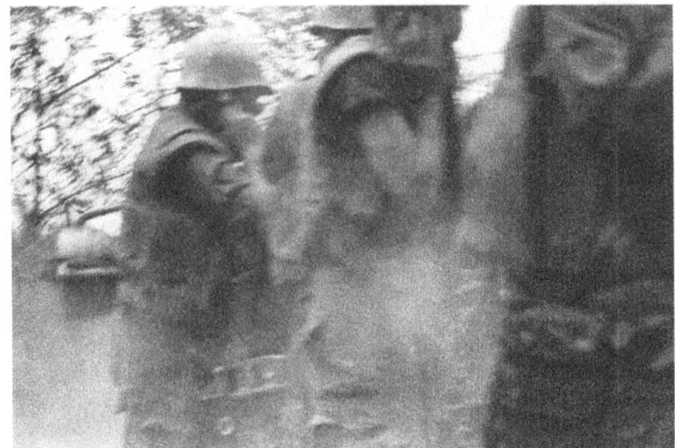

A 106mm recoilless rifle crew braces for the blast and overpressure from their guns as they fire on an enemy position east of Hue during Operation Baxter Garden in April 1968. PHOTO BY CPL. DENNIS FISHER

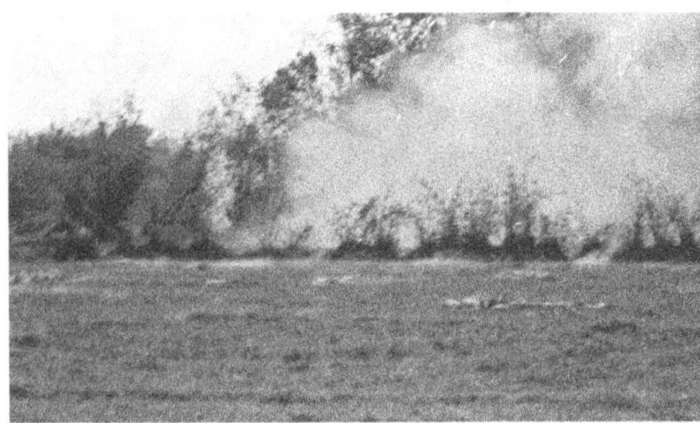

An HE round from a 106mm recoilless rifle impacts an enemy position in a tree line east of Hue during Operation Baxter Garden in April 1968. PHOTO BY CPL. DENNIS FISHER

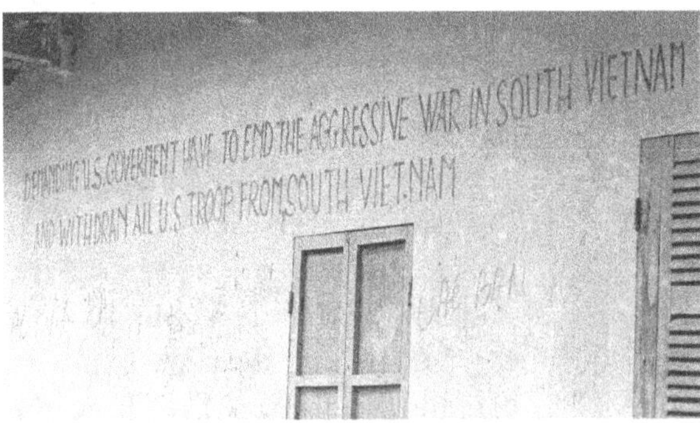


North Vietnamese propaganda written in English on the side of a building east of Hue during Operation Baxter Garden in April 1968. PHOTO BY CPL. DENNIS FISHER

This morning went badly for the Marines, and I knew as I photographed them bringing in their dead and wounded that this op wasn't going to be a walk in the park. By my count, there were eight dead and a dozen or more wounded. The survivors who were bringing back the dead were very distressed and had a sort of "what the hell just happened" look about them. They were none too happy to see me taking photos of them and their deceased friends, either. While I never liked photographing our own dead, my job was to document the whole operation as it happened. My only concession when photographing our dead was to avoid showing their faces. Whether the mission went good or bad, I shot it all.

As things were quieting down with Bravo Company, I continued following the directions from the grunts on my trek to join up with Hotel 2/5. Passing a building that the enemy had defaced with their version of psychological warfare propaganda, I paused to take a photo. These messages in English were often found in areas occupied by the enemy, as well as some in Vietnamese that were directed toward the locals.

I heard a lot of firing in the general direction I was heading and began to think that Hotel was engaged in something. As I was leaving to find my unit, one of the Marines from Bravo told me that

Hotel had set up a blocking force and had been sending out patrols during the morning to try and locate the enemy. It sounded like one of those patrols had made contact. The sound of LAWs being fired, small arms fire, bloopers, and artillery rounds exploding rolled across the paddies. Continuing to move toward the sound of guns, I noted that firing became more sporadic and seemed to quiet down before I reached them.

When I finally did reach Hotel 2/5, I checked in with Captain Hendrickson, the company CO, and let him know I'd been assigned to cover his unit. It was important to always let everyone in the chain of command know where you were, or where you planned to be, so that they could include you when ordering rations, account for you if you were wounded, or look for you if you didn't show up by nightfall.

I was reported missing in action on Operation Allen Brook when the company radio operator failed to pass on my message to the CO that I had run out of film and was taking a resupply chopper back to our lab. Upon arriving at the lab, they had already heard I was MIA and were greatly relieved to see me still among the living. After that experience, I always made sure to personally inform the CO of my movements.

Traveling with them for the rest of the day had been relatively uneventful until early afternoon when a couple of the men set off booby traps as we were entering a small village. Three men were wounded as a result, but none were killed. Two of them were medevacked, and the corpsman patched up the third, who was well enough to continue the mission. The company had continued on the sweep when about an hour later, a nearby Marine tripped another booby trap, wounding himself. He had received a head wound and was bleeding badly. A corpsman was quickly on the scene with another Marine, and the wounded Marine was quickly bandaged with a battle dressing and moved to the rear to be medevacked.

During this patrol the Marines captured some enemy gear and laid it out so I could photograph it. Not a whole lot of stuff, but at least the mortar shells and B-40s they retrieved wouldn't be raining down on us at night. By now the day was winding down, when just before sunset there was a lot of shooting to the north of us. One of the patrols from Echo was engaged in a firefight but they were too far away for me to join them, and it was getting to the point where there wasn't enough light to take photos anyway.

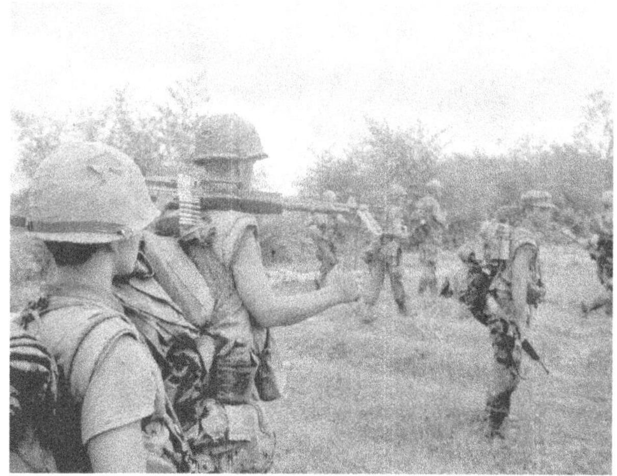

Marines from Hotel 2/5 move toward their next objective during Operation Baxter Garden along the coast, east of Hue, in April 1968. PHOTO BY CPL. DENNIS FISHER

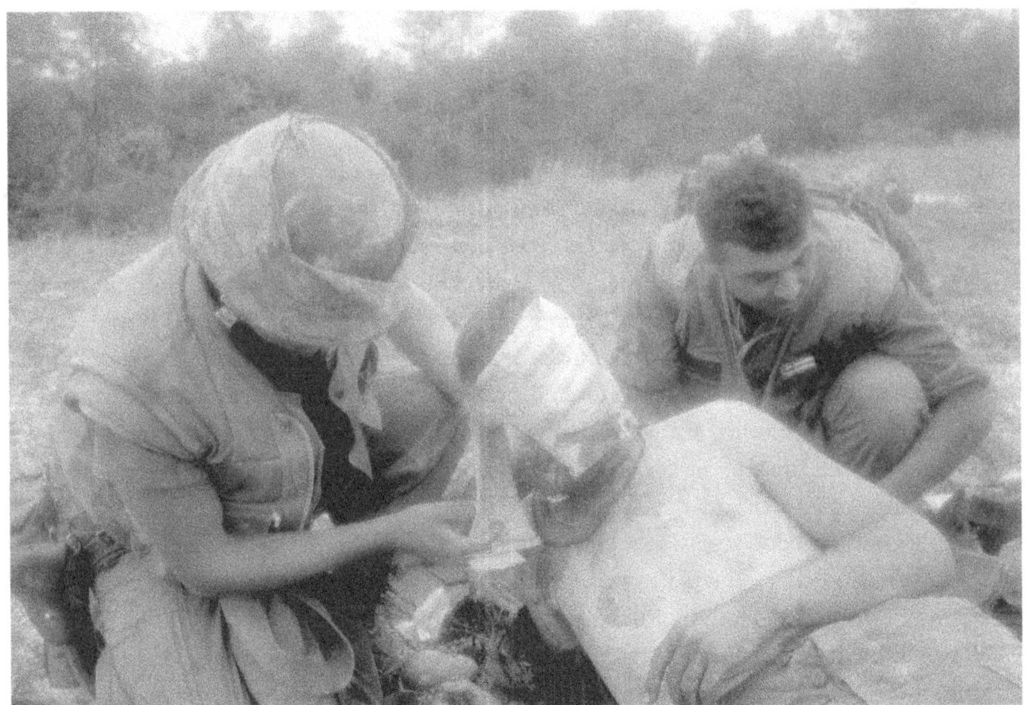

A wounded Marine from Hotel 2/5 being treated in the field before being moved to the battalion aid station for medevac during Operation Baxter Garden, along the coast, east of Hue, April 1968. PHOTO BY CPL. DENNIS FISHER

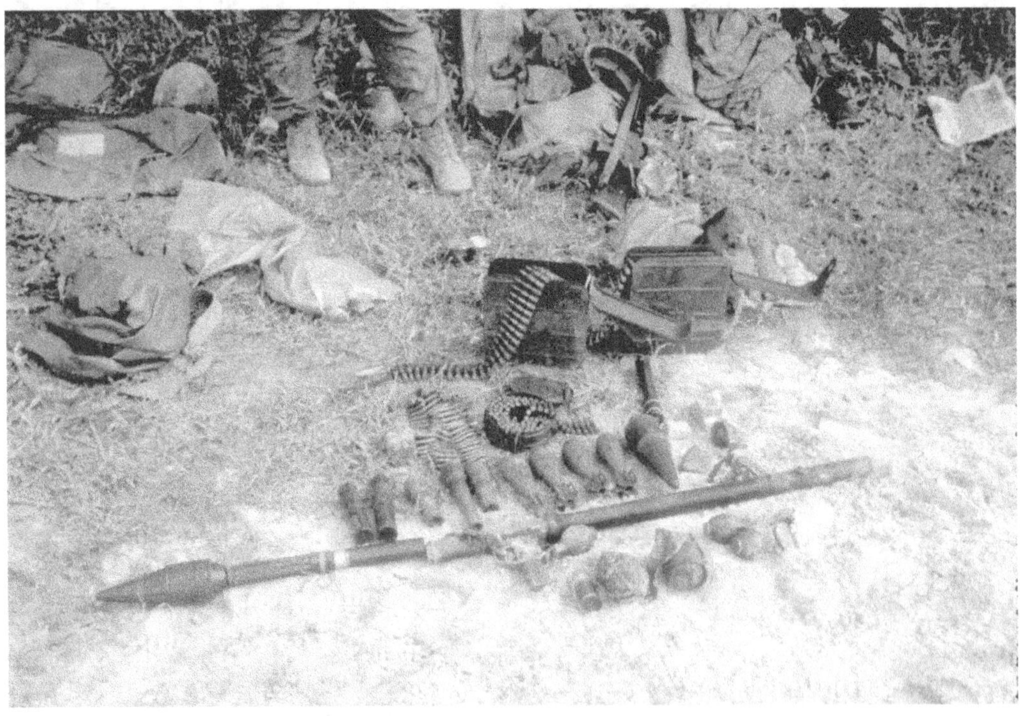

A small cache of enemy equipment and weapons captured by Hotel 2/5 during Operation Baxter Garden, east of Hue, April 1968. PHOTO BY CPL. DENNIS FISHER

The enemy had plenty of time to prepare fighting positions in the several months they had occupied this area. Spider holes, trenches, and bunkers were scattered around and had to be identified and neutralized as we moved through. Marines used everything from hand grenades to air strikes to reduce these threats.

Taking advantage of what light was left to clean my cameras and get my caption sheets up to date ended my day. Cleaning the Nikon F was nothing more than using a small camel-hair brush to clean the dust and dirt out of the eyepiece and removing the pentaprism and focusing screen to do the same. The reflex mirror was also given a dusting off. The front elements of the lenses were treated to a little lens cleaner and lens tissue to get them back in shape. My Nikonos, which was designed as an underwater camera, required little more than cleaning the front of the lens, since it was a sealed unit.

I set my cameras aside, broke out my P-38, and opened a can of "Ham, Sliced, Cooked" from a B-3A C-ration unit for dinner, along with a can of fruit cocktail. I was too tired and hungry to warm the ham up and just ate it cold. I have often been asked about C-rats, especially with regard to taste and what types of food were in them. Here is the short version: First off, they were supplied to us in the field in heavy-duty cardboard cases, bound with wire that held a dozen meals. The meals were individually boxed and came in different varieties meant for breakfast, lunch, and dinner. Each meal was labeled with its contents, such as "Beefsteak," "Turkey Loaf," "Chopped Ham and Eggs," etc.

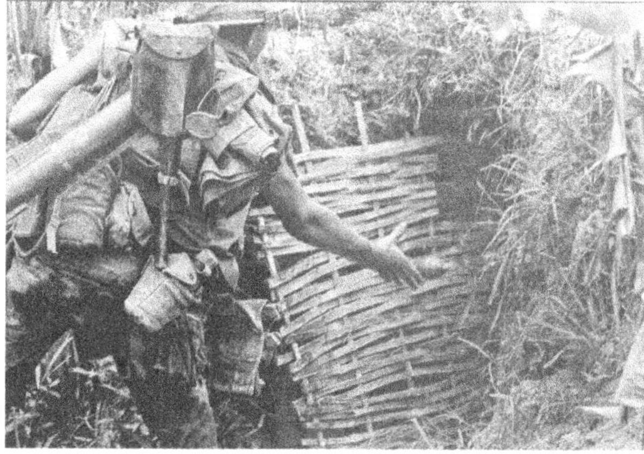

A Marine from Hotel 2/5 neutralizes an enemy bunker with an M26 fragmentation grenade during Operation Baxter Garden along the coast, east of Hue, April 1968. PHOTO BY CPL. DENNIS FISHER/COURTESY OF NARA STILL PICTURE BRANCH

An opened case of C-rations showing the selection of meals. The rations got their name from a large letter "C" that was on the front of the case. They were more correctly known as meal, combat, individual, or MCIs. PHOTO BY CPL. DENNIS FISHER

Each Marine had his favorite, so to keep the selections fair, the opened cases would be turned upside down so the labels faced the ground. Each man would then get to pick out two or three meals at random. After finding out what you got, it was time to start trading to try and acquire what you really wanted. The least popular meal was the Ham and Lima Beans (or "Ham and Motherf*ckers," in Marine parlance). With the exception of Marines who hailed from the Southern states, the rest of us would rather go hungry than eat those.

Included in the meal box was an accessory pack that had matches, chewing gum, toilet paper, cigarettes, instant coffee, powdered cream, sugar, and salt. There was also a nylon plastic spoon included. We were usually supplied with the blue-colored Trioxane heat tabs to warm up the rations. Frequently C-4 plastic explosive was used to heat water for coffee or cocoa. When it was lit, it burned very hot and fast, which precluded using it for food, but for liquids it was fine.

Everyone carried a "stove" fashioned from one of the smaller C-ration cans, which was perforated around the bottom with a can opener to allow airflow to the heat tabs. Remember, cans were all made of steel back then, no aluminum, and there were no pop tops or self-opening cans. Everyone carried a "church key and a John Wayne"—a combination bottle/can opener and a P-38 C-ration opener. The P-38 was usually kept on your dog tag chain so it was easily available when needed. Plus, we never kept the C-rations in the boxes. They would be dumped out and put in our pack loose. I usually picked out what I wanted to eat next and stowed it in a pocket on my pack where I could find it easily. Some guys would put them in a sock tied to their pack.

With the light fading, it was time to dig in for the night. This could mean a number of things with regard to preparing a way to protect and defend yourself from incoming small arms fire and mortars. Everyone carried an E-tool (entrenching tool), which was a small multiuse folding shovel to prepare their night defensive position. Providing some sort of protection from mortars was the primary concern; you might actually dig a foxhole, but that took a lot of time and effort. Another option was to utilize trenches or fighting holes abandoned by the enemy, although you had to check them carefully for booby traps. Making use of existing terrain features or man-made structures would work too. Whatever you chose, it had to fall along the defensive perimeter that the commander had chosen. As a photographer, I didn't have to stand guard at night and could set in at a place of my choosing. I normally tried to stay in the vicinity of the CP group so I could find out what was planned for the next day and keep informed about what was going on with our sister companies.

Around 0930 on the morning of April 21, Hotel Company headed out toward a new objective, and this time we were joined by some The M48 Patton tanks from the Alpha Company of the 1st Tank Battalion. It was pretty easy going for them in most areas, and I photographed them on the move. One tank did get hung up in a particularly heavy hedge line, but only for a moment. It was always nice to have the tanks along, because they could directly engage enemy threats with their big gun at a moment's notice. We finally broke

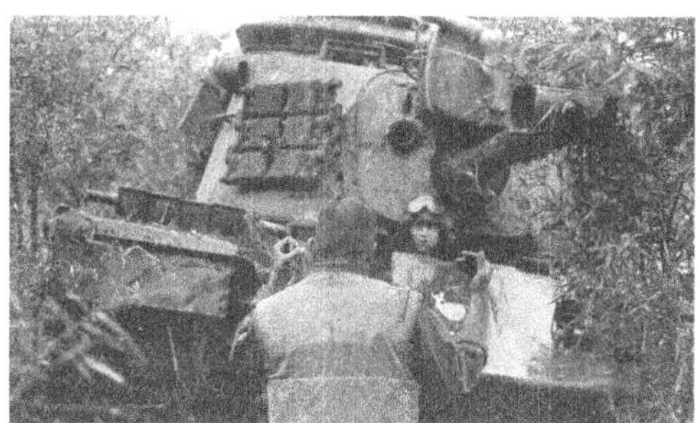

An M48 Patton tank from the 1st Tank Battalion moves carefully through heavy vegetation during Operation Baxter Garden in support of Hotel 2/5, east of Hue, in April 1968. PHOTO BY CPL. DENNIS FISHER

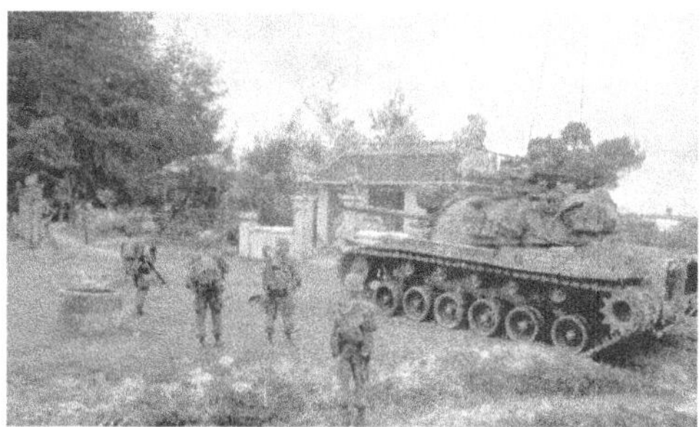

The M48 Patton tank "Eve of Destruction" from the 1st Tank Battalion moves into position to support Hotel 2/5 during Operation Baxter Garden along the coast, east of Hue, in April 1968. PHOTO BY CPL. DENNIS FISHER

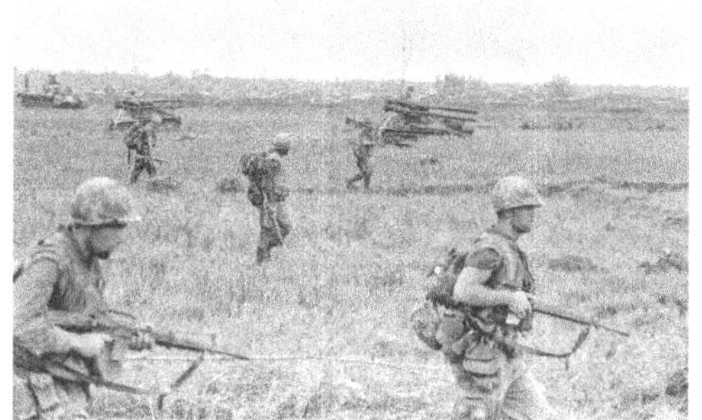

Marines from Hotel 2/5 spread out on line as they advance on the enemy with support from tanks and Ontos vehicles during Operation Baxter Garden, along the coast, east of Hue, in April 1968. PHOTO BY CPL. DENNIS FISHER

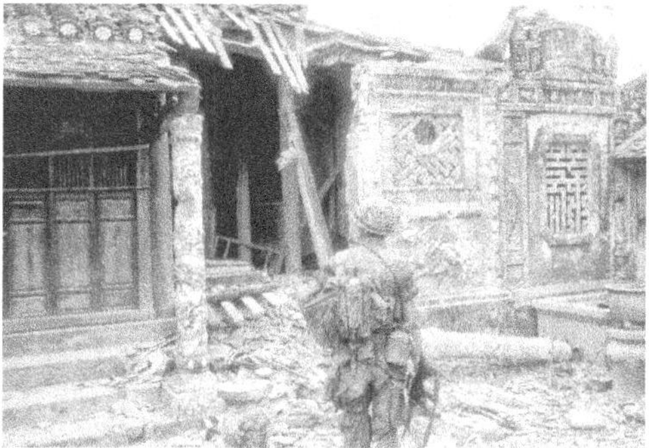

A Marine from Hotel 2/5 examines the destruction to the position that had been neutralized by 90mm HE rounds from supporting tanks during Operation Baxter Garden in April 1968. PHOTO BY CPL. DENNIS FISHER

out into an open sandy area and I could now see the infantry on line, the tanks, Ontos vehicles, and Amtracs sweeping across the battlefield, which ran adjacent to a huge cemetery. We were not receiving any fire at this time, and the advance went smoothly.

I think they pulled Bravo Company from the op that morning, or at least I didn't see them in the field anymore. There were so many helicopters flying around, bringing in supplies and taking out wounded, it was hard to tell from a distance exactly what was going on. In the midst of all this, one of the other platoons caught a VC hiding in a spider hole and killed him that afternoon, capturing his weapon and some documents. However, the rest of that afternoon didn't go well at all. Several booby traps were tripped, and four more men from Hotel Company were medevacked. It seemed like mines and booby traps littered the landscape and were causing most of the casualties, with no end in sight.

At this point I pretty much lost track of how many men had been killed or wounded, but the toll was definitely rising and continued to mount during the day, with men from a number of companies being wounded. We had been moving generally in a southeast direction, paralleling the coast for most of the day, and around 1700, word was passed to halt and set in for the night. We hadn't really covered a lot of distance due to the frequent encounters with mines and booby traps, but it was nice to finally sit down and take a break.

One thing I remember about Vietnam was the noise. It was noisy day and night. You would think things would quiet down at night, but this was generally not so, even in the rear. Between the air strikes, helicopters, trucks, tanks, artillery, mortars, and all the infantry small arms, it was a huge cacophony of sound. One did get used to it after a fashion, or you never would have gotten any sleep. There was no ear protection, and even if it had been available, no one would have worn it because your eyes and ears were the main senses you needed on the battlefield.

That night wasn't too bad until an early-morning explosion roused me and everyone else who wasn't already awake. At first I thought it was an incoming mortar, but it turned out to be another booby trap, which wounded eight more men, seven of whom had to be medevacked. And so it continued all day, one mine or booby trap after another. The Marines were good at spotting them, and many were blown in place by the engineers, but the sheer number of them and the enemy's ability to conceal them was proving costly.

We had barely begun moving on the morning of April 23 when yet another booby trap wounded two men from the company. I

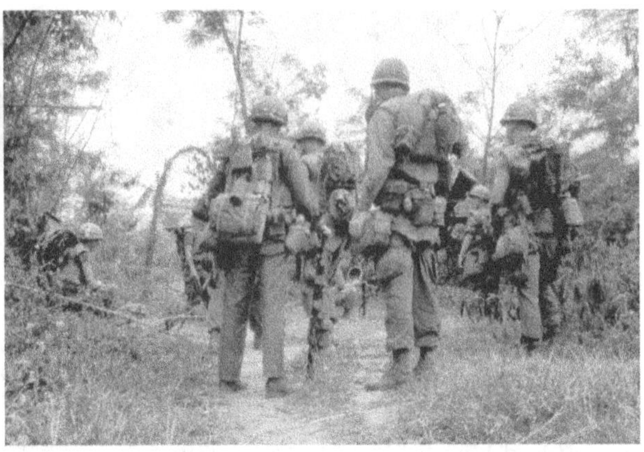

Marines from Hotel 2/5 pause prior to moving toward their next objective during Operation Baxter Garden along the coast, east of Hue, in April 1968. PHOTO BY CPL. DENNIS FISHER

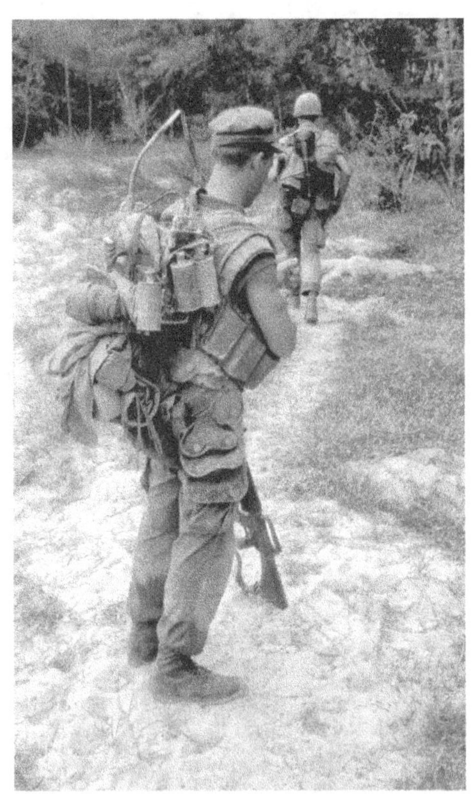

A radioman from Hotel 2/5 pauses to monitor radio traffic as his unit moves into a wooded area recently occupied by the enemy. PHOTO BY CPL. DENNIS FISHER

heard the explosion but was some distance away. A little later that morning I heard a lot of automatic weapons fire from what sounded like AKs and RPDs, followed by firing from the platoon on our flank. Soon after I saw a huge plume of black smoke rising several hundred yards away in the direction of the firing, and I suspected that one of our flamethrower teams had opened up on the enemy position. I found out later that it was actually one of the flame tanks. Most of the tanks had names painted on their gun barrels; I remember one was called "Crispy Critters." This was the name of a breakfast cereal back then, but it was given a whole new meaning here when applied to a flamethrower tank.

Photographically the activities that day were what would be considered routine on this type of mission. As a photographer, I always wanted to be at the scene of the action, but it was just the luck of the draw. Sometimes the unit I was with would go all day and never fire a round, and other times they would be involved in several heavy firefights. If the action was happening within a hundred yards or so, I would move to the sound of the guns, but running down the trails here, in light of all the mines and booby traps, was just plain stupid.

Setting in for the night on this day came with word that we would be moving out for a night march. It seemed the enemy had reoccupied one of the places we had previously cleared, and the unit needed to be in place by daybreak for an early-morning assault. Since I couldn't take photos at night, I was back to being a grunt for a while. The assault in the morning was anticlimactic, as the enemy had spotted our approach and moved out.

The big news on April 24 was that two Marines from H&S Company were missing. An immediate search on the ground and by air was undertaken, but to no avail. Most of us assumed they had somehow become separated from their unit and were captured or killed by the enemy. I never learned their fate, and to this day don't know what happened to them.

Around sunset on April 25, Echo ran into thirty or forty enemy, engaged them in a firefight, and called in artillery and gunship support. The enemy took off with Echo right behind them, and about a half-hour later they were driven into a blocking force of tanks, which opened up with their 90mm main guns, as well as their machine guns. I wasn't present, but could hear the 90mm guns from the tanks firing, along with a lot of machine-gun fire. As the sun set, the enemy fled, leaving seventeen dead on the field and numerous blood trails.

One other incident that sticks in my mind with regard to Baxter Garden was the use of an E-8 CS gas launcher. This was a backpack launcher unit that contained a number of inch-and-a-half-diameter rockets equipped with CS tear-gas warheads. I followed the crew that carried one around for an afternoon, hoping to get some photos of it being fired, but it wasn't employed when I was with them. When they finally did have an opportunity to use it, a bunch of us were downwind and the gas blew our way. We were far enough away that it was only mildly irritating. I had my gas mask along but didn't feel the gas was strong enough to warrant putting it on. The E-8 seemed like more of a riot-control munition than something to be used in combat, but I guess that someone somewhere decided it would be a good thing to try out.

The next day Operation Baxter Garden wound up and I flew with 2/5 back to their base at Cao Doi. The CH-46 slid out of the sky for a smooth landing, and the Marines quickly deplaned down the rear ramp. We were only on the ground long enough for them to exit and then were airborne again. I remained the lone passenger as the chopper quickly lifted off and headed for Phu Bai to refuel and drop me off. Sitting there alone, I was watching the door gunner scanning the ground below for muzzle flashes, wondering how many times he had done this. Would this flight be uneventful, or would it suddenly devolve into a fight for survival in the air? Although I'd flown many times, I never lost the fear that things could go bad real fast while landing or taking off.

As we gained altitude and moved beyond the range of ground fire, the gunners relaxed, and there was nothing to do but sit back and enjoy the cool air rushing in the windows for the short hop back to Phu Bai. It seemed like the adrenaline was finally wearing off, and all of a sudden I was tired. I just wanted to get back to my hooch and sleep for a day in the relative safety of the base.

Thirteen Marines were lost on that operation, but only one with the company I covered. In the end, I don't know how successful we were in driving the enemy out of that area. They were tough and resourceful, and there was no doubt the Marines would be encountering them again.

I walked from the airfield across the base, heading for the ISO hooch, but first detoured across the street to Division Headquarters, where they had a walk-up window to sell sodas and snacks. I was straight in from the field, still carrying all my gear, and all I wanted was a cold Pepsi. The office pogue who was manning the window looked down at my boots and said that they had a rule you couldn't buy anything unless your boots were shined. I

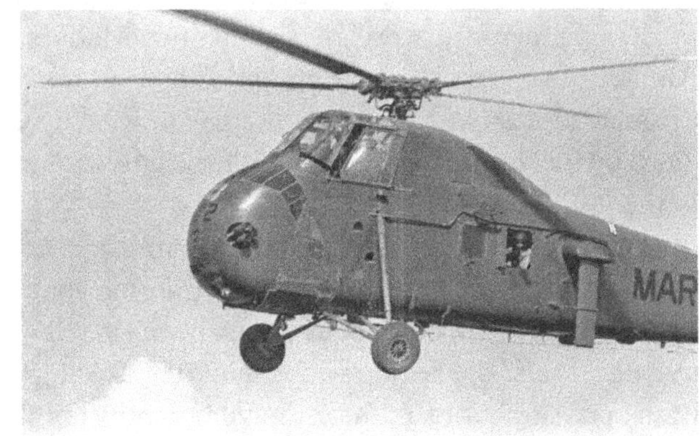

A UH-34 helicopter arriving to transport troops back to base following the completion of Operation Baxter Garden in April 1968. PHOTO BY CPL. DENNIS FISHER

tried explaining my situation to him but he wasn't having any of it. I considered unlimbering my grease gun and sending his sorry ass home in a body bag, but felt it would hurt my chances for promotion to sergeant.

As the discussion rapidly progressed into a heated argument, a Marine lieutenant colonel on his way into the building walked up and quickly resolved the situation by suggesting that the private either sell me the soda or be transferred to a line company, so he could better appreciate my request. This officer had obviously spent time in the field with line companies and didn't have any more use for these REMFs than I did. I often wondered why those Marines who were lucky enough to serve in rear-area positions didn't have more empathy for those who served in the field. This antipathy was pretty widespread and a constant source of irritation among Marines.

It is events like this that taint my thoughts about those who served "in the rear with the gear." Yes, they served in Vietnam, but I have no respect for those who enjoyed all the privileges that such an assignment afforded while using their position to screw over the men who actually faced the enemy in the field. I don't want to imply that all rear-echelon Marines were like this, but the few that were gave the rest a bad rap.

Leaving the headquarters building and crossing the dusty dirt road, I arrived at the ISO hooch and stopped there for a few minutes to check in, let the lieutenant know I was back, and see what was going on. A few of the correspondents were working on stories and welcomed me back. After a brief conversation, they went back to work and I headed for my hooch.

# CHAPTER 14

# Tank and Infantry Sweep along Route 545

BACK AT THE BASE, IT WAS TIME TO PROCESS FILM, MAKE PRINTS, GET NEGATIVES READY for submission to HQMC, and make prints to go with correspondents' stories. This routine was repeated with each return from the field. It was also time to catch up with the other photographers and correspondents to find out what was going on with the units they covered.

Most importantly, it was time to collect my mail. Staff Sergeant Upton came up from the lab at Da Nang, bringing the latest batch of mail with him. I watched with anxious anticipation as Martinez handed out the mail, thrusting a handful of letters my way. Suddenly he pulled back, having to take another look at one of Nancy's crazy-looking envelopes. I don't remember his exact words, but it was something expressing surprise, at which point he held it up in the air for everyone in the office to see. I snatched it away, along with my other letters, telling him he should be so lucky, and retreated to a quiet corner to read it.

Mail was our lifeblood, the only connection with people back home. As I read Nancy's letter, my morale shot through the roof. For a brief moment my mind was transported back to the real world and far away from the hardships of Vietnam. I don't believe the folks back home could ever know what these letters meant to their loved ones. There weren't any telephones, and this was years before the Internet, e-mail, and social media. Going weeks without receiving any mail was disheartening in a way that only men at war in a remote part of the world could understand. When "Mail call" was announced, everyone from the platoon would gather as the mail orderly called out names. If yours was called, a response of "Yo" was shouted in reply, and your letter would be thrown or

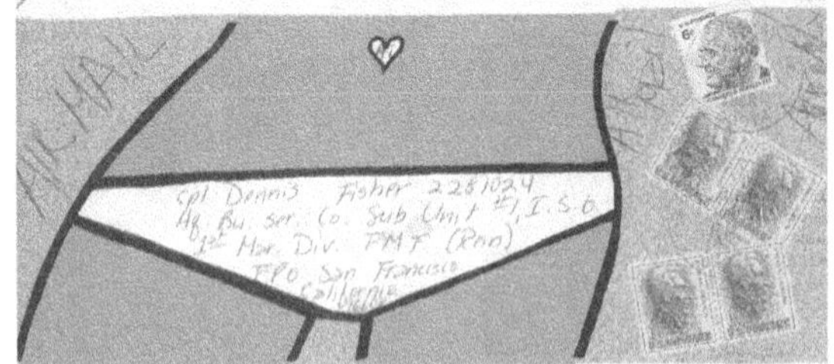

Mail was an important morale booster, especially when a letter arrived in an eye-catching envelope, such as this one from Nancy Van Mater to Cpl. Dennis Fisher. PHOTO BY CPL. DENNIS FISHER

handed back. Nothing hurt more than walking away empty-handed, wondering if anyone back home cared about you or what you were going through. To twist the knife a little more, you were left watching as others left to read their mail. Eventually the day would come when a letter arrived from someone dear to you, and your whole attitude would change.

As April rolled into May, I was back down with Lieutenant Green and Delta Company 1/5 on another tank infantry sweep along Route 545, southeast of Phu Bai. These sweeps and other patrols run by the Marines were meant to detect and deter the enemy from getting too close to our base. Constant patrols were needed to protect against surprise ground attacks. The base at Phu Bai served as the headquarters for a number of outfits, including the 3rd Marine Division. The army had a presence there, too, as well as some civilian contractors. It was also the site of a significant airfield, large ammunition dump, and artillery batteries. Thus it was a prime target for rocket and mortar attacks. I think the enemy thought it too well defended to try a ground assault, or they would have given it a try during the Tet Offensive.

Having mentioned these sweeps with Delta 1/5 on several occasions, I thought I would describe one in more detail so the reader could get a better appreciation of how they were conducted, some of the things that happened, and how the photos were used. On this particular sweep, Sergeant Rick Lavers from the ISO shop was along as a combat

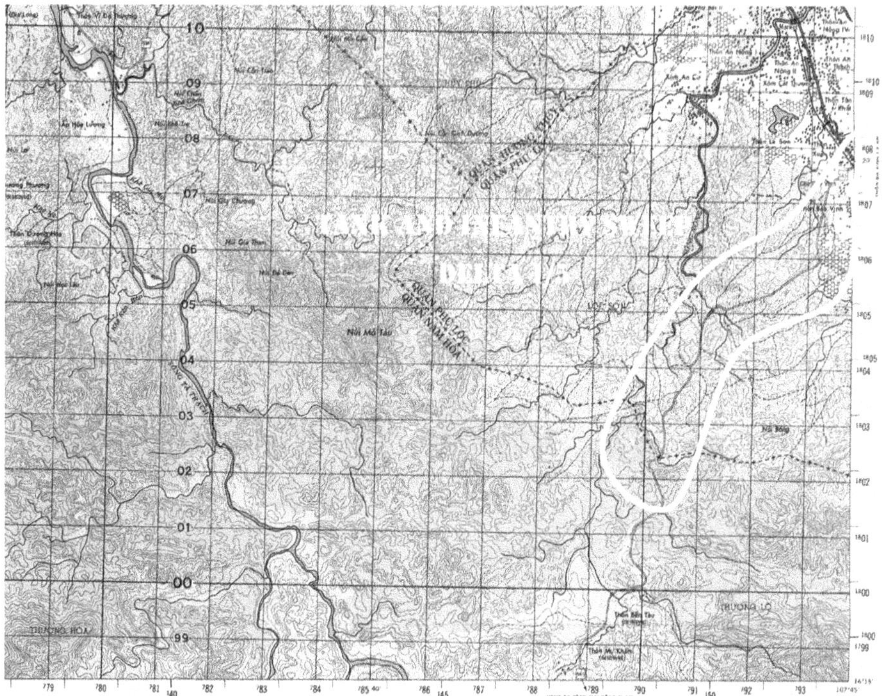

A map depicting the location of several tank and infantry sweeps along Route 545 south of Phu in the spring and summer of 1968. This combat sweep was conducted by Delta 1/5 and elements of the 1st Tank Battalion.

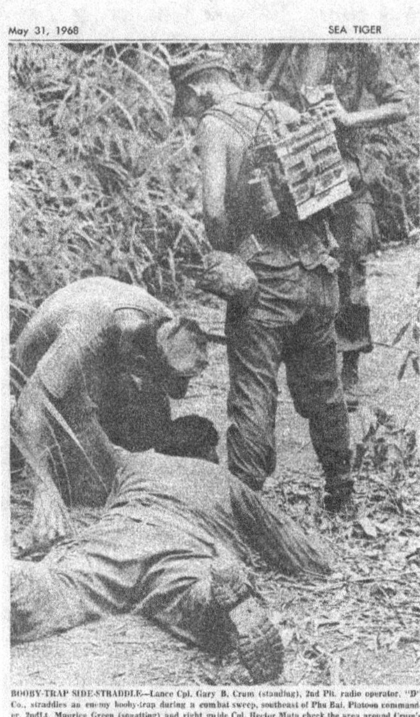

May 31, 1968 — SEA TIGER

BOOBY-TRAP SIDE-STRADDLE—Lance Cpl. Gary B. Crum (standing), 2nd Plt. radio operator, "D" Co., straddles an enemy booby-trap during a combat sweep, southeast of Phu Bai. Platoon commander, 2ndLt. Maurice Green (squatting) and right guide Cpl. Hector Mata check the area around Crum's feet for contact with the arming device.  (Photo by Cpl. Dennis Fisher)

A photo published in *Sea Tiger* (May 1968) to accompany the story of a booby-trap incident during a tank infantry sweep with Delta 1/5. NEWSPAPER CLIPPINGS/AUTHOR'S COLLECTION

Page 5

## Marine Straddles Booby Trap . . . But Not For Exercise

By: Sgt. Rick Lavers

PHU BAI—From the beginning of his military physical training, a Marine becomes proficient in the "side straddle hop", but rarely does he find use for the "booby-trap side-straddle", a position recently tested by a Michigan Marine.

LCpl. Gary B. Crum, (2514 Bannister, Wayne, Mich.), radio operator for 2nd Plt., "Delta" Co., 1/5 completed the test, then wiped the sweat from his brow and said, "Even if I spend the rest of my active duty in Vietnam, I never want to go through that again!"

Crum straddled a Viet Cong booby trap for several minutes during a company-size combat sweep near Nui Bong, southeast of Phu Bai.

"My platoon commander had just stepped over it," added Crum. "As I took a step, I glanced down, and there it was, staring at me between my legs."

2ndLt. Maurice Green (Birmingham, Ala.), platoon commander, ordered the rest of his platoon back down the trail. He and his right guide carefully cleared leaves and dirt from around Crum's boots.

"It was an old 'pineapple' style grenade," commented Lt. Green, "tied to a strip of bamboo. It didn't look armed, but we couldn't take chances."

The right guide, Cpl. Hector Mata (El Cerrito, Calif.), searched the area for a trip wire or some other arming device.

"I couldn't find anything," recalled Mata, "so we had Gary slowly lift each foot and step away from it."

When Crum was clear of the area, the lieutenant placed a fragmentation hand grenade next to the booby trap and pulled the pin.

"I knew I should have been a track star in school," laughed Green. "I couldn't make it to the bend in the trail in time, so I jumped for a ditch on the side."

Fortunately, no one was hurt in the incident, but LCpl. Crum learned one good lesson — the "booby-trap side-straddle" will never replace the good ol' "side straddle hop"!

### Canisters Saved From Explosion

By L/Cpl. Louis Barajas

DA NANG — "Those thirty to forty miles seemed like a lifetime," said L/Cpl. David W. Thacker, (3208 Hornsea Rd., Chesapeake, Va.), as he talked about his actions during an ammunition fire at the Ca Lu Marine Base.

Thacker was serving as part of an eight-man communications team at the Force Logistic Command Ca Lu Logistical Support Activity (LSA) south of the DMZ, when it came under enemy attack. Several rounds landed and set off secondary explosions in the ammunition hook-and-sling area where the ammo was staged to be helicopter-lifted to requesting units.

"Some flares had gone off and were landing all over the place," said Thacker. "When one landed on a crate of powder canisters, we knew that we had to put out the fire quickly or the exploding powder would start bigger fires and ignite the ammunition."

The powder canisters were in a crate on top of a trailer, but the wire bands used to hold the crates in place could not be broken by hand. Seeing a 6,000 pound fork lift near by, Thacker jumped into the seat. He had never operated the machine, but quickly familiarized

An article by Sgt. Rick Lavers, ISO Task Force X-Ray, published in *Sea Tiger* (May 1968), about a booby-trap incident that occurred during a tank infantry sweep with Delta 1/5. NEWSPAPER CLIPPINGS/AUTHOR'S COLLECTION

correspondent, and summarized one of the key events that happened in a story for the May 31, 1968, edition of the *Sea Tiger*, accompanied by one of my photos. Photographers and correspondents frequently paired up on operations, and this was no exception. By splitting the duties, the photographer could concentrate on getting the best photos while the correspondent gathered all the details needed to support his story.

Route 545 was a paved single-lane road that ran from Route 1 west into some low, rolling hills. The sides of the road were heavily overgrown with elephant grass, which really limited visibility and provided the enemy with

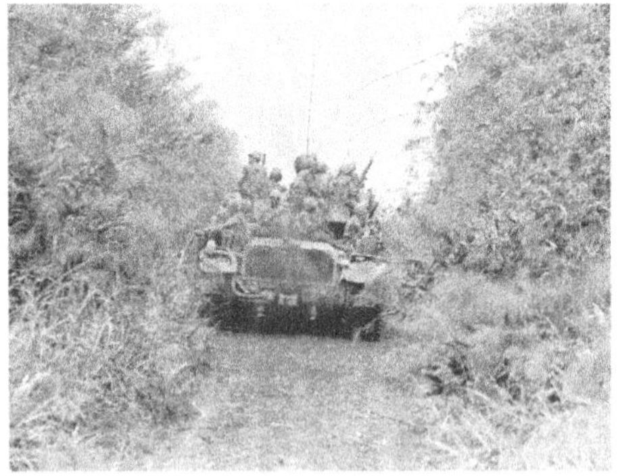

A tank from the 1st Tank Battalion transports Marines from Delta 1/5 into the operational area of a tank infantry sweep along Route 545, southeast of Phu Bai, in May 1968. PHOTO BY CPL. DENNIS FISHER

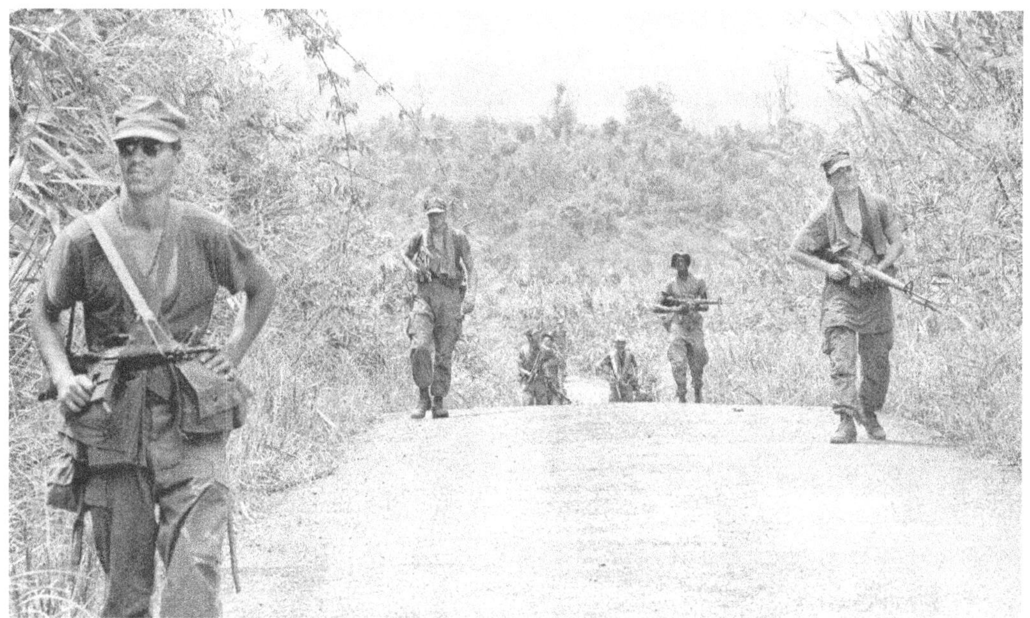

Marines from Delta 1/5 sweep Route 545 and the hills near Nui Bong, southeast of Phu Bai, during a tank infantry sweep in May 1968. PHOTO BY CPL. DENNIS FISHER/COURTESY OF NARA STILL PICTURE BRANCH

good ambush locations. The tanks went ahead as the Marines moved forward. Some of the infantry went down the road in a staggered column while others moved off to either side to protect the flanks. A lot of the hills were covered with tall grass and the going was slow. It was a hot humid day, and since we were only going to be gone for the day, everyone was traveling light, with only their arms and ammunition along with water and some snacks.

The sweep was going along uneventfully with the exception of a few sniper rounds when Lance Corporal Gary Crum, the 2nd Platoon radioman, froze in his tracks. He looked down just as his boots came down on either side of a suspicious device. Its serrated appearance through the leaves that camouflaged it made it easy to mistake for an old World War II pineapple-type hand grenade.

Lieutenant Green and Corporal Mata immediately came to his aid. The lieutenant began probing around the device with his KA-BAR while Corporal Mata went prone on his stomach, his face just a foot away. He began gently removing the leaves and debris that had been used to camouflage the booby trap. It rapidly became apparent this was a mine, not an old hand grenade.

Photographing the cautious procedure, I realized that no one was familiar with this particular type of mine or, more importantly, how to disarm it. The trip wire that emanated from a bamboo handle was similar to a ChiCom grenade, and it was assumed that if the trip wire was pulled it would detonate. But as we all knew, you never assume anything when dealing with booby traps. We did not have combat engineers or EOD people along, so Lieutenant Green took charge and moved everyone back.

With an abundance of caution he had Gary slowly remove his foot from the proximity of the mine, which had now been fully exposed. To our great relief, this was all accomplished safely, and after the platoon had moved down the road, the lieutenant placed a hand grenade next to the mine, pulled the pin, and ran back to join us as the explosion blew the mine in place.

I think the delay with resolving the booby-trap incident gave the VC a chance to maneuver on us, and we started taking more

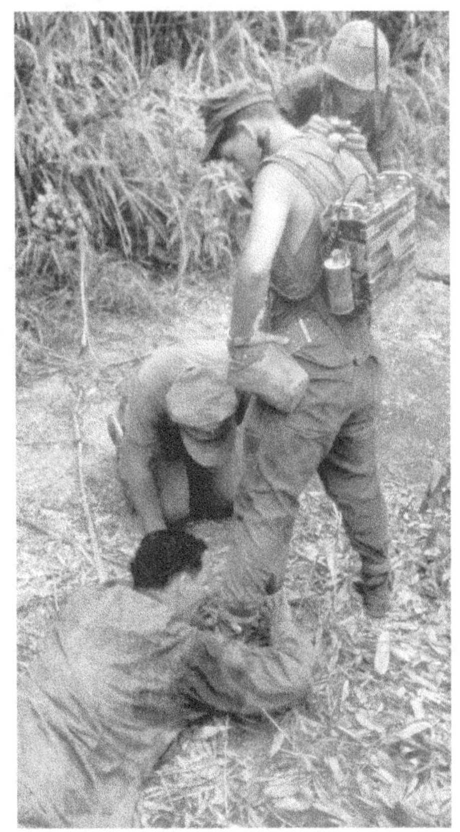

L/Cpl. Gary Crum (standing), 2nd Platoon radio operator for Delta 1/5, straddles an enemy booby trap during a tank infantry sweep southeast of Phu Bai in May 1968. Platoon commander 2nd Lt. Maurice Green (kneeling) and right guide Cpl. Hector Mata (prone) check the area around Crum's foot for contact with an arming device. Sgt. Rick Lavers, combat correspondent with Task Force X-Ray, is seen standing in the back with a camera. PHOTO BY CPL. DENNIS FISHER

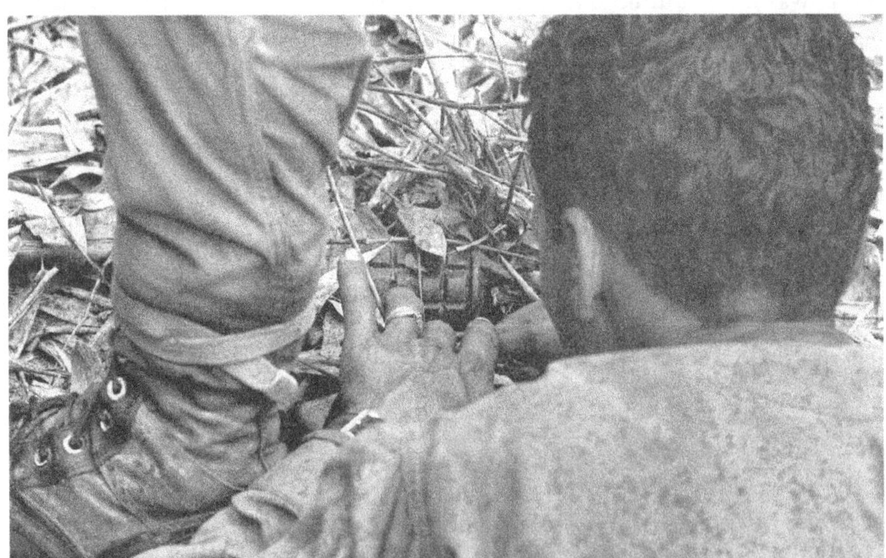

Cpl. Hector Mata, right guide with Delta 1/5, 2nd Platoon, removes camouflage from what they learned was a Z-10 mine at the foot of L/Cpl. Gary Crum, 2nd Platoon radio operator for Delta 1/5, during a tank infantry sweep southeast of Phu Bai in May 1968. PHOTO BY CPL. DENNIS FISHER

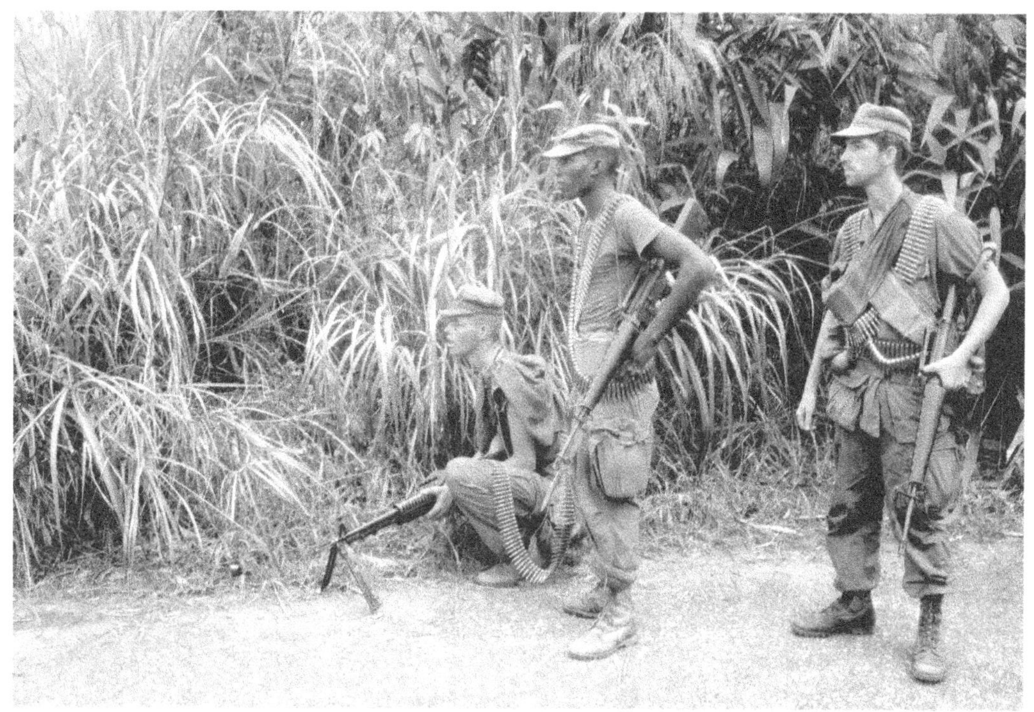

An M60 machine-gun team with Delta 1/5, 2nd Platoon, scans the road ahead for enemy movement during a tank infantry sweep southeast of Phu Bai in May 1968. PHOTO BY CPL. DENNIS FISHER

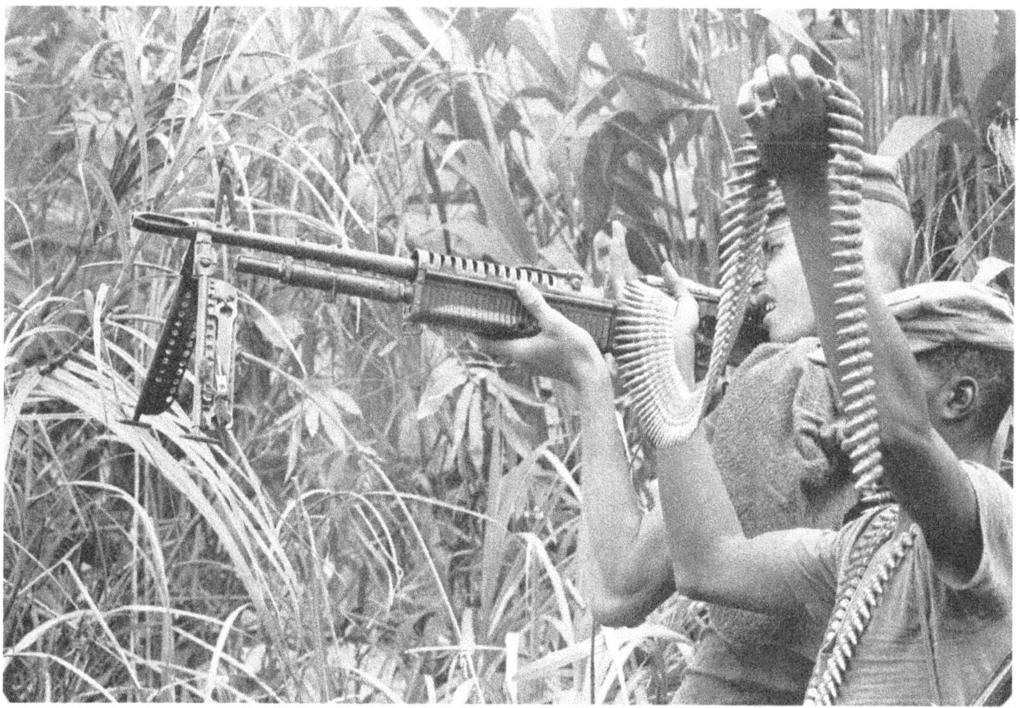

An M60 machine-gun team with Delta 1/5, 2nd Platoon, opens fire on an enemy sniper position during a tank infantry sweep southeast of Phu Bai in May 1968. PHOTO BY CPL. DENNIS FISHER/COURTESY OF NARA STILL PICTURE BRANCH

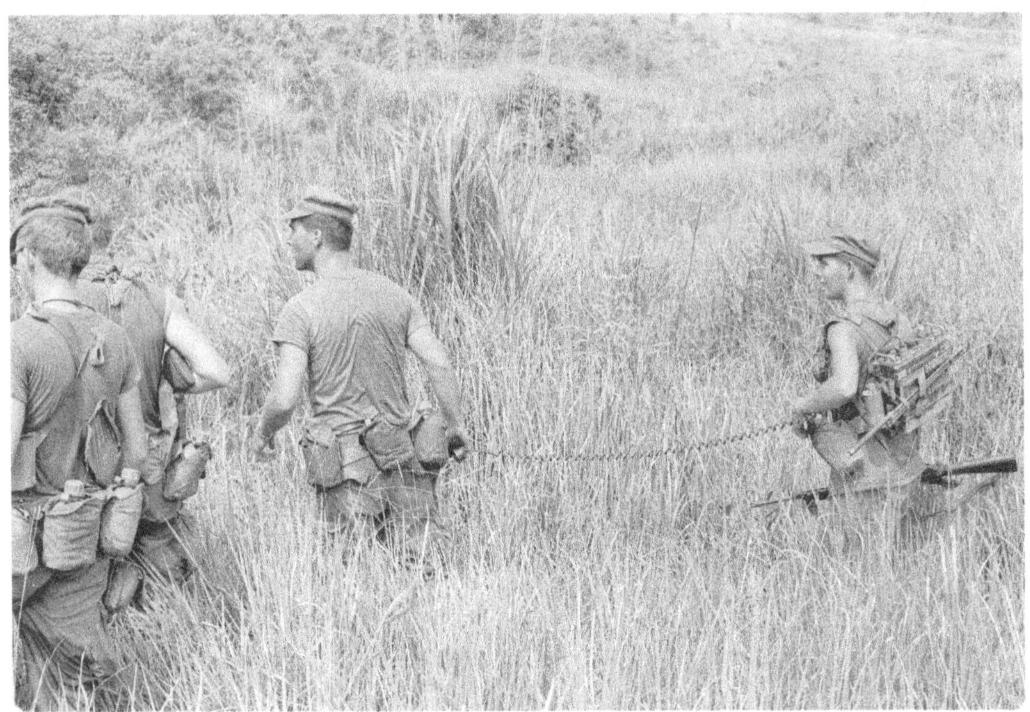

2nd Lt. Maurice Green, 2nd Platoon commander, Delta 1/5, prepares to call in artillery on an enemy position during a tank infantry sweep in the hills near Nui Bong, southeast of Phu Bai, in May 1968. PHOTO BY CPL. DENNIS FISHER/COURTESY OF NARA STILL PICTURE BRANCH

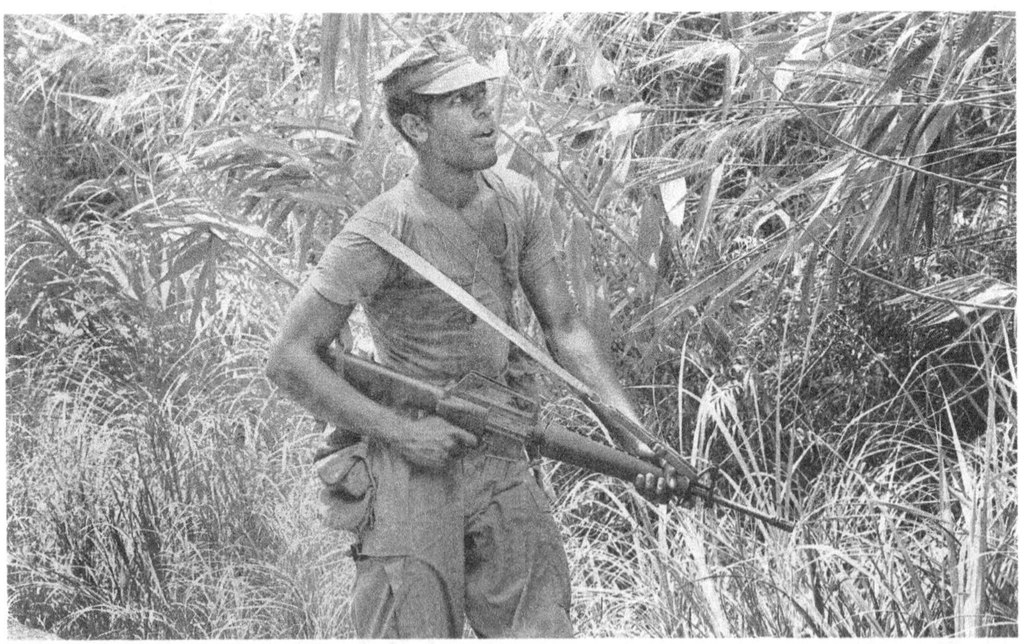

A rifleman with Delta 1/5, 2nd Platoon, scans the trail ahead for an enemy sniper position during a tank infantry sweep southeast of Phu Bai in May 1968. PHOTO BY CPL. DENNIS FISHER

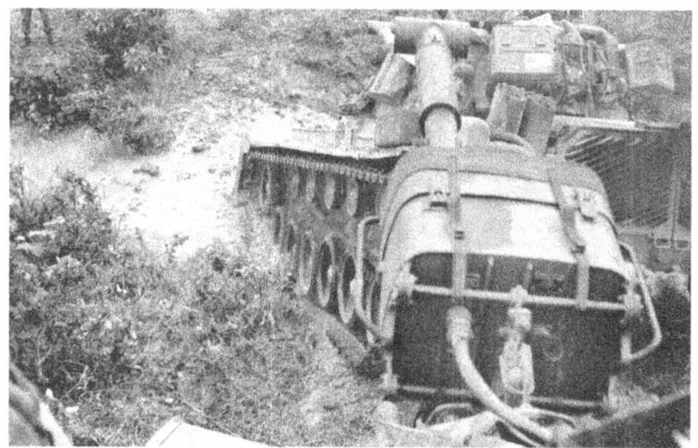

An M48 tank from the 1st Tank Battalion, 1st Marine Division, becomes stuck at a stream crossing during a tank infantry sweep in support of Delta 1/5, southeast of Phu Bai, in May 1968. PHOTO BY CPL. DENNIS FISHER

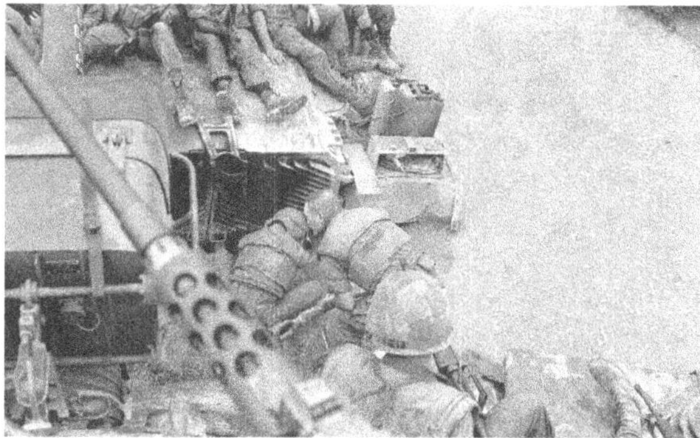

A tank crew attached a tow cable to an M48 tank from the 1st Tank Battalion, 1st Marine Division that had become stuck at a stream crossing during a tank infantry sweep in support of Delta 1/5 southeast of Phu Bai in May 1968. PHOTO BY CPL. DENNIS FISHER

sniper fire. Our M60 gun team returned fire, and I heard some of the riflemen firing too.

Lieutenant Green immediately brought the platoon up on line and sent the tanks forward toward the source of the firing. The sniping was quickly squelched and the sweep continued. We came to a bridge over a small stream that was neither wide enough nor strong enough to support the fifty-ton tanks, so they decided to ford the small stream. Unfortunately, the lead tank got stuck and had to wait until two other tanks, including one I was riding on, came to his aid. They hooked onto him with a big braided-steel tow cable, and after some effort, were able to free him.

The rest of the sweep was quiet, and when it was time to head back, everyone climbed aboard the tanks for a ride. Even though we had just swept through this area, every Marine was alert to the possibility that the enemy may have circled around to ambush us on our return. Whenever possible these patrols never returned by the same route they took going out, in order to avoid just this type of situation. But the terrain here kept the tanks confined to the road and the infantry was their only protection, so we retraced our path back to Route 1.

This sweep was typical of those I went out on with 1/5. There were no big pitched battles, just occasional snipers and the ubiquitous booby traps. The snipers were not the highly trained assassin variety, but rather some local villagers with carbines. Luckily they were not very good shots, and after firing a couple of rounds they would retreat before the Marines could locate them and return fire. So ended another day in the life of a combat photographer.

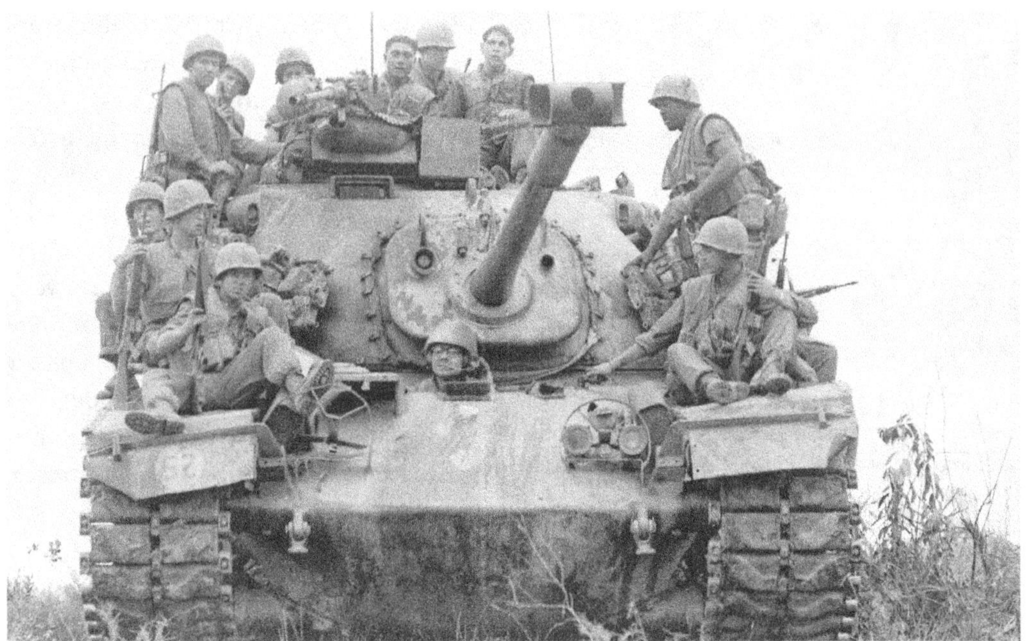

A tank from the 1st Tank Battalion transports Marines from Delta 1/5, 2nd Platoon, out of the operational area following a combat sweep along Route 545, southeast of Phu Bai, in May 1968. PHOTO BY CPL. DENNIS FISHER

It should be mentioned that Lieutenant Maurice O. V. Green was a Marines' Marine; he never hesitated to run toward the sound of the fighting. When I met him on this tank sweep, he had only recently returned from the hospital after being wounded while leading his platoon into Hue. He was involved in a number of hard-fought battles, and would be awarded the Navy Cross and Silver Star for his heroic actions, in addition to several Purple Hearts. He went on to have a distinguished career in the US Marine Corps, rising to the rank of major.

# Chapter 15

# Civic Action Programs

Earl Gerheim, Gus Hasford, Bill Dickman, and I went out on a number of MEDCAPs and civic action missions to help the Vietnamese in between combat operations. Our assignment was to get the story and take photos, but we usually ended up pitching in to help. There were all types of these events, meant to assist local villagers and build goodwill. This was all part of the US strategy to "win the hearts and minds" of the Vietnamese. The Marines didn't need any official policy to carry out these projects; we would have done them anyway. Some involved medical aid, others, personal hygiene; some were for distribution of donated goods and food, while others were to help build things. The people were always glad to see us, and even before our trucks stopped, we were swarmed with children.

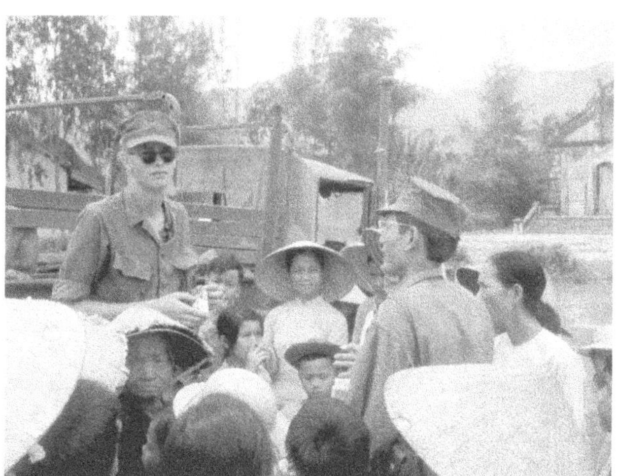

A hospital corpsman from 3/5 and an interpreter surrounded by villagers upon arriving to conduct a MEDCAP near Phu Bai in May 1968. PHOTO BY CPL. DENNIS FISHER

Most of the civil affairs events that I covered were very positive and welcomed by the local population. Earl Gerheim and I covered a number of these programs during the summer of 1968 when we were back in from the field. Several were with 2nd Lieutenant Weyman Dodson, the civil affairs officer with 3rd Battalion, 5th Marine Regiment (3/5), to provide medical care, demonstrations on how to make hush puppies with donated cornmeal from the United States, and hygiene instruction. Lieutenant

Dodson worked very well with the Vietnamese, and they seemed glad to see him arrive. A corpsman always accompanied the team to provide medical care, and his help was especially welcomed by the locals. An interpreter was provided to make things run smoothly, as few of the Vietnamese spoke English. This was especially helpful when working with medical problems.

I must admit that covering these events was a welcome relief from the combat operations that were our bread and butter. Most were conducted in secure areas with little chance of being shot at; plus it gave me a chance to interact with the Vietnamese in a more relaxed environment. Encounters with them on combat operations were quite different, as they were scared or nervous about being caught in between the VC and the Americans. "Caught" in the sense that they didn't want to be seen as government sympathizers in the eyes of the VC, or as VC sympathizers in the eyes of the Americans. These civil affairs programs helped in numerous ways, but primarily they helped cement relationships with the locals.

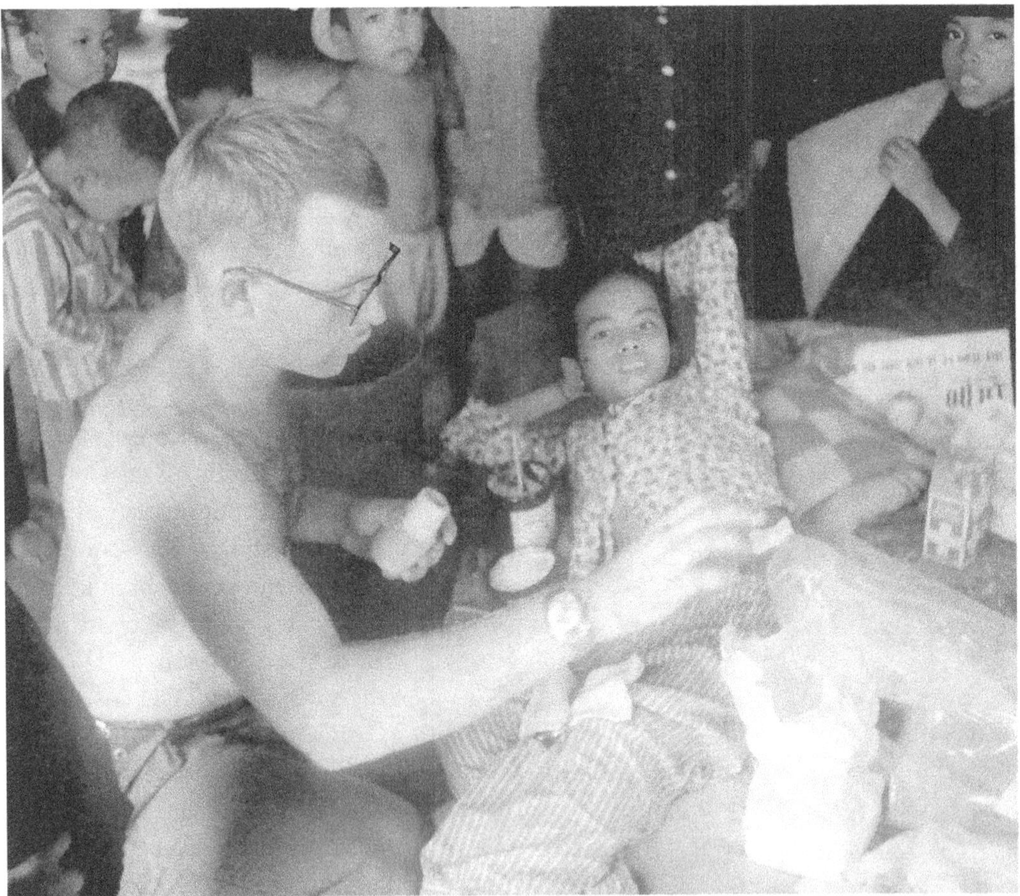

A hospital corpsman from 3/5 treating a young boy during a MEDCAP near Phu Bai in May 1968.
PHOTO BY CPL. DENNIS FISHER

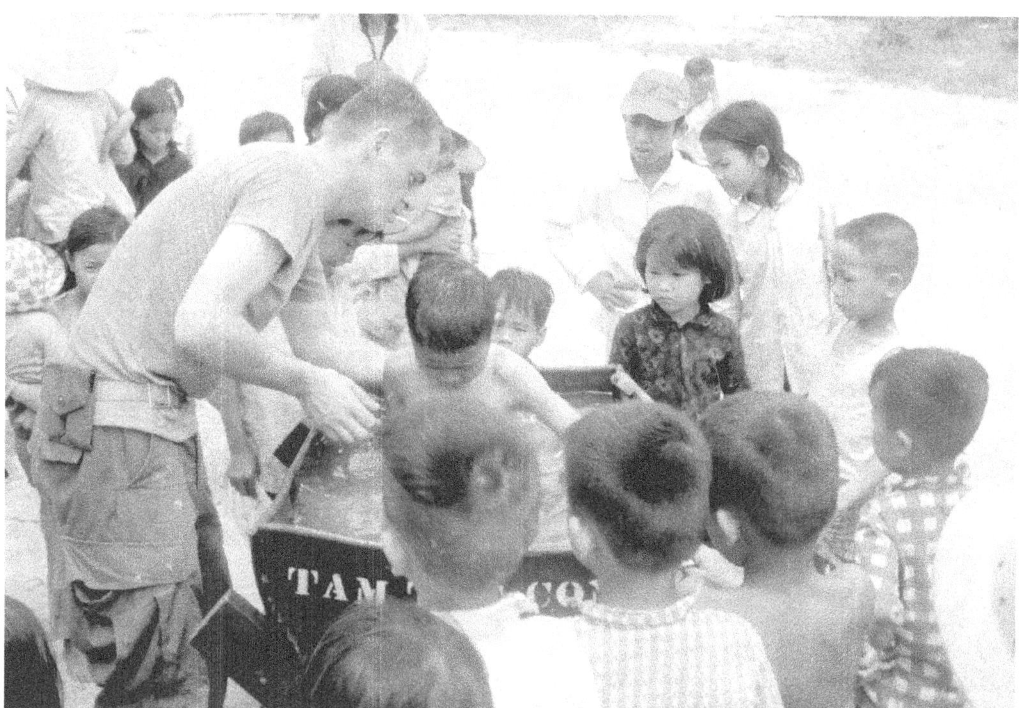

2nd Lt. Weyman Dodson, the civil affairs officer for 3/5, bathes a Vietnamese child during a MEDCAP, south of Phu Bai. Basic instructions were provided to the villagers to improve hygiene and prevent skin infections. PHOTO BY CPL. DENNIS FISHER

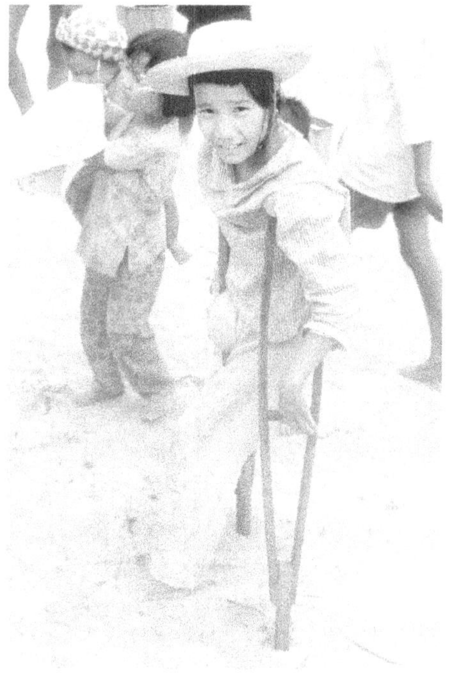

A casualty of war, this Vietnamese girl attended a MEDCAP, hosted by 3/5's Civil Affairs Office near Phu Bai in May 1968, to seek treatment for the stump of her amputated leg. PHOTO BY CPL. DENNIS FISHER

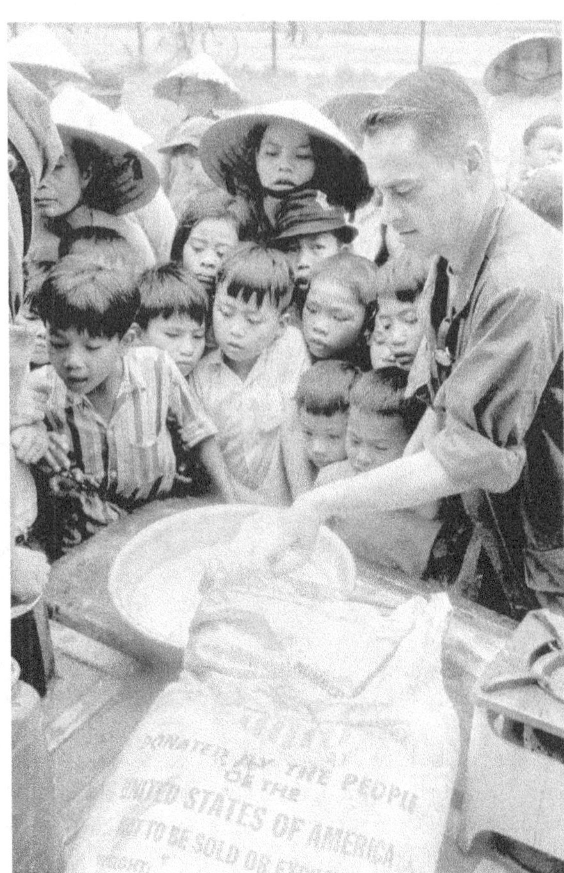

2nd Lt. Weyman Dodson, civil affairs officer for 3/5, demonstrates how to make hush puppies out of donated cornmeal from the United States during a MEDCAP, south of Phu Bai. PHOTO BY CPL. DENNIS FISHER

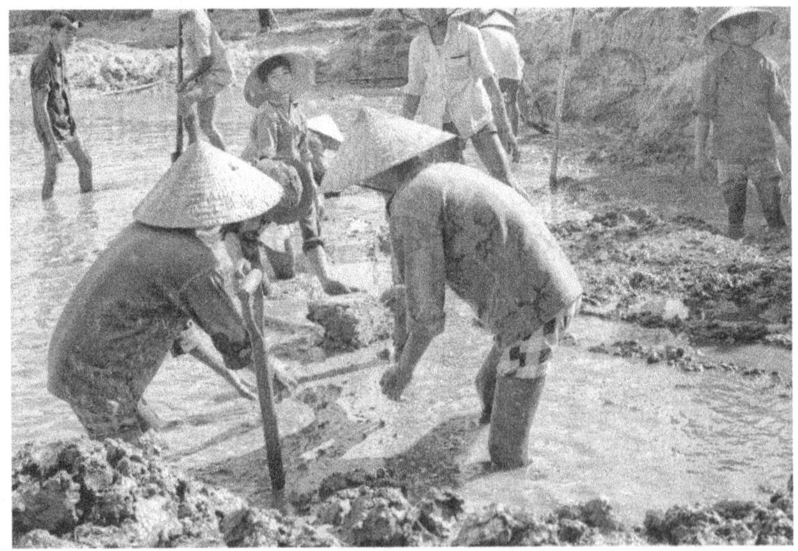

Local villagers prepare a site prior to pouring concrete for a dam on the Phu Bai River. American-provided supplies assisted in this project to improve irrigation for nearby agriculture in June 1968. PHOTO BY SGT. DENNIS FISHER/COURTESY OF NARA STILL PICTURE BRANCH

An interesting event occurred during a civil affairs project when Lieutenant LaPage sent Gus Hasford and me to meet with Lieutenant Robinson from the 1st Medical Battalion's S-5 office. Robinson was going out in the bush to deliver family boxes to some needy Vietnamese; although not typically conducted by the Med Battalion, as it wasn't strictly medical in nature, it was greatly appreciated by the locals nonetheless.

The day before the mission Gus and I met with Lieutenant Robinson to get some background for Gus's story and my caption material. He emphasized that this could be dangerous, and he wanted everyone in helmets and flak jackets. I was surprised that these 1st Med guys were even leaving the base. The only navy medical personnel that I ever saw in the field were the corpsmen, and once in a while, the battalion surgeon. I guessed there was a first time for everything.

We boarded two deuce and a half trucks loaded high with boxes on May 12, 1968, along with a squad of infantry for security, and headed out the main gate. After driving for only a few minutes, we stopped at Thuy Chau, a local village just up the road from the base. I saw the officer in charge, a doctor, ordering everyone out of the trucks and having the Marines set up a security perimeter. I figured the lead truck had broken down or something. This was one of the vills closest to the base where Marines and army personnel would hang out in their spare time. Some of the local girls were talking with the Marines they knew, offering to sell them beer or sodas.

The Marines began unloading the boxes as a delegation arrived from the village. There were twenty-five big family boxes that were being jointly distributed by the 1st Medical Battalion/1st Marine Division Civil Affairs Office. Each box was loaded with clothes, personal hygiene items, and toys for kids. It finally dawned on me that this was the doctor's idea of going out in the bush. To top things off, Gus had thrown his helmet and flak jacket in the back of the truck and put on his soft cover while he was taking some notes.

The doctor saw him and threatened to have him court-martialed for disobeying a direct order. Gus gave him his best boot camp "Aye-aye, sir," did an about-face, grabbed his gear, and walked back to the base, muttering "What's he going to do, send me to Vietnam?" He caught hell the next day from our lieutenant, but nothing ever came of it.

CHAPTER 16

# Operation Allen Brook

### *Go Noi Island*

THE TET OFFENSIVE WAS IN THE REARVIEW MIRROR BY NOW, AND MOST OF US THOUGHT that with the tremendous losses suffered by the NVA and VC, the war would be winding down soon. But it seems the enemy had other ideas and was looking for a redo, which resulted in what would come to be called Tet II, or Mini Tet. In I Corps their main targets in our area appeared to be the Da Nang air base, logistics support activities, and 1st Marine Division Headquarters. I'm sure military historians have a better appreciation today of what was going on, but at the time I only had the scuttlebutt that filtered down.

One of the enemy's main staging areas for this upcoming attack was Go Noi Island, which was only an island during the rainy season. The Song Thu Bon was a west-to-east-flowing river that emptied into the ocean near Hoi An, about thirteen miles south of Da Nang. The main part of the river had a secondary channel that branched off to the south and then ran parallel to it for about nine miles, where it reconnected. This created an island about two miles wide and nine miles long. During Allen Brook, the secondary channel was mostly dry, leaving a sandy riverbed. The whole island was a warren of bunkers, tunnels, trenches, and spider holes separated by thick bamboo hedge lines and rice paddies.

The 7th Marines kicked off the operation in early May, and then the 27th Marines were brought in. Around the middle of May we got word that 3/5 was joining the fight and would replace 3/7 in the battle. The 26th Marines were soon involved. This was turning out to be a bigger fight that anyone had anticipated. This "two-week" operation would continue for about three and a half months, until August 24, and was actually part of the second phase of the Tet Offensive.

Up at Task Force X-Ray we were aware of the operation. It looked like the 7th Marines were going to be the unit taking on the mission. Covering operations in that part of I Corps would be the job of the 1st Marine Division Combat Photo Section, so we weren't surprised when they deployed still photographer Corporal R. J. "Del" Del Vecchio

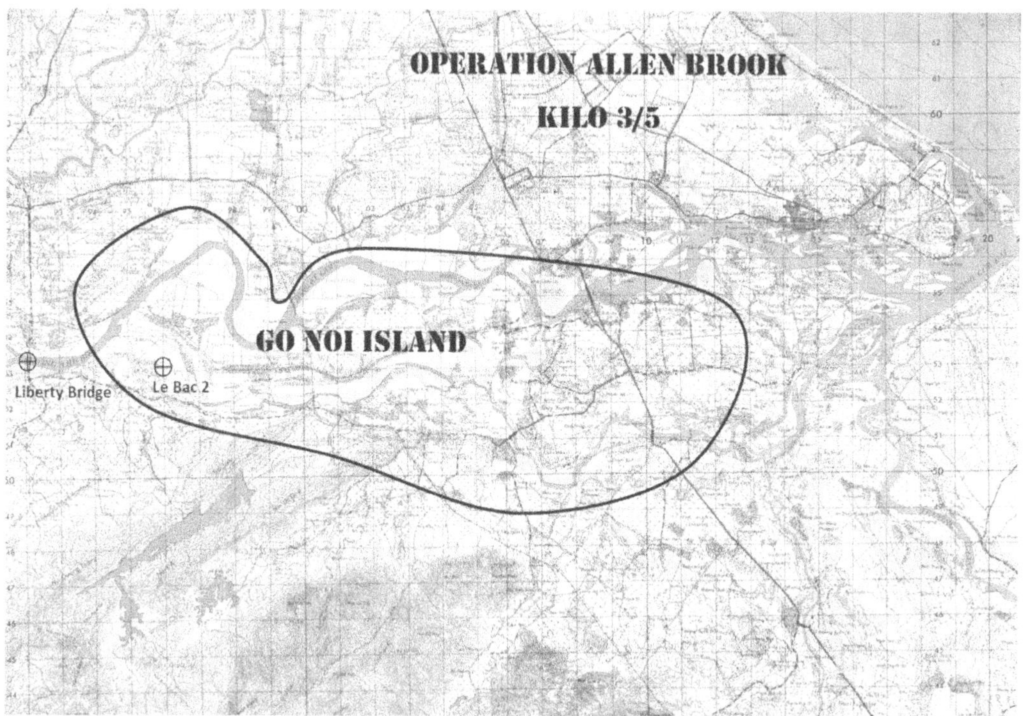


Go Noi Island, located about 15 miles south of DaNang, was the scene of heavy fighting during Operation Allen Brook from early May to late August 1968 as Marines fought to dislodge heavily entrenched Viet Cong and PAVN troops from this staging area. Elements of 7th, 5th, and 27th Marine participated in this operation along with artillery and air support.

and mopic photographer Corporal John "Penny" Pennington to accompany 2/7 as they kicked off the operation. Enemy resistance was strong from the beginning, and they were right in the middle of it, covering the men of Gulf Company.

Del's experiences of May 7, 1968, were unique, even for a photographer, but they are illustrative of the challenges faced by combat photographers and their tenacious dedication to getting the job done. Here he recounts the events of that day in his own words.

*In early May '68 the 1stMarDiv Photo Lab was notified that the 7th Marines had started a major operation which was under way on Go Noi Island. John Pennington and I were sent out to provide coverage, arriving on the island by chopper on the 5th to join with 2/7. The first day was not too eventful, but on the 6th heavy contact was made with VC forces. John and I slept that night in a shallow hole and watched tracer bullets streaking past a few inches over us.*

*The next morning there was no firing and everyone opened their C-rats for breakfast. A platoon was sent out from the open ground where the company was located to cut through a jungle area to get to an LZ for more supplies. Late in the morning they radioed back they were under attack and surrounded by enemy troops. Immediately*

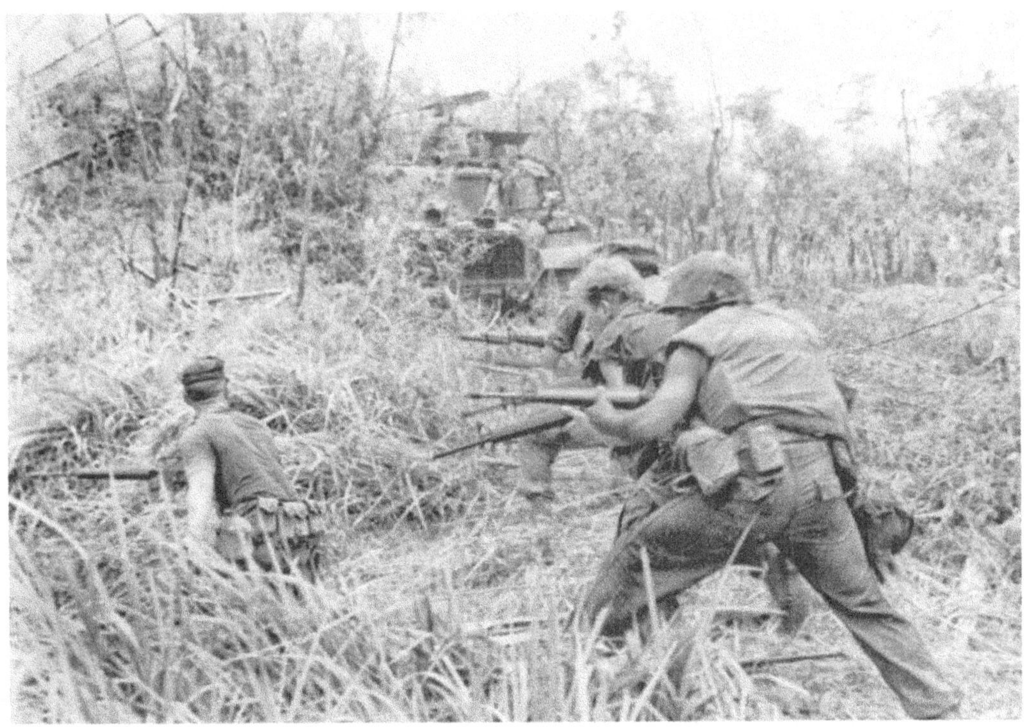

Marines of Golf 2/7 charge into an NVA ambush on May 7, 1968, during the opening phase of Operation Allen Brook on Go Noi Island, south of Da Nang. PHOTO BY CPL. R. J. DEL VECCHIO/COURTESY OF NARA STILL PICTURE BRANCH

*everyone was alerted to get ready to move, and within some minutes the company was strung out on the road toward the jungle area. It was already a very hot day, probably over 100 degF, so when everyone arrived at the edge of the heavy vegetation, permission was granted to drop helmets and flak jackets if anyone wanted to.*

*Golf Company then got online and proceeded slowly into the thick vegetation where we could hear the faint popping of rifle fire coming from the trapped platoon's location. Penny had remained behind to see what other areas might develop into combat.*

*As we proceeded forward, accompanied by a tank that could only proceed through the somewhat open areas, everything was very quiet, and tension kept rising.*

*Then in a split second everything went to hell as a prepared ambush was sprung. It was a V-shaped ambush with machine guns on both wings spraying bullets in a wide pattern of overlapping fires, some RPGs coming in and exploding—the noise was totally deafening—bullets were ricocheting off the tank armor, Marines were firing M16s, blooper 40mm grenades, and M60 MGs [machine guns]. Some Marines were hit.*

*The tank turned to the right and got bogged down in a heavy bamboo thicket. A Marine trying to fire the turret .50 cal was shot by a sniper and fell back. I started tak-*

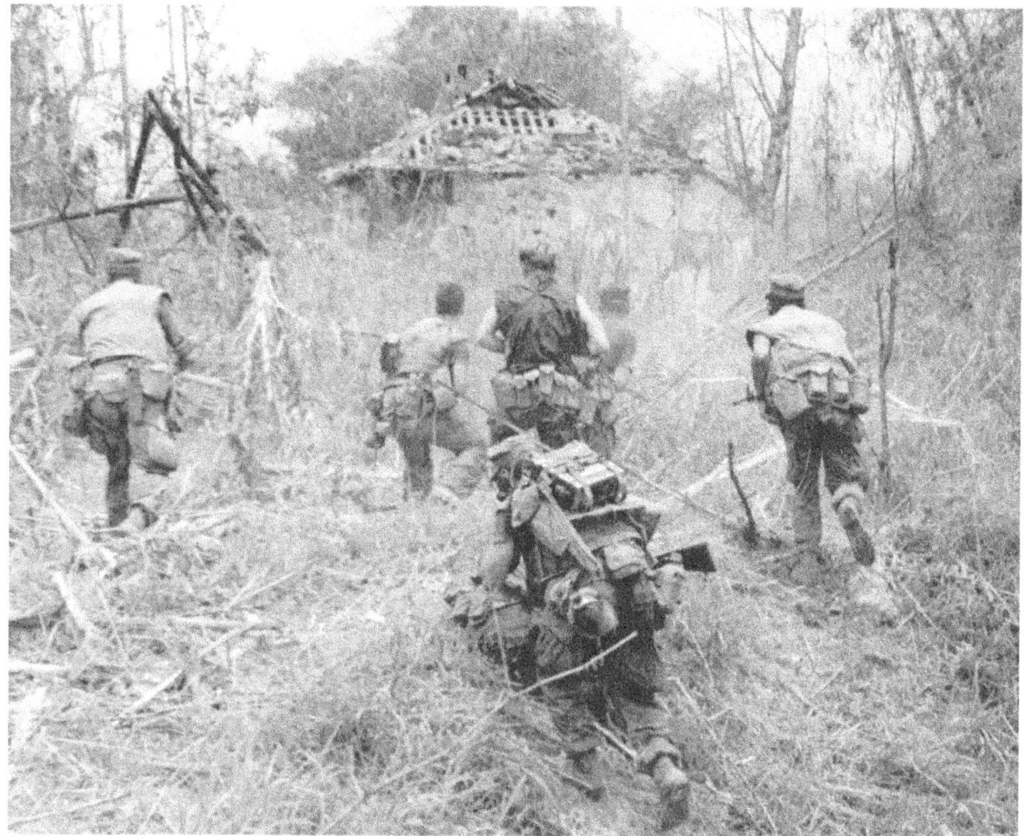

A team of Marines from Golf 2/7 advance toward an enemy machine-gun nest to neutralize it on May 7, 1968, during the opening phase of Operation Allen Brook on Go Noi Island, south of Da Nang.
PHOTO BY CPL. R. J. DEL VECCHIO/COURTESY OF NARA STILL PICTURE BRANCH

*ing pictures, got one of a team of Marines charging past me that was later on the cover of the* Sea Tiger *newspaper.*

*I continued to move forward in kind of a crouch as the sharp snap of passing bullets hit my ears. The action was unfolding all around me as I took a series of images of a team moving to suppress the fire of an enemy MG and drop a grenade into their position.*

*That finished the roll of B&W film, and I stayed low and loaded a roll of color film. As I finished, a small group of Marines ran past me, moving toward the left, and I followed them. We came to what appeared to be a cleared path in the trees and plants, which turned out to be a firing lane for an enemy MG, and as the Marines in front of me ran across, the M60 gunner was hit in the thigh and dropped. The assistant gunner grabbed the gun and kept going.*

*I took cover behind a tree on the edge of the cleared area and took some pictures. When I looked up, everyone was gone except the wounded Marine, who saw me and asked for help.*

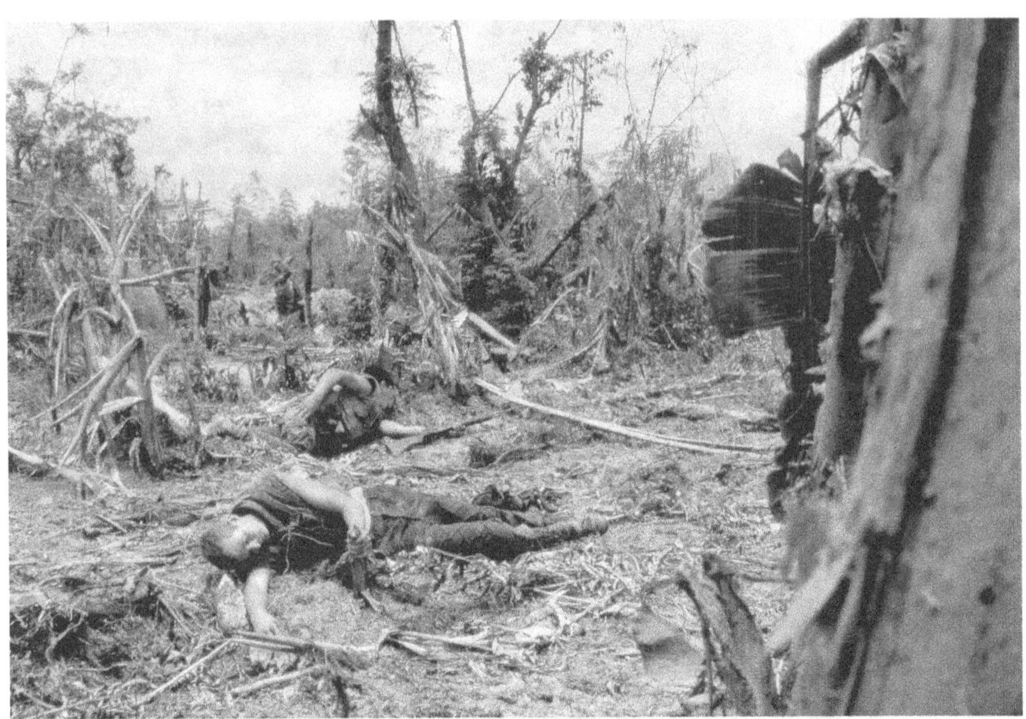

A wounded Marine from Golf 2/7 lies in the enemy's firing lane awaiting medical assistance after receiving a wound to the thigh on May 7, 1968, during the opening phase of Operation Allen Brook on Go Noi Island, south of Da Nang. This particular image was saved from Cpl. Del Vecchio's bullet-riddled camera. PHOTO BY CPL. R. J. DEL VECCHIO/COURTESY OF NARA STILL PICTURE BRANCH

*I looked for someone else to send, and there was no one. So it had to be me. I ran out, did not take the time to do a fireman's carry, since the MG was firing, and dragged the wounded man into safety.*

*There was a bomb crater just next to us, about fifteen feet wide and five feet deep, and the gunner and I slid to its bottom. Bullets were still cracking over our heads. There were two other men in the crater; one was a corpsman with symptoms of heat stroke, which disabled him, and the other clearly a very new guy and very young. We all rested for a few minutes.*

*Then we heard the tank coming and thought if it passed by the crater we could get up and use it for cover. But the next thing we saw was the bow of the tank appearing at the edge of the crater and we realized it was going to come down through the crater. The driver could not see us, and we were right in the tank's path.*

*We galvanized, and I told the young grunt to pull the corpsman up over the edge of the crater, away from the direction of incoming fire. Then I pulled the wounded Marine to that side of the crater and then had the young Marine grab him and help pull him up as I pushed upwards. As we got him clear, the tank came down into the crater and the tread went over my left foot, which I had extended behind me as I pushed the Marine up.*

*At that point I heard screaming and realized it was me as I felt my foot being crushed down. They heard me in the tank and backed up, which hurt just as much. Then I collapsed into the crater and the other three men came back down into it as well. They helped cut my left boot off as the instep rapidly swelled up into a big blister-like lump, but there was no blood. The soft sand at the bottom of the crater had saved me from having the foot totally destroyed.*

*After a while I could see [that] the wounded man and the corpsman needed help, so I decided to get back to where there were more Marines and tell them about the crater. I started slowly crawling back to the right and, after maybe fifty yards or so, found the tank again with a small group of Marines and corpsmen next to it. I told the corpsmen about the guys in the crater and they went to get them.*

*I then settled into a shallow crater in front and to the right of the tank, with a couple of wounded Marines. Someone looked out and said "There are gooks moving over there in the brush," so I saw an opportunity to get a very rare image of the enemy during combat. I raised up and put the camera to my eye, held vertically in my left hand. As I began to look for the enemy there was another burst of firing, and suddenly a baseball bat came and slammed the camera out of my hands—at least, that's what it felt like.*

*I dropped back down in shock and then went to reach for the camera, which was still on its strap around my neck. I realized my left hand hurt a lot and looked at it. The little [pinkie] and ring fingers were broken and hanging from their lower section by some flesh, and blood was dripping out. Using my right hand I grabbed the camera and realized it had a bullet hole in it. It was clear the bullet had hit my fingers holding the base of the camera and then pierced it and knocked it flying.*

*Up until then I had been able to stay focused on doing my job, but now I had no camera, one smashed foot, and one wounded hand, and it didn't seem to be a good idea to hang around. At that moment the tank fired the 90mm cannon, and I was in the blast cone, where the energy wave bounces you off the ground and your ears feel like each one has had an ice pick jammed into it. That made me sure I needed to leave, so I turned my body around and started crawling back out of the combat zone. Crawling with one bad foot and one bad hand is not easy, but bit by bit I covered maybe one hundred yards to get into the clear again.*

*At that point I saw Penny coming toward me, and when he saw me his first reaction was obvious shock. But then he pulled himself together and his ability to handle anything with humor came out, as he said to me, in a very exasperated tone, "Can't I leave you just for a minute?" Then he helped me get up and get back to what had become the LZ for medevac choppers to wait for my ride to a hospital. I gave him my exposed film, the camera, and my .45 to take back, and went on for the rest of a very long day.*

A day or two after Del was wounded, word filtered up to Task Force X-Ray (TFX) that he was hospitalized with non-life-threatening wounds. I wouldn't know the full story until sometime later when I ran into him down at the Photo Lab. A week later we started hearing reports about the fighting on Go Noi Island and began to realize that Allen Brook was becoming a significant battle. The scuttlebutt also led me to believe that the 5th Marines, which were one of the units I regularly covered, may be joining the fight. The scuttlebutt proved correct for a change, and 3/5 was scheduled to replace 3/7 on May 18. Since our TFX photographers and correspondents covered most of the 5th Marines actions, Corporal Earl Gerheim and I teamed up on this op with Kilo 3/5.

Earl was already on the ground with 3/5 down at Lang Co, and convoyed with them down to Hill 55. A night march brought them to the river where they crossed over to Go Noi Island. Coming from Phu Bai, it took me a little longer to get there, but I flew in on a CH-46 with some of the grunts two days later, on May 21, 1968. Enjoying the cool air we experienced while flying at around six thousand feet soon gave way to the exceedingly oppressive heat and humidity on the ground. I was glad I'd brought along extra canteens, three in all, because I was going to need them.

The helicopter descended rapidly toward a rising column of yellow smoke and dropped us off. Following a scout dog and his handler down the ramp, I started asking around for the location of Lieutenant Fred Smith, the CO of Kilo 3/5. With some rudimentary directions, I left the LZ to find Lieutenant Smith. On the way, I passed a field battery of 81mm mortars that were busy supporting Lima 3/5 at the time. The mortar tubes were nearly vertical, and I could tell they were shooting at something relatively close by—by their account, around five hundred meters. I photographed them in action in both color and B&W and made a few audio recordings of the action before I continued on, moving from one unit to the next. The terrain here was a patchwork of rice paddies and bamboo hedge lines, with small villages scattered around. This was the perfect place for booby traps, or an ambush.

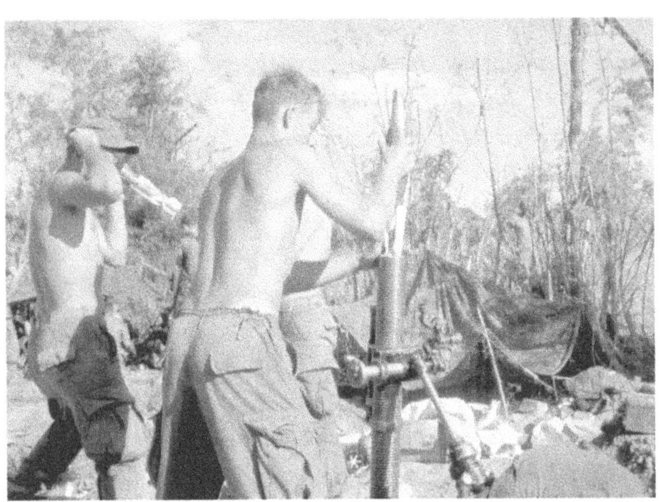

Mortarmen from 5th Marines fire in support of Lima 3/5 during Operation Allen Brook south of Da Nang in May 1968. PHOTO BY CPL. DENNIS FISHER

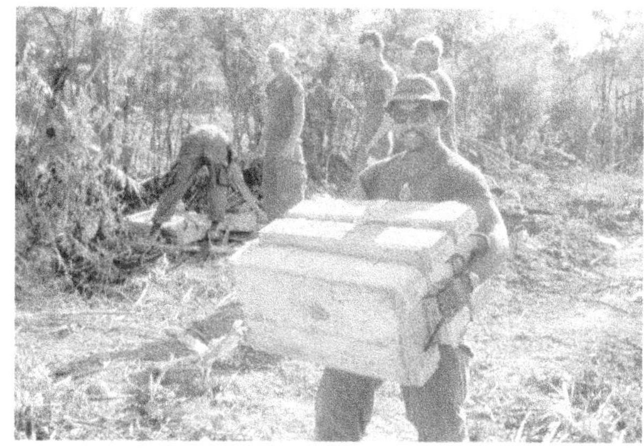

Mortarman bringing up additional 81mm mortar rounds to support his battery in heavy fighting during Operation Allen Brook, south of Da Nang, May 1968. PHOTO BY CPL. DENNIS FISHER

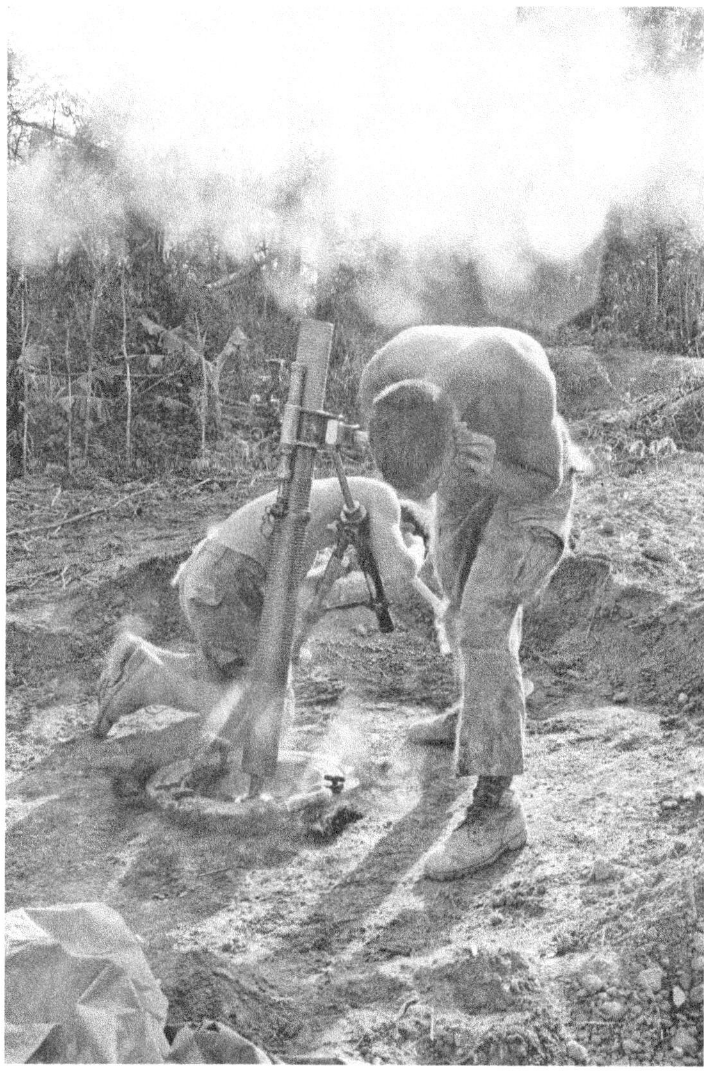

Mortarmen from 5th Marines fire in support of Lima 3/5 during Operation Allen Brook, south of Da Nang, May 1968. PHOTO BY CPL. DENNIS FISHER/COURTESY OF NARA STILL PICTURE BRANCH

Continuing on for another couple hundred yards, I found the lieutenant and his radioman in the midst of calling in a fire mission from the 81mm mortars that I had just left. When things settled down I introduced myself, and he gave me a brief rundown of what had happened so far and where his platoons were located at the time. He also told me there was already a correspondent with 3rd Platoon, which I assumed was Earl. He had his radioman check to confirm, and we finally got together later in the day.

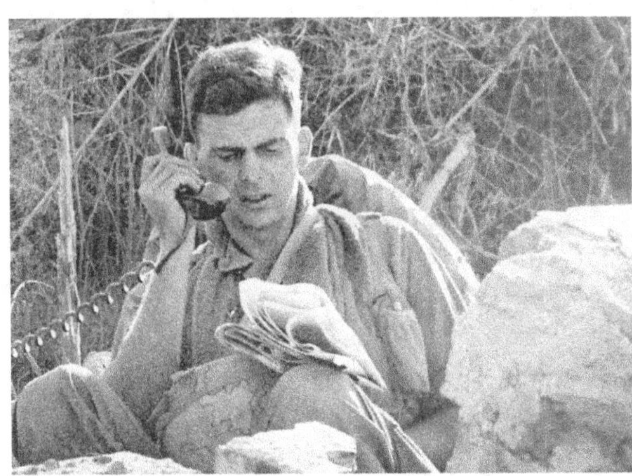

1st Lt. Frederick Smith, CO of Kilo 3/5, calls in 81mm mortar fire on the enemy positions as his men advance during Operation Allen Brook in May 1968. PHOTO BY CPL. DENNIS FISHER

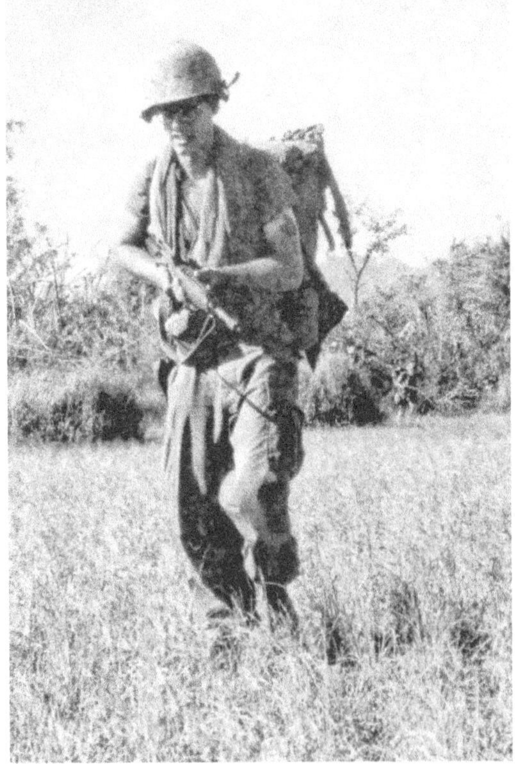

Cpl. Earl Gerheim, a combat correspondent with the 1st Marine Division Task Force X-Ray, advances with the infantry from Kilo 3/5 during an assault on the Le Bac village complex during Operation Allen Brook on Go Noi Island in May 1968. PHOTO BY CPL. DENNIS FISHER

Almost immediately he radioed his platoon commanders and had them prepare to move toward their next objective, which I believe was Le Bac 2, a small village complex. The vill was quiet; many of the people had already fled to safety, and the Marines took advantage of a communal well to fill up their canteens. Fresh, cool, clean water was a rare treat in the field. (Even so, we treated it with iodine or Halazone water purification tablets, just to be on the safe side.)

I was carrying my normal complement of equipment, but had added a cassette tape recorder to capture some of the sounds of battle. This was the only op I carried it on—I found it too big and awkward—but I did get some good recordings. Listening to them now really takes me back to that time and the sounds of battle: Lieutenant Smith calling in a fire mission, helicopter gunships, fighter planes, booby traps exploding, corpsmen being summoned, intense firefights, and much more, allow me to recall those moments with crystal clarity.

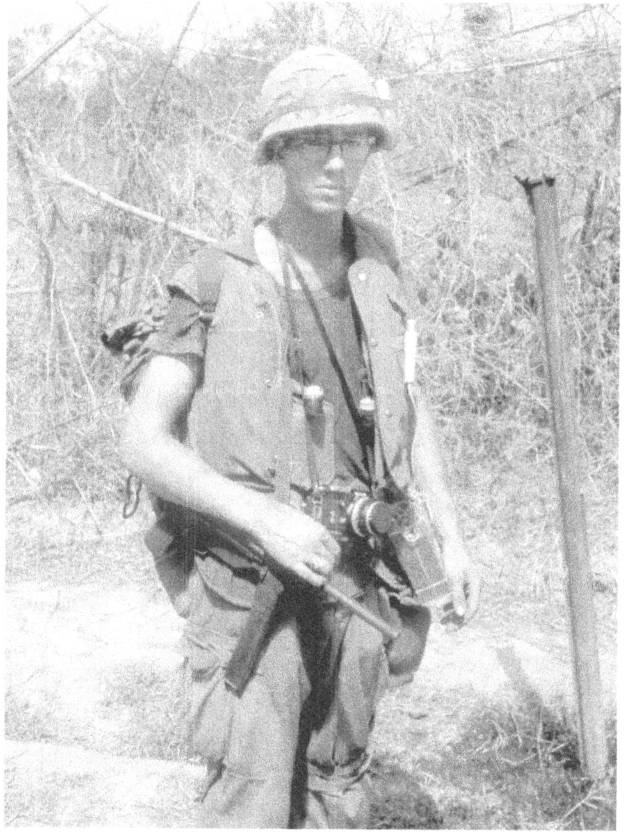

Cpl. Dennis Fisher, combat photographer with Task Force X-Ray, 1st Marine Division, pictured here with his cameras and tape recorder during Operation Allen Brook, south of Da Nang, May 1968. PHOTO BY CPL. EARL GERHEIM/AUTHOR'S COLLECTION

Earl and I were sort of poaching this op that was rightfully being covered by our buddies at 1st Division Headquarters. I remember we encountered Corporal Bob Bayer, one of the ISO combat correspondents from Da Nang covering 3/27. He seemed surprised to see us down there, and asked us outright, "What are you guys doing down here?" The implication was that they had it covered and didn't need our help. I responded that we were doing the same thing they had done during Operations Hue City, Ford, and Baxter Garden in our area. It was all part of the good-natured ribbing frequently heard among those of us jockeying for position on the big ops.

As the operation dragged on from early May through late August, the rifle companies were rotated in and out of the field every couple of weeks, to rest and recruit. The same thing happened with the photographers and correspondents, with nearly everyone in the shop participating in Allen Brook at one time or another.

This operation resulted in some heavy fighting for the Marines from 1/27 who I had covered up near Hue on Operation No Name II. They were in the thick of it and taking heavy casualties along with many other units I had photographed. My recollections of Allen Brook are a series of vignettes recalled from the photos that I took there. My notes, caption sheets, and negatives from that op disappeared many years ago, and the photos I do have are scans from original prints that I made back in the lab, or scans of negatives that were submitted to the National Archives. I did find a few 35mm color slides, but not many.

It was really hot and humid, and 3/5 was starting to take a number of heat casualties. The CO called frequent stops in shady areas to try and keep people cool, which helped. The corpsman was passing out salt tablets to everyone, pills that were meant to help the body retain water. He gave me a bottle and I stuck them in my helmet band for ready access.

If all else failed, a field treatment area had been set up to handle heat casualties. It consisted of a one-and-a-half-ton cargo trailer from a deuce and a half that had been lined with plastic and filled with ice and water. The casualties were submerged in it to bring their body temperature back down. There were two men being treated in it when Earl and I happened by. I suffered from the heat on this op, too, but it was primarily because I wasn't drinking enough water. This resulted in severe migraine-like headaches. I conserved my water, not knowing when I would get more, which is what caused the problem. The corpsman read me the riot act about drinking more water and taking the salt pills he gave me, and that resolved the issue.

I photographed Corporal Morgan, a forward observer for the 81mm mortars, as we stopped for a break. He told me his sister Paula was stationed at Camp Lejeune and asked me to look her up when I returned there in August. (I would meet up with Paula when I eventually returned to Camp Lejeune, where she served as a woman Marine. She wanted to know more about her brother and what it was like for him in Vietnam. While I recounted the events of Allen Brook, I couldn't provide much more than that.)

The familiar sound of helicopters foretold the arrival of our resupply. I was able to top off my C-ration supply and get fresh water, along with two cans of Pepsi.

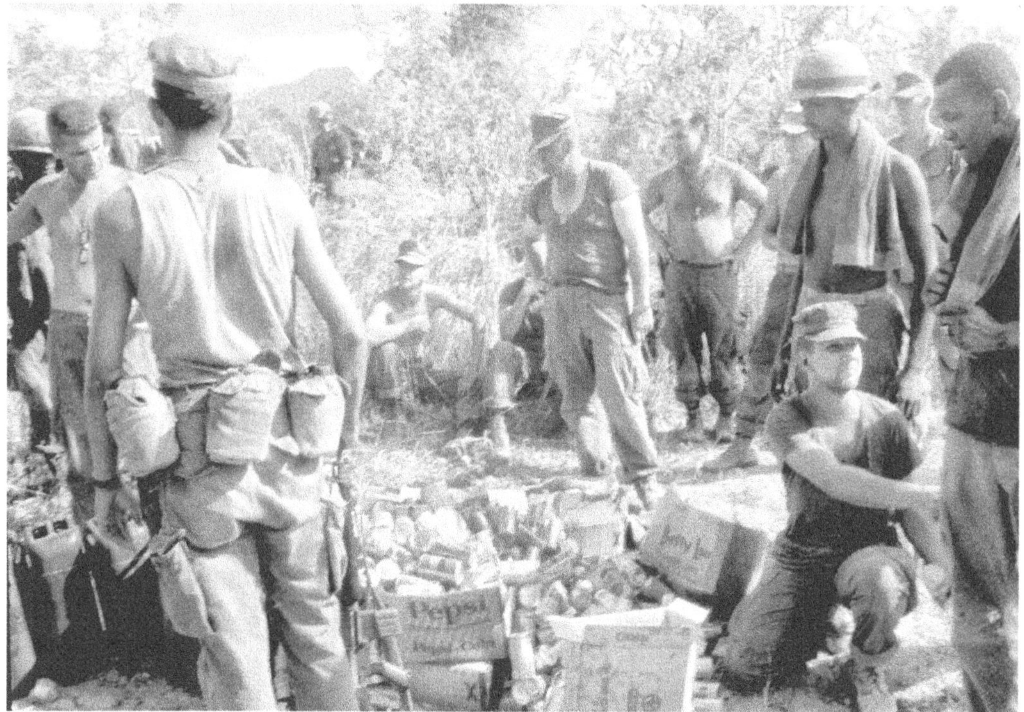

Marines from Kilo 3/5 were resupplied with soft drinks and C-rations during Operation Allen Brook, south of Da Nang, in May 1968. PHOTO BY CPL. DENNIS FISHER

After all the rations were divvied out, Lieutenant Smith began preparing his platoon's move to their next objective, which involved crossing an open expanse of rice paddies. At this time of year the rice paddies were dry, but full of growing rice, which was harvested in the fall. On the far side of the rice paddies was a substantial-looking bamboo hedge line that offered a perfect place of concealment for the enemy. The lieutenant wasn't going to send his men out there, especially in light of all the recent ambushes that had beset other companies.

I photographed and recorded him as he called in a fire mission from the 11th Marines' 105mm artillery battery over near Hill 55. After a few spotter rounds, he had the range dialed in and they began firing for effect. My recorder captured the sound of ninety-eight HE rounds working their way down the hedge line. They were VT-fused for air bursts that explode at treetop level and project a cone of shrapnel down on the enemy. The barrage shredded the hedge line and the troops advanced unmolested. Lieutenant Smith told me that artillery shells were cheap compared to the life of a Marine, and thus he didn't use them sparingly.

I continued photographing events as they unfolded. At one point, we had stopped for a few minutes when I heard the sound of an explosion and the call "Corpsman up!" I knew someone had triggered a booby trap. At almost the same time a Marine spotted the enemy and started firing with his M16. Others joined in, and we could hear the distinctive sound of AK rounds coming back at us, along with green tracers from an enemy machine gun. It soon became a general firefight that kept growing in intensity as the red tracers from one of our M60s could be seen raking a nearby bamboo hedge line. One of the grenadiers began firing on the same position, and you could see the gold-colored HE rounds arcing toward the target. Next the helicopter gunships began firing rockets and machine guns, followed by an F-4 dropping 250-pound bombs. I captured the sound on my recorder and still marvel at the intensity of that engagement.

When 3/5 was pulled off the op for a while, Earl and I returned to the 1st Division Headquarters area to visit our respective units. On the way back from the op I stopped by Freedom Hill PX for some food at the USO, and took in a movie. It wasn't so much that I wanted to see a movie; it was air-conditioned inside, and I think I slept through most of it.

From there I stopped by the lab to see what was going on. Both Corporal Del Vecchio and Corporal Bill Tuor were back from the hospital. As Del described earlier, he had been out on Allen Brook with the 7th Marines when he was shot through two of his fingers, the bullet lodging in his camera. The doctors had done their best to put his fingers back together, but they were not completely healed yet.

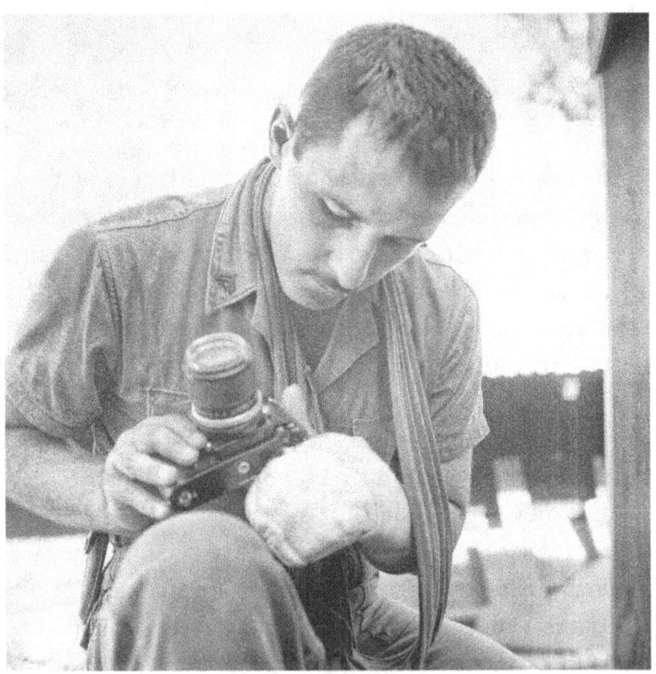

Cpl. R. J. Del Vecchio, combat photographer attached to 1st Division Photo, inspects the bullet hole in his 35mm camera. The round pierced Cpl. Del Vecchio's fingers and lodged in the film compartment of the camera during Operation Allen Brook. PHOTO BY SSGT. MAURICE UPTON/COURTESY OF NARA STILL PICTURE BRANCH

Bill Tuor had taken about five pieces of shrapnel from a mine while covering Operation Pegasus, but he seemed to be doing okay. I also heard that Sergeant Gelb, a photographer with the 3rd Marine Division, had drowned trying to rescue a wounded Marine while crossing the Cua Viet River up near Dong Ha. Records made available after the war indicated he died as the result of an explosive device. I don't know which account is the truth. I didn't know him personally, but he was the third Marine photographer to be killed in action so far in 1968: Brown was lost in February, Steward in March, and now Gelb in May. All were from the 3rd Division and operating in the northern part of I Corps near the DMZ.

Top Brown interrupted our reunion, took me aside, and told me that when it got close to my rotation date, he would pull me in from the field and have me transferred back to the lab. This was good news, although he never really specified what "close" meant. I was hoping it would be a month before I was due to leave. I still had two and half months before wheels up on the Freedom Bird so there was still plenty of time to get hurt, or worse. The closer I got to leaving, the more nervous I got about being in the field.

Earl stopped by the lab and told me there was a convoy heading up to Phu Bai the next day and inquired if I wanted to go with them, or fly back. I think he wanted to stop and visit with some of his 5th Marines buddies at Lang Co, on the north side of Hai Van Pass. I begged off and told him I wanted to get back and process my film at Phu Bai. I grabbed all my gear and headed down to the helipad, where I was able to catch a ride on a CH-46 back to Phu Bai.

I would later learn that Corporal Geoffrey Rowson—an M60 machine gunner from Delta 1/27 who I had photographed firing his gun from the top of a pagoda on Operation No Name II—had been killed, along with his assistant gunner, during Allen Brook. The 27th Marines were involved in some the heaviest fighting on that op. I would also learn some fifty years later that Lieutenant Fred Smith would leave the US Marine Corps and go on to found FedEx, enjoying a successful career as president and CEO of that company.

CHAPTER 17

# Tragedy Strikes

By May 30, I was back at Phu Bai, processing and printing my film from Allen Brook and wondering what I would be shooting next. I had no sooner got caught up when two of my friends from the Division Lab at Da Nang stopped by to say hi.

It was early June, and Corporal John ("Penny") Pennington and PFC Edward ("Sully") Sullivan were on their way up to Khe Sanh and had a little time to chat while their convoy stopped at Phu Bai. Penny had been out on Allen Brook with Del Vecchio and gave me an update on his recovery. We had a nice time catching up on the latest events. Sully was kind of quiet, but did relate some news from Boston, his hometown. Penny was telling me about his girlfriend, Jacky Lachmann, and a recent letter he'd had from her. Del, Penny, and I were really close, and always spent time together when we were in from the field, discussing all manner of things, but mostly our plans after returning home.

Looking back on it, I guess we talked about all the things young men talk about: girlfriends, family, hobbies, recent books we'd read, plans for the future, cars, and motorcycles. Reading books, writing letters, and talking to each other were our main forms of entertainment in Nam. Oh, and an occasional movie at our outdoor theater with its sandbag seats and screen stretched between a couple of poles.

One other topic of discussion concerned the number of combat photographers being killed in action as the fighting had increased during the Tet Offensive. Three of those lost in 1968 were with the 3rd Marine Division, serving up in Quang Tri Province near the DMZ. This was not a good year for combat photographers. Penny and Sully were going right into the heart of this area, and although nothing was said, it was understood they were heading into dangerous territory.

After about a half-hour they had to leave to rejoin the convoy, so I walked over to the waiting trucks with them, we shook hands, and they promised to stop by on their way back. Being up in Phu Bai with Task Force X-Ray, I didn't get to see my friends from Division Photo very often, unless I happened to run into them on an operation, so this was an unexpected and pleasant surprise. I hoped to be in Phu Bai when they returned, when we would have a little more time to talk. I waved good-bye as the convoy rolled out of the base and headed north.

Although I don't know all the details, their convoy continued north for about sixty-five miles to Dong Ha, and then west along Route 9 for the last forty-mile stretch to Khe Sanh. At some point along that last section of travel, tragedy struck as the convoy was ambushed, resulting in fifteen Marines killed, including both Penny and Sully. Their lives ended in an explosion when a satchel charge was thrown into the back of the truck in which they were riding. In an instant, all their hopes and dreams vanished. Their families would be devastated, their lives changed forever.

I found out about all of this the next day when word came into the ISO office about their deaths. One of the gunnery sergeants from Division Photo was on his way up to identify the bodies and escort them back to Da Nang.

I was dumbstruck by this turn of events. While many of us with 1st Division had been wounded, no one had been killed. As I mentioned earlier, 1968 proved to be the deadliest year for Marine combat photographers. Of the ten Marine photographers who were killed in action during the war, one was lost in 1966, two in 1967, and seven in 1968. I had seen many Marines killed during my tour, but I didn't have a close friendship with them. This was different. It was personal, and really took the wind out of my sails. It brought home the fact that not only could the worst happen, but it could happen to my friends—or to me if I wasn't careful. Hell, even if I *was* careful, there was no end to the ways you could get yourself maimed or killed, and not just by the enemy. Friendly fire incidents accounted for many of those killed and wounded during the war, from misdirected artillery, bombs dropped on our own men, rockets, and even rifle fire.

I traveled down to Division Photo on Saturday, June 15, to attend memorial services for Penny and Sully on Sunday, a week to the day after they died. When I arrived the whole lab was in a state of shock. Knowing that I was the last one from Photo to see them alive, they had a lot of questions for me, although I didn't have many answers. My last meeting with them had been routine, with nothing of much import discussed. The thought of losing a photographer had never crossed my mind, and the idea that we could lose *two* on the same day seemed beyond the pale.

It was strangely quiet in the lab that day. The sadness of what had happened weighed on everyone in the unit as the full extent of our loss was finally sinking in. As we prepared to attend the memorial service the next day, everyone spoke in hushed tones, if they spoke at all. I think most of us were lost in personal introspection as we walked to the CP Chapel. Despite all I had been through, June 16, 1968, was the day the war finally touched me in a way I'd managed to avoid for a year and a half. The full impact of what it meant to lose a friend to war had finally reached in and torn at my heart. I remember little of the memorial service; my mind was elsewhere. I do remember singing the Navy Hymn ("Eternal Father, Strong to Save") at the end.

Earl and some of the ISO guys also attended the service. Penny was widely known and universally liked by photographers and correspondents alike. I didn't know Sully that well but had been out with him on Operation Baxter Garden. Both he and Penny were dedicated to capturing the best coverage of our men in action. After we returned to the lab, Earl stopped by and asked if I wanted to ride back to Phu Bai with a convoy. He was always on the lookout for a story; he always said you never knew what might happen en route. Ambushes were not too common along the stretch of Route 1 between Da Nang and Phu Bai, but land mines were frequently encountered. So with a little reticence, I relented. Even though I wasn't looking forward to sitting in the back of a deuce and a half on those hard benches, over fifty miles of rough road, we still had a war to cover.

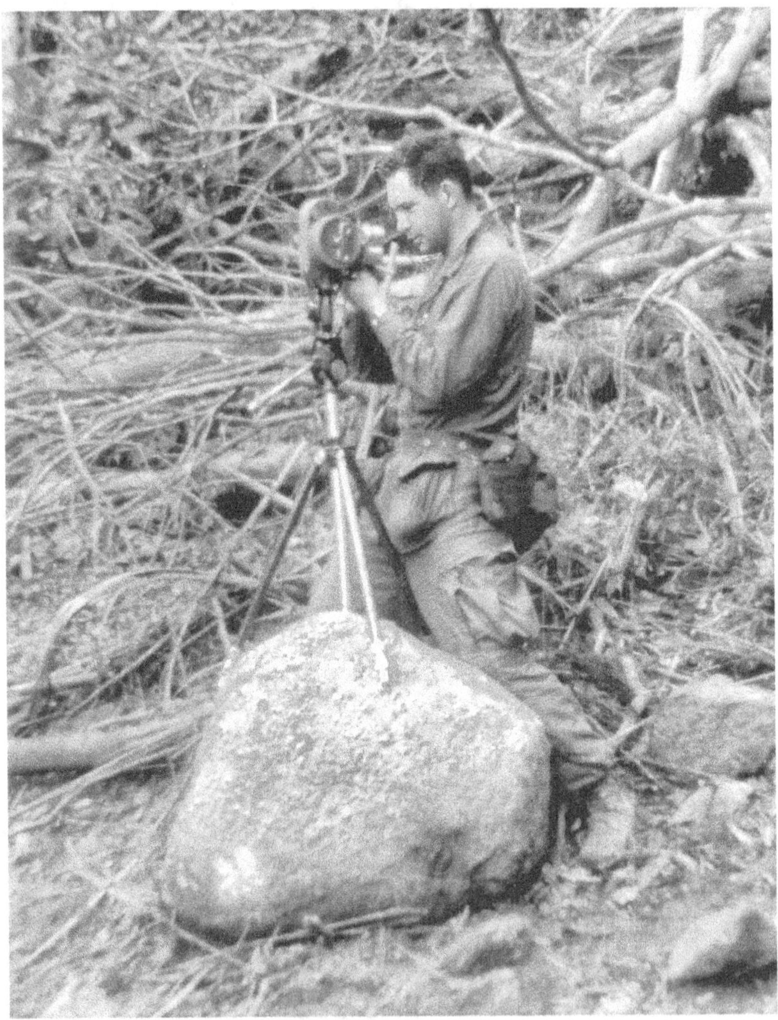

Combat photographer Cpl. Penny Pennington adjusts settings on his 16mm mopic camera during a combat sweep near Da Nang in the spring of 1968.
PHOTO BY CPL. R. J. DEL VECCHIO/AUTHOR'S COLLECTION

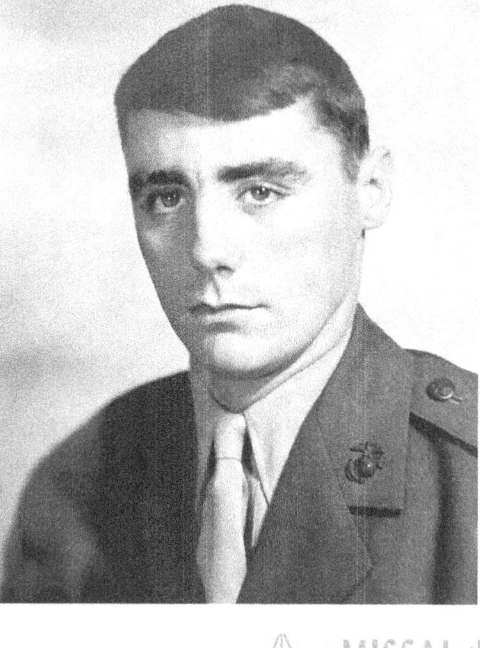

Combat photographer PFC Edward Michael Sullivan, who was killed in action on June 9, 1968. OFFICIAL USMC PHOTO FROM AUTHOR'S COLLECTION

The church bulletin from the memorial service for Cpl. John C. Pennington and PFC Edward M. Sullivan in June 1968 at the 1st Marine Division Headquarters CP Chapel in Da Nang.
AUTHOR'S COLLECTION

MISSAL~BULLETIN

June 16, 1968

Second Sunday after Pentecost

HEADQUARTERS
FIRST MARINE DIVISION (REIN), FMF
DA NANG, VIETNAM

SUNDAY — 1st MarDiv — CP Chapel 1000
(Confessions before Mass)

OTHER MASSES IN AREA: 0800 Security Platoon
0815 1st Eng. Battalion
1100 1st Hospital Company
1530 1st Recon Battalion

DAILY MASSES: 1st MarDiv CP Chapel — 1130
1st Hospital Company — 1630

* * * * * * * * * * * * * * * * * * * * * * * * * * * * * * * * * * *

I N   M E M O R I A M

Corporal John Charles Pennington, USMC
Division Photographic Section
Service Company, Headquarters Battalion
1st Marine Division (Rein), FMF

Enlisted 8 September 1966
Killed in action 9 Jun 1968

Private First Class Edward Michael Sullivan, USMC
Division Photographic Section
Service Company, Headquarters Battalion
1st Marine Division (Rein), FMF

Enlisted 31 October 1966
Killed in action 9 Jun 1968

REMEMBERED AT THIS SUNDAY MASS are Corporal John Pennington of Roy, Utah and PFC Edward Sullivan of Dorchester, Massachusetts. They were attached to the Division Photographic Section and were on a photo mission in the Khe Sanh area when their truck convoy was attacked at approximately 1100 on 9 June.

We pray that God will lighten the burden of sorrow for their parents and families and that God will have mercy on John and Edward. May they and all the souls of the faithful departed rest in peace.

* * * * * * * * * * * * * * * * * * * * * * * * * * * * * * * * * * *

CHANGE IN LOCAL MASS SCHEDULE is planned beginning next Sunday. The 1700 Mass the CP Chapel is cancelled. There will be an afternoon Mass at 1530 in the Recon Chapel.

* * * * * * * * * * * * * * * * * * * * * * * * * * * * * * * * * * *

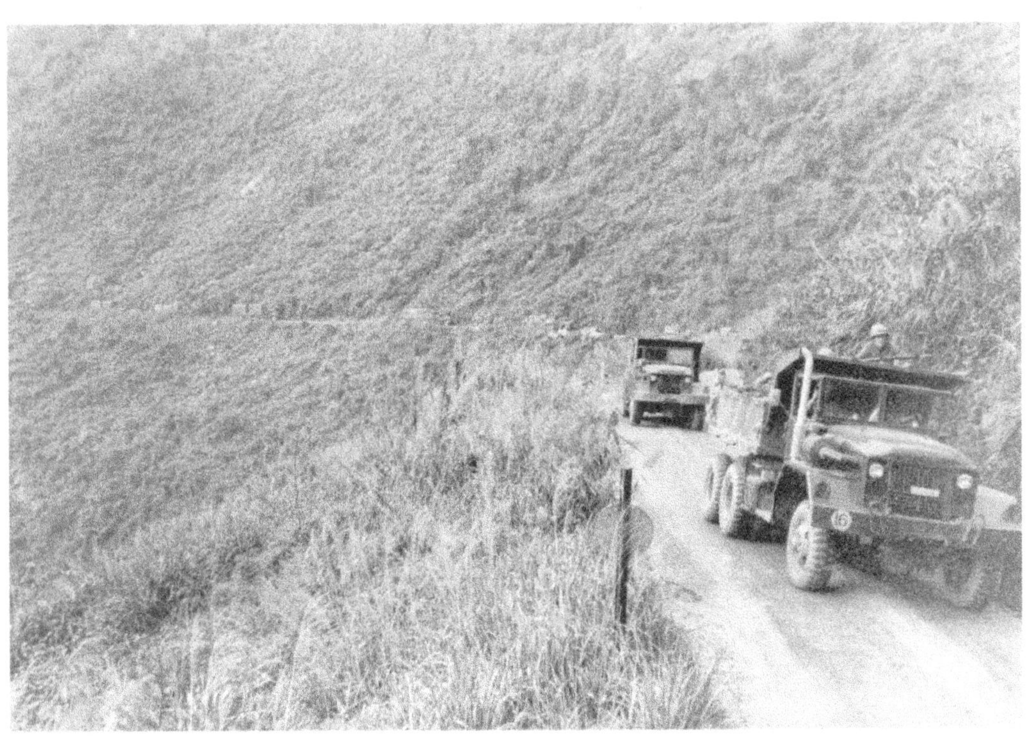

A Marine convoy traversing Hai Van Pass north of Da Nang en route to Phu Bai during the summer of 1968. USMC PHOTO/AUTHOR'S COLLECTION

# Chapter 18

# Back to Phu Bai

The ride from 11 Motor Transport to Lang Co, our first stop, was uneventful, although on an earlier trip one of the trucks had hit a mine. We had a gun truck with a quad-50 mounted on it for rear security. It was also loaded with war souvenirs, mostly captured enemy gear and a few SKS rifles, to trade with the supply guys at Lang Co for some things that we had a hard time getting through the regular supply system.

We arrived without incident, and out of curiosity, I followed the driver over to the supply point to see what they had to trade. Since I didn't have any trade goods, I was basically a looky-loo, but I was seeking some ammo for my grease gun. The supply sergeant directed me to the ammo point.

Leaving the horse trading behind, I found my way to the small arms ammo supply point and asked if I could scrounge four boxes of .45 ammo for my grease gun. The supply sergeant told me that he didn't actually have much call for .45 ammo, and was glad to provide as much as I wanted. All the while he had been eyeing my grease gun, and finally asked if he could shoot it. "No problem," I said, and we walked down to the nearby beach to shoot out into the water.

I threw an empty C-ration can out in the water as a target, but it immediately sank, so I picked up a small hunk of two-by-four and tossed it out. He handed me his M16 to do some plinking while he opened up with the grease gun. He did amazingly well with it as a steady stream of .45 slugs pounded the water and the board until the thirty-round magazine was empty.

With his curiosity satisfied, we headed to the supply point and he handed me a .50 caliber ammo can that was full of fifty-round boxes of ammo for my gun. Although I really didn't need it all, I took it anyway, figuring I could share it with the ISO guys who carried .45 pistols. We headed back to the trucks for the last leg of our trip up to Phu Bai. I didn't see Earl anywhere and was wondering if he'd decided to stay, but he appeared just as the trucks were firing up their engines and climbed on board.

I had lucked out and got a seat in the cab next to one of the drivers, which beat the heck out of riding in the back on wooden bench seats on these rough roads. We were making good time and everything was going smoothly as we passed some little vill about halfway to Phu Bai.

All of a sudden the gunner on the ring-mount .50 caliber Ma Deuce right above my head opened fire. The noise was deafening, and hot brass was showering down on me. What the hell was going on? My first thought was an ambush, and having just come from the memorial service for two photographers who were killed when their convoy was attacked, that possibility wasn't lost on me.

I brought my weapon up and began scanning my side of the road for muzzle flashes, but didn't see anything. Almost immediately I heard someone yelling "Cease fire, cease fire!" followed quickly by "What the hell are you shooting at?" It turned out that the gunner had seen something suspicious on the driver's side of the road and did what we called "recon by fire," meaning you see something that doesn't look right and you shoot at it to see if you get a response. If no one shoots back, you continue on your mission. If they shoot, then the fight is on. No one shot back, so we continued on.

The last ten miles or so to Phu Bai were uneventful, but my ears were still ringing. The convoy pulled into the base and paused until all the trucks were safely in the gate. While they were stopped, Earl and I jumped down and walked to the ISO hooch to check in with the lieutenant. He said things were slow right now, and that Hasford and I, who were getting short, should start thinking about getting all our household goods (personal non-issue things) packed up. The government shipped them for free to our next duty station or home of record, but I would need to get them down to Shipping & Receiving at Da Nang to make the arrangements. I really didn't have much and figured it could wait until late July, but I did start scrounging around for a suitable box to pack everything in.

At dinnertime I headed over to the chow hall and saw a sailor in his dress white uniform with a sea bag on his shoulder, walking in from the LZ. Definitely a new guy. As I got closer I recognized him: It was Ward, one of the corpsmen from the naval hospital on Guam. We were surprised to run into each other. I invited him to join me in the mess hall to get some chow and catch up on what had brought him to Phu Bai.

Now, you have to realize that Ward had been pulled from a safe and secure billet on Guam and dumped right into the middle of I Corps, with combat operations going on continually. He looked a little nervous from the continued firing of the nearby artillery battery's 105s, but I assured him it was just outgoing rounds. Entering the mess hall with its shrapnel-riddled walls from incoming mortars and rockets didn't exactly bolster his confidence. I could tell he realized he was really in the war now, and would soon find out how guys like me had ended up in that hospital on Guam. Ward told me he'd been assigned to one of the line companies as corpsman. I really felt sorry for him. He talked about some of the other orderlies I knew, and I gave him the lowdown on what to expect as a corpsman with an infantry company.

After we finished eating, I wished him luck and we parted company. I never saw him again, but his name is not on the Vietnam Veterans Memorial, so I guess he made it back.

Rockets and mortars fell on our base semi-regularly, and the primary protection we had were sandbag bunkers. They would protect us from nearby hits of both rockets and mortars, but not from a direct hit by a 122mm rocket. The best protection was patrolling the area around the base for enemy activity and keeping them out of range. Under the heading of "You Can't Fix Stupid," I observed some Marines climbing up on the roofs of their hooches to watch a mortar attack. These were obviously rear-echelon troops who lacked both common sense and an understanding of how deadly these attacks could be.

One day in late June of 1968, I was over at the ISO hooch working on some photo captions when I heard a loud explosion and immediately ran outside to our bunker, which was adjacent to our shop. I saw a plume of smoke rising from the direction of the ammo dump, so I ran back inside and grabbed my camera, flak jacket, and helmet and ran toward it.

It wasn't far away, and I arrived on the scene in short order. Marines were running away from the explosions and looking for any shelter they could find. The exploding artillery shells were sending tons of shrapnel into the air, which was now beginning to fall back to earth in a shower of hot jagged metal. Since all of this was occurring in the middle of the afternoon, I suspected this was some kind of accident and not an enemy attack. I heard later that a helicopter had crashed into the ammo dump while attempting to lift a pallet of artillery shells. Like so many events that happened during the war, within a few days it was old news, and something else had become the main topic of discussion.

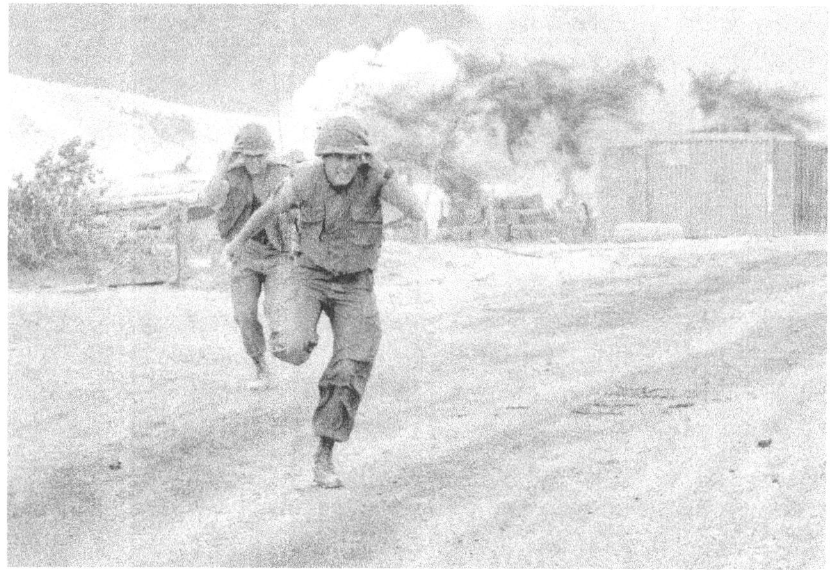

Marines run for cover as the ammunition dump explodes behind them in the summer of 1968 at Phu Bai. PHOTO BY SGT. DENNIS FISHER

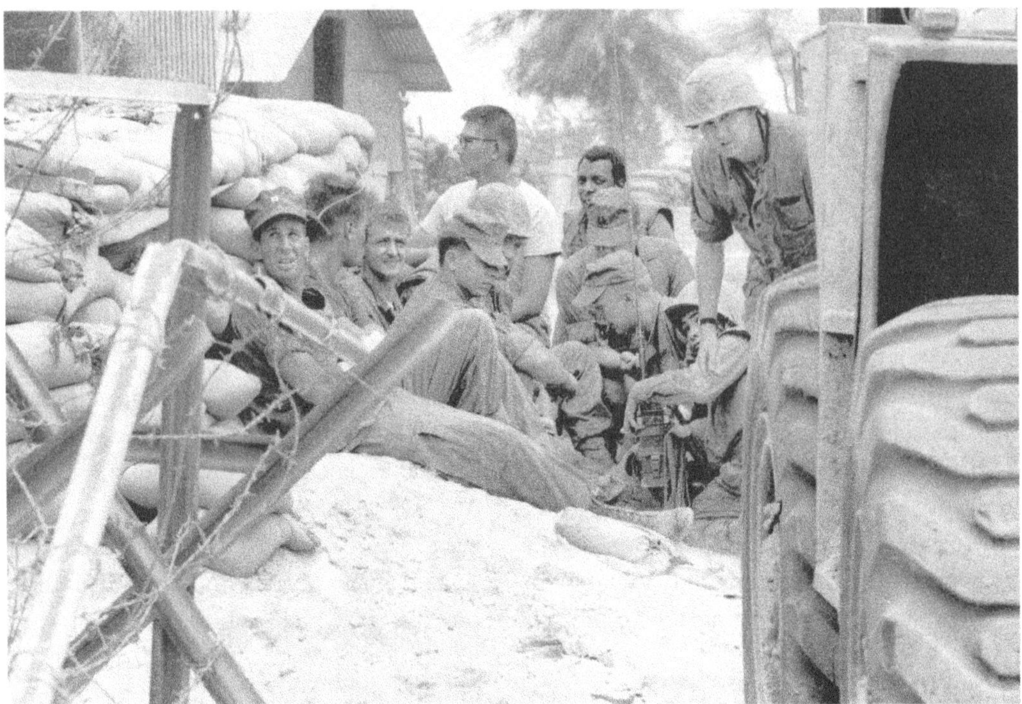

Marines seek shelter as the ammunition dump at Phu Bai explodes in the summer of 1968. PHOTO BY SGT. DENNIS FISHER

The next day, Corporal Gus Hasford brought me a 35mm negative I had shot of him earlier and asked me to make up some 8x10 glossy prints. It was a head-and-shoulders shot with his rifle on his shoulder, looking real gung-ho. He told me he needed about twenty prints. Noticing I looked a little perplexed, he said he'd picked up a bunch of letters from some college girls in a box of treats on his last op; he wanted to write to them, and include a photo. I think he'd seen the response I got when writing to Nancy and wanted to see if he could find someone to write to as well. He had eight or nine manila envelopes all addressed and ready to go, and just needed photos to add to them.

Gus and I were pretty good friends. In fact, we shared the same hooch for a while, and had been on several ops together, so I printed up the photos for him and he sent them off. A few weeks later I checked with him to see what kind of response he'd gotten, and he said he hadn't heard anything back yet. Rick Lavers, another correspondent, told me he didn't think anyone would answer his letters. When I asked why not, he said that Gus had gone down to Repo and had them print up a stack of letters for this mass mailing effort, handwriting their name at the beginning and then signing his at the end. We agreed that trying to start a relationship with a form letter was probably not the best idea he'd ever had, but Gus being Gus, we weren't surprised.

After leaving the Marine Corps, Gus would go on to have a career as an author. His book *The Short-Timers*, the first of a planned trilogy on the Vietnam War, would be brought to the big screen by Stanley Kubrick as *Full Metal Jacket* (1987). His second book, *Phantom Blooper*, was not as successful.

Gus had a run-in with the authorities in 1989 over a large number of stolen and overdue library books in San Luis Obispo, California, and was sentenced to six months in the county jail. I only lived forty miles away in Santa Maria and tried to visit him, but he had used up all his visiting hours with his lawyer. We wrote instead. Shortly after his release he sent me a copy of *The Phantom Blooper* with an inscription to me on the flyleaf. This was the last communication I had with him before he left for the Greek islands, where he lived and wrote as an expatriate until his death at age forty-five, from a combination of diabetes and heart disease.

Gus led a storied life with more than his share of quirks, but the bonds he formed with his fellow correspondents and photographers in Vietnam remained unbroken until his passing.



An inscription to the author by former Marine combat correspondent Cpl. Gustav Hasford, on the flyleaf of his book, *The Phantom Blooper*. AUTHOR'S COLLECTION

CHAPTER 19

# Getting Short

JUNE 1968 WAS IN THE REARVIEW MIRROR, AND NOW THAT IT WAS JULY, I COULDN'T STOP thinking that I was going home next month. I had been in Vietnam so long that it seemed like home, and I'd come to accept the hardships of war as normal. It was a surreal experience when the realization hit me that my tour was really just about over and I was going home soon. The thing I had been anticipating and dreaming of was now in sight. But the war was still going on and I would continue to cover it up until my last few days in the country.

It was now July 25 and I hadn't been on any named ops for a while, and frankly, I was just as glad. I kept busy shooting small patrols, aerial jobs, and assignments around the base. I had expected to be transferred back to Da Nang by this point but hadn't heard anything from the lab. So I decided to take all my personal stuff down to Da Nang to the Household Effects Section and get everything shipped off in preparation for my return home. I had traveled down with a convoy and the driver of the truck was good enough to drop me off at Household Effects. I showed them my orders, filled out the necessary paperwork, and was off to the Photo Lab.

Stopping by the lab, I checked in with Warrant Officer Huntley and asked when they were going to bring me back to the lab. He told me that I could leave Phu Bai at my discretion anytime during the first week in August. In the meantime he said I should finish up anything I was working on there. That was only a week away. He said I didn't need any orders for the move and that I would be checking out in Da Nang where all my records were. In fact, I already had my orders to go back to the States and was only waiting to be assigned a flight date. This was really good news.

As I was leaving the office WO Huntley held up a copy of *Leatherneck* magazine and asked me if I had seen my photo in it. I told him I hadn't, and he opened it up to show me. It was the photo I'd taken on a tank/infantry sweep in May of the M48 tank with Marines from Delta 1/5 sitting on it and holding their ears as the main gun was fired. I

158

was really proud that some of my work was actually being seen back in the States. As a Marine, there was also a bit of cachet associated with having your photos published in *Leatherneck* magazine. In the long run, this photo "had legs," as we said of images that saw repeated publication. Most recently the National Archives and Record Administration, where the original is housed, featured the photo as the lead on their DocsTeach website for educators in their "The War in Vietnam: A Story in Photographs" series.

It was time to head back to Phu Bai and begin wrapping things up. I caught a helicopter for the ride back and began letting everyone know that I would be returning to Da Nang the following week. The next few days were a series of good-byes with all of my friends.

Hasford noted that I still had my KA-BAR and asked why I hadn't shipped it back with my personal belongings. Marines have a special affection for those knives, and I was kicking myself for not throwing it in with my household goods. The problem with trying to hand-carry it back to the States was that Marines didn't go directly home from Vietnam. We flew to Okinawa first, and upon arriving there we were checked for contraband. Everything you had was dumped out on a six-foot-square table and gone through by inspectors. They were looking for live ordnance, drugs, war souvenirs that didn't have proper paperwork, machine guns, and a whole host of other things. My KA-BAR would have been confiscated had I tried to hand-carry it back. Gus offered to get it back to the States for me, and true to his word, he showed up at my apartment in Santa Barbara with my KA-BAR, in 1973.

I was glad to finally be headed back to the States, but at the same time I felt like I was abandoning my friends. These were men I had been with through numerous operations, close calls, and all the hardships of war. We had shared our personal feelings, stories of our families, the ups and downs of relationships, and our hopes and dreams for the future. I knew that I would most likely never see them again, and all these years later, that has more or less held true. I have kept in touch with five: "Del" Del Vecchio, Earl Gerheim, Bill Tuor, Dale Dye, and Gus Hasford (until he passed away).

But forget all that—I was starting to take on a FIGMO (F*ck It, Got My Orders), or short-timer's, attitude. I was ready to head home in a few weeks. I just had to concentrate on keeping my head and ass wired together, as the saying went, and not doing anything stupid that could get me hurt again, or worse. This was no time for a rookie mistake.

CHAPTER 20

# Short-Timer

So here it was, the beginning of August, and I was ready to ship out in a couple of weeks. Being back at Division Photo with all my buddies was like a homecoming. Each time I had traveled down to the lab from Phu Bai or stopped on my way back from an op, a few new faces appeared, while others had rotated back to the States. Although I knew I wouldn't be there long, I figured I could coast along, shooting local assignments until I received my flight date.

But the gunny wasn't ready to keep me in the rear quite yet. The day after I got back, he sent me out to cover a gunship crew that was conducting a sampan interdiction mission out near An Hoa. I grabbed my gear and went down to the airfield to meet up with the crew.

Two Huey gunships were sitting on the ramp, all loaded with 2.75-inch folding-fin rocket pods, external M60 machine guns, and more M60s manned by the door gunners. The crew had been notified I was coming, and as soon as I climbed aboard the number-one ship they spun up the turbines and began doing some checks prior to takeoff. I didn't have a headset so I couldn't hear exactly what was going on, but in a few minutes we were taxiing out to the runway and began climbing out to the west.

A lot of the NVA's rockets and other supplies were brought in via sampan by the enemy, but this was usually done at night. I don't know where the intel came from—perhaps from one of our recon units—but a boat was reported to be traveling in broad daylight. They could have been fishermen, but since a couple of gunships were being sent out, something must have aroused suspicion.

We approached the area of the sighting and saw a sampan that appeared be beached, or perhaps had run aground in the night. The river in this area is broad and shallow and changed channels frequently, so navigating it could be tricky in the dark. The pilot dropped down to have a look, and as we neared it the door gunner opened up with his

M60. The pilot adjusted his angle of attack to bring the guns to bear and I could see the tracers cutting across the water and into the sampan followed by the rockets.

I began getting photos of everyone as the action progressed. The door gunner brought his gun to bear as we flew by, sending an arcing stream of red tracers into the boat. The external guns on the right side seemed to have run out of ammo or jammed, and the door gunner, after securing his gunner's belt, went out on the skid to fix the problem as we climbed away. In the meantime, the number-two ship made a rocket run on the boat and it seemed to disappear as a huge plume of water erupted from the rocket impacts. We made one more pass to confirm that it had been destroyed and then headed back to Da Nang. Mission accomplished.

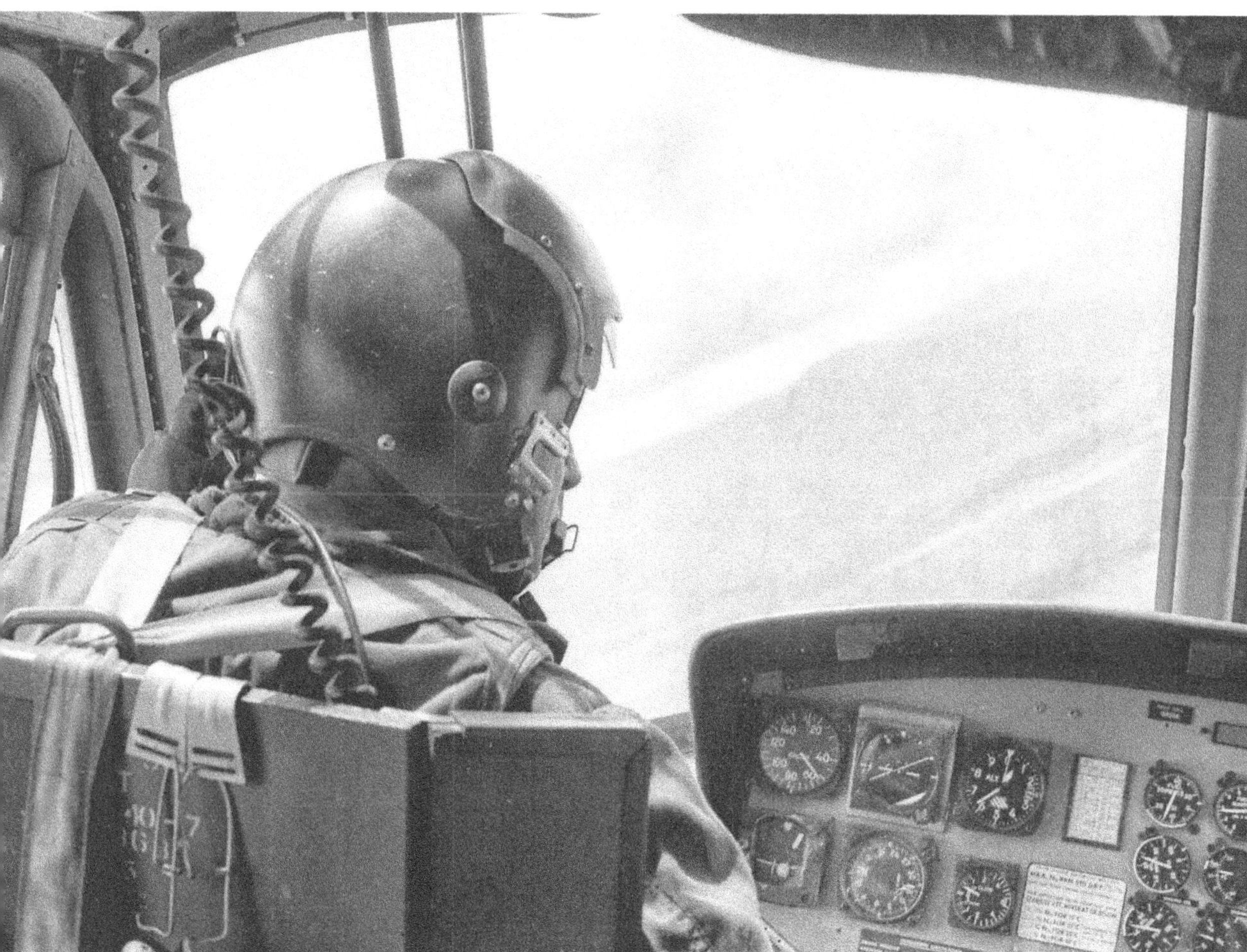

A gunship pilot rolls in on a target for a rocket run during a sampan interdiction mission near An Hoa in August 1968. PHOTO BY SGT. DENNIS FISHER

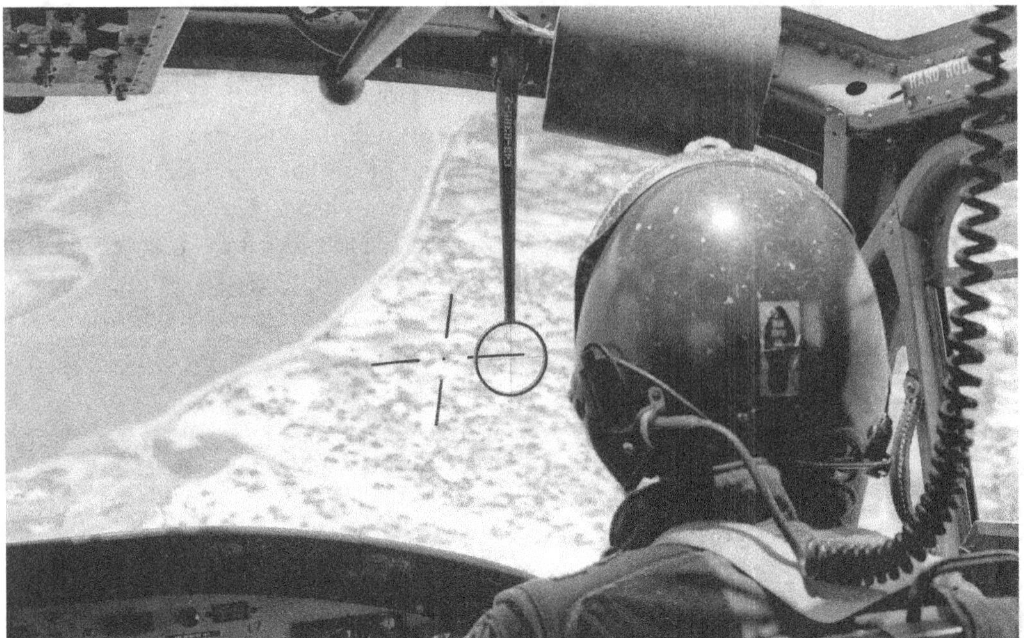

A gunship copilot lines up sights for a rocket run during a sampan interdiction mission near An Hoa in August 1968. PHOTO BY SGT. DENNIS FISHER

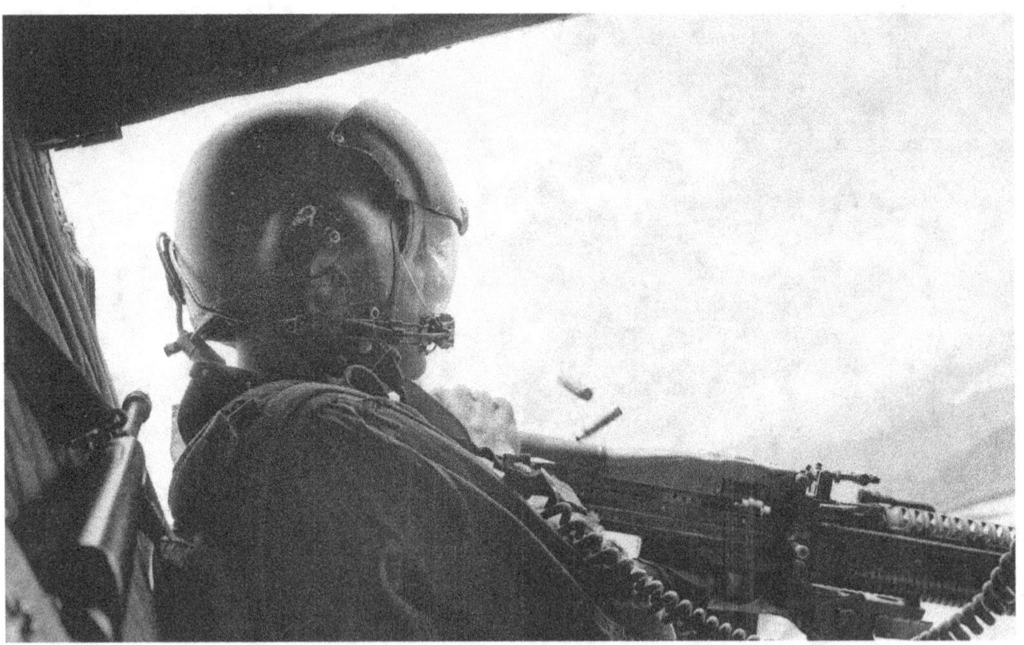

A UH-1 Huey door gunner opens fire with his M60 machine gun during a sampan interdiction mission near An Hoa in August 1968. PHOTO BY SGT. DENNIS FISHER

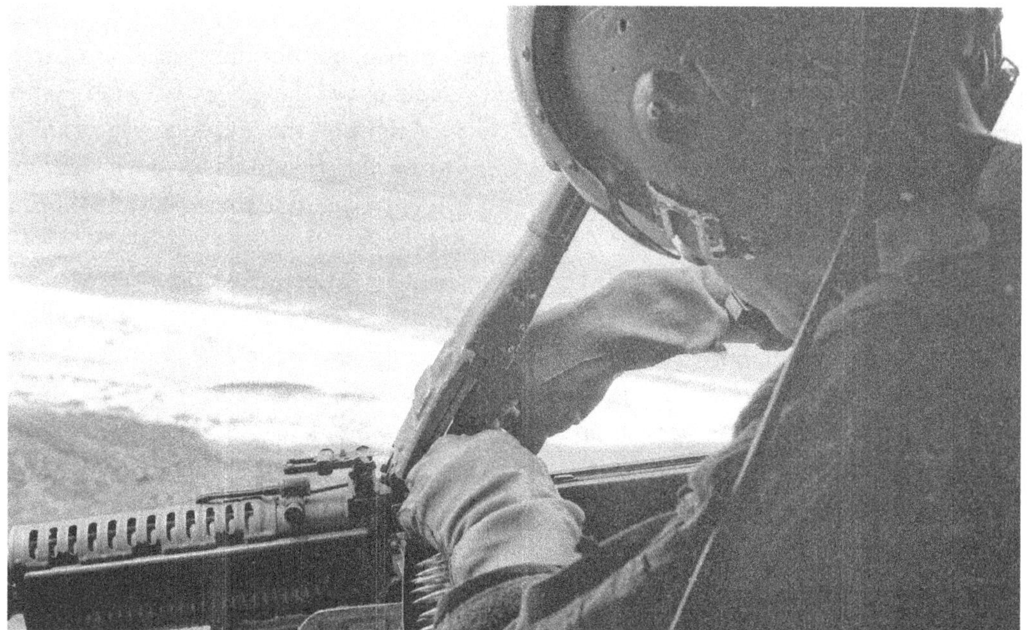

A UH-1 Huey door gunner reloads his M60 machine gun during a sampan interdiction mission near An Hoa in August 1968. PHOTO BY SGT. DENNIS FISHER

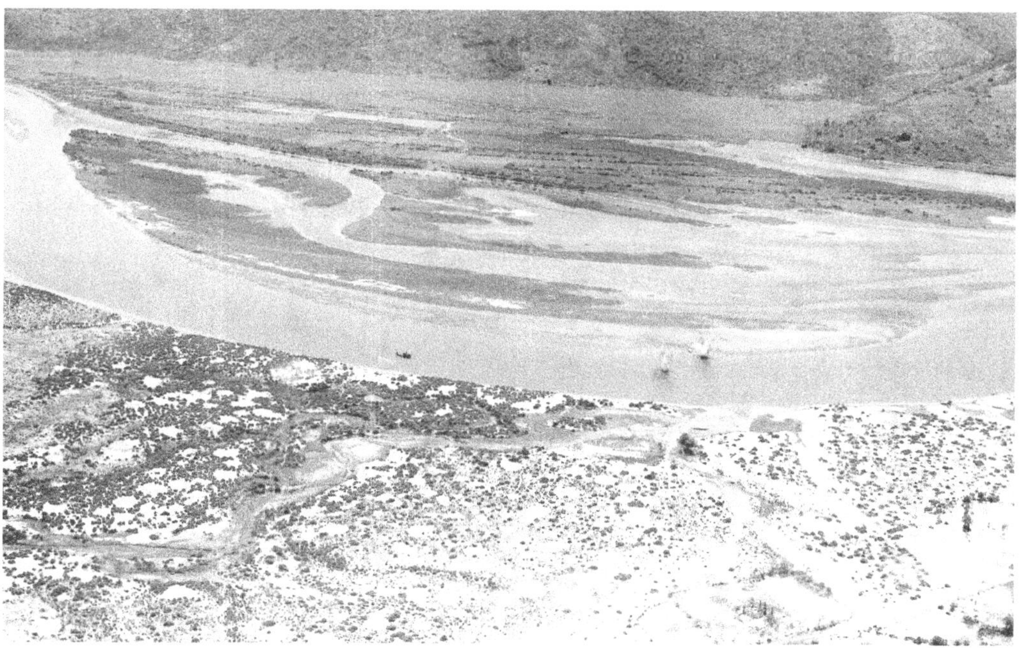

A number-two Huey gunship firing 2.75-inch rockets during a sampan interdiction mission near An Hoa in August 1968. PHOTO BY SGT. DENNIS FISHER

The door gunners were still on alert and scanning the riverbank for muzzle flashes as the ship climbed out after the gun run on the sampan, but our departure from there proved to be uneventful. The helicopter climbed rapidly out of the range of ground fire to around five thousand feet. Cool, refreshing air flowed through the open doors, providing a welcome relief from the summer heat awaiting us on the ground. The crew relaxed as we climbed out of the range of small arms fire and I got as comfortable as I could on the bench seat for the ride back.

The *whop whop whop* of the rotor blades provided a comforting sound as we headed back to Da Nang. As I saw the airfield appear in the distance, I knew this could be one of my last field assignments. Thoughts that my tour of duty was coming to an end in a couple of weeks continued to race through my head. I was ready to go.

I was aroused from my reverie as one of the crewmen tapped me on the shoulder with a set of headphones and motioned for me to put them on. I did so and adjusted the mic so I could speak. The pilot's voice came through loud and clear above the engine whine and rotor noise.

"Are you Fisher?" he said. I told him I was. He said that my CO had requested they drop me off at the 1st Division LZ instead of the airfield, with instructions for me to return to my unit at once. The pilot said they had another mission and couldn't divert to Division but that they could get someone to drive me back to the lab from the airfield. I thanked him and said that I'd send over some copies of the photos I had taken in a week or so.

As soon as we landed, the ground crews came out and began re-arming the gunships as I went into the operations shack to check on a ride back to the lab. One was quickly arranged, and we wound our way along a now-familiar route around the end of the runway, through Dog Patch, and past the Freedom Hill PX, arriving at the Photo Lab in less than a half-hour. I thanked the Marine for driving me back and went inside.

I had no idea what was so urgent, but a quick chat with the gunny answered my question. He said my rotation date had been moved up a week and I was going home a little early; I needed to get checked out and ready to leave in a couple days.

That was good news indeed, and I told him I would get on it right away. But first I needed to soup my film from this mission and make some prints. I had only exposed one roll of film and decided to process it immediately and hang it up to dry so I could start making prints in the morning.

The whole time I was in the Nam, I'd been marking off days on my short-timer calendar. I knew exactly how many I had left. With each combat operation, I'd wondered if I would actually complete my tour in one piece, especially after being wounded and spending two months in the hospital. Realizing that I was now truly a short-timer, I feared that something would happen to me with only days left in the country. I'd heard many times about some poor grunt who stepped on a mine or was shot with only a week left in country.

It wasn't until I walked into the Photo Lab on that hot August day and the gunny told me to pack my bags and get ready to leave that I felt the weight of a thousand possible tragic what-ifs lifted off my shoulders. I wasn't short anymore; I was next.

CHAPTER 21

# The Freedom Bird

I WAS ORIGINALLY SCHEDULED TO DEPART VIETNAM ON OR ABOUT AUGUST 15, BUT that date had been moved up to August 7. This required showing up at the Transit Facility by 1630 on the day prior to departure to be manifested on the flight.

The next few days were spent finishing up my lab work, saying good-bye to my friends, and checking out. My tour was finally over, and after a final stroll around the lab and a round of hand-shaking, the time had come to shove off. The hot and humid weather took a little break that day, August 6, when a thunderstorm and some light rain cooled things off. A mud-splattered Mighty Mite arrived from the motor pool to take me to the airfield. The driver confirmed my name and destination and made some entries on his trip ticket as I tossed my gear in the back. I climbed aboard and off we went.

My last trip to the airfield was bittersweet. What seemed like a lifetime of memories flooded in as I passed by the Security Platoon, Division Headquarters, Charlie Med, 1st Recon, and the Freedom Hill PX complex for the last time. As we neared the Transit Facility I saw stacks of metal coffins that would soon be filled with Marine KIAs for shipment back to the States. For those families there would be no joyous homecoming— only a lifetime of sorrow and grieving over the life of a loved one lost. A son, a husband, a father . . . a life cut short, far from home. It was one last grim testament to the horrors of war as I prepared to leave. I was one of the lucky ones.

The driver dropped me off in front of the facility and I headed into the building amid a throng of other anxious but happy homeward-bound Marines. All were lean and heavily suntanned. They stood in stark contrast to the pale-looking, newly arrived replacements who were awaiting transportation to their units. But that wasn't the only difference. The countenance of the veterans betrayed all the hardships they had suffered during their tour. Yes, they were happy to be heading home, but there was a somberness behind the smiles that came with thoughts of all those who'd been lost. The new guys had no idea what they were in for, and there was no way to explain it to them. With luck, they would be standing here in our place in a year.

I really don't have any detailed recollection of the check-in that afternoon, or of waiting to board the Freedom Bird the next day. There were so many things running through my mind at the time that there wasn't any room to store new information. The one event I recall was climbing the stairs to the plane and watching as each step brought me closer to the door. Finally, I crossed that threshold and was greeted by a lovely stewardess who welcomed me on board. It was like I had entered an episode of *The Twilight Zone*, and the door was a portal to a new world.

As we taxied out for takeoff, there was still a bit of apprehension in the air. After eighteen months in Nam, I knew that any number of things could go wrong and delay our departure. But once we were airborne and the wheels could be heard retracting into the wheel wells, a cheer went up, and true excitement was in the air.

So ended my tour in Vietnam.

I made it. I was alive, and headed home. Well, not exactly home. First we had to make a stop in Okinawa for a few days, to get ourselves cleaned up and our uniforms up to snuff. Back then we traveled in our dress uniforms, and after a year in storage they needed to be cleaned and pressed. Plus, our rank insignias and ribbons required updating. The thing I remember most about my stay in Okinawa, though, was that one of my Nikon cameras was stolen, and since I was on a Marine base, it was most likely stolen by another Marine. Not all Marines are noble warriors; we had our share of bad apples.

The time passed quickly, and at last I stood along the flight line at Kadena AFB waiting to board my flight home. I was lost in thought about my final return to the States, and the timing of everything. In Vietnam it seemed as if time didn't matter, but now I was back on the clock. I had been given five days of travel time, four days of "proceed," and I had put in for twenty days of annual leave. This meant I had twenty-nine days from the time I left Vietnam until I had to report to Camp Lejeune, my next duty station, to finish off my enlistment.

As I scanned the runway looking at the planes landing and taking off, a long black futuristic aircraft without any markings taxied out on to the active runway. I had no idea what it was, but it looked like something out of a sci-fi movie. I immediately brought my camera into action and began photographing it. Out of nowhere an MP stepped in front of me and asked what the hell I was doing. I pulled out my Marine Corps photographer ID and told him I was photographing that airplane. He told me in no uncertain terms that I was not, and demanded I remove the film from my camera and give it to him. I complied, because I didn't want to get involved in some squabble that would make me miss my flight home.

By now the plane was roaring down the runway and off on its mission. The MP told me "No more pictures on the flight line, and especially none of the 'Blackbird.'" I was stunned by this airplane. I thought the F-4 Phantom was the top of the line in those days and had no idea that Lockheed had developed the SR-71 Blackbird reconnaissance aircraft. Apparently the air force didn't want anyone else to know about it either. Little did I know that two years later, I would be working for Pratt & Whitney Aircraft, photographing the overhaul and repair of the engines for those very same aircraft.

After a long flight I arrived in San Francisco, at night. I wasn't greeted by antiwar protesters or spit on, but rather by a deserted airport. After a change of flights I was back in the air on my way to Florida. This 747 red-eye cross-country flight was nearly empty, with row after row of vacant seats. A stewardess came by to see if I needed anything and we chatted for a few minutes. She could see I was tired and handed me a blanket and several pillows from the overhead compartment. I stretched out on the row of seats, made myself comfortable, and was soon fast asleep.

My homecoming was great, although being with family again seemed a little strange at first. Plus, I didn't know anyone in New Smyrna Beach. It wasn't like going back to Ligonier after I got out of the hospital. I had a lot of friends there and ran into them everywhere. My father had taken a job on the Eastern Test Range in Florida and had moved the family there after I'd returned to Vietnam following my trip home after being hospitalized. I was returning to a place I had never been before.

Slowly but surely I was getting back into life in the States, enjoying my leave. Actually, I was enjoying everything about being back in the States, especially living near the beach and cruising up and down A1A on my Triumph Bonneville. Before long I ran into another Triumph rider at the local Whataburger. His name was Jerry Fromann, and we became friends and riding buddies. He grew up in New Smyrna, knew everyone, and began introducing me to all his friends. He had a lot of questions about my time in Vietnam. Jerry had signed up for a warrant officer program in the army to become a helicopter pilot. He went through basic training, completed helicopter flight school, was deployed to Vietnam, severely wounded, medically discharged, and back riding his Triumph on the beach in Florida, all in about one and half years.

My leave seemed to run out too fast, and before I knew it I was on my way to Camp Lejeune and life as a stateside Marine. The tedium of duty in the States was decidedly different from the excitement of combat operations in Vietnam. The Marine Corps instituted a program to let those who were not going to reenlist muster out two months early. I went over to the career advisor's office to sign up, but he was still trying to entice me into reapplying for Officer Candidate School (OCS).

In fact, I was no longer interested in a career in the Marine Corps. The taste of stateside duty after being in a war seemed mundane and petty, filled with never-ending training exercises and inspections. While these things were necessary to keep Marines on their toes in case another conflict arose, I was ready to call it quits. On top of that, Marines were not allowed to have motorcycles on base, and that was my only means of transportation. The biggest disappointment was being assigned to the Headquarters Battalion, Headquarters Platoon, Communications Company instead of to the Photo Lab. I didn't have a Communications MOS, and they weren't sure what to do with me there, so they made me the mail orderly. At the end of September, I put in an AA form requesting a transfer to the Photo Lab, which was approved after a few months, but I could see that without getting my primary MOS changed to photographer, I would continue to have this problem.

During my seven months at Camp Lejeune I met up with Ron Sarron, my old friend from the University of Miami, who was now in the Marines and flying CH-46s out of Cherry Point. The crews flew cross-country training flights on the weekends, and he asked if I wanted to fly down to Florida with him. I took him up on that, and we had a chance to catch up on what had happened in our lives since we'd last met at the U of M. Not long after that he was deployed to Vietnam.

Back on base I had been nominated for Marine of the month for my actions apprehending two thieves in a jewelry store holdup, but I lost out to one of the cooks who had been baking cookies for a charitable group downtown. The one good thing that came out of the holdup was that I was given a week's free leave to go testify at the trial in Miami. As it turned out, I didn't have to testify, as the guys pled guilty at the last minute. So it was mainly a free trip to visit friends and family for a few days before heading back to base.

I failed to talk my way out of being sent to the rifle range for two weeks to qualify with the M16. I told them I was getting an early out and it was just a waste of time, but since I didn't have it approved in writing, it was off to the range. As much as I enjoy shooting, my heart just wasn't in it, and I did just enough to qualify.

As soon as I returned from the range, the paperwork for my early out was approved. I was now counting down the days until I would be released from active duty and returned to civilian life. One would think that once you were out, that was it. But I was actually placed on inactive reserve status, which meant I could still be recalled in case of a national emergency. I wouldn't be officially discharged until I had served six years of combined active and inactive service.

The day finally arrived—April 18, 1969. I left the base for the last time and headed home to Florida. So long to J'ville and Camp Lejeune, hello to civilian life. I might have left the Corps, but the Corps would never leave me. My training, and especially my experiences in Vietnam, are still with me. Perhaps more importantly, it was what I learned about problem-solving, working as part of a team, the self-confidence and never giving up, always having a plan B and plan C in case plan A goes south, and pushing yourself to do things you never thought possible. These lessons shaped my approach to life. You never know what you are capable of until you are put to the test, and Vietnam was a major testing ground where failure was not an option. Well, actually it was, but you didn't want to go there. Vietnam and all I experienced there will always be with me. The events of that odyssey are seared into my memory, and I will carry them to my grave.

*Semper Fi*

CHAPTER 22

# Reflections on Combat Photography

It is said that combat is days of boredom interrupted by minutes of sheer terror. And so it seemed to be on many occasions. I've been asked if I was scared being out in the fighting. The answer to that is easy: Yes—but only momentarily. I was usually more surprised than scared when fighting erupted, as happened when we were ambushed on Operation Rock. I can say that I was initially scared, but once I realized I was uninjured, I set about my job. Corporal Earl Gerheim and I were carrying ammo to Operation No Name II when we were taken under fire and heard rounds snapping close by us. The realization that someone is shooting at you in particular can trigger fear rather quickly. Everyone was afraid, but it's what you did to overcome it and revert back to your training that kept you alive. That being said, you could do everything right and still be killed or wounded. On the other hand, you could mess up and come out without a scratch. Luck or providence seemed to play a big part.

War photography is photojournalism at its most dangerous level. Vietnam was no different, with the Marines losing ten photographers killed in action, and the civilian media losing a dozen, including a number of famous names: Larry Burrows, Dickey Chapelle, Sean Flynn, Henri Huet, and Dana Stone. It's a tough and dangerous job not meant for the faint of heart.

As a photographer, I used my infantry experience to anticipate what men would do next so that I could be in a good position to capture the action. You had some control over the composition of the photo, but Mother Nature's lighting could leave a lot to be desired. Technical mastery of your equipment was essential and had to be second nature so that you could trip the shutter at just the right time, with confidence that your setting and focus were correct. There were no motor-drive cameras for us; it was up to the photographer to capture the peak of the action, all while trying to avoid being shot by both sides.

Photographing combat with a still camera was an aesthetic challenge, as the photographer had little or no control over many elements of composition. Point of view, lighting, angle of view, rule of thirds, depth of field, and many other technical aspects for creating a good photograph had to be evaluated on the fly. Your ability to move around the battlefield to achieve the best photos while avoiding getting hit was always a consideration. Once you got into a favorable position, you could then concentrate on framing your shot and choosing the right instant to press the shutter release. Doing this under combat conditions while trying to minimize one's own exposure to enemy fire was a challenge.

Motion picture documentation and sound recordings preserve more of the original experience but only give you a fleeting glimpse of the event. An iconic example would be the flag-raising on Iwo Jima. The motion picture coverage of that event portrays the Marines raising the flag, all over in a few seconds. The still photo by Joe Rosenthal captured the key moment of that event in a fraction of a second and created a photo that is one of the most recognizable ever taken.

Two photos from Vietnam civilian correspondents that stick out in my mind are Eddie Adams's photo of the Viet Cong prisoner being shot in the head by General Nguyen Ngoc Loan, and Nick Ut's photo of Phan Thi Kim Phúc, the napalm girl. It seems ironic to me that neither of the two most recognized photos depict the bravery or suffering of our troops.

Photographers lived like the grunts and endured all the same hardships and dangers out in the field. But after finishing an op, we could go back to the rear and get a shower and some hot chow. Then it was into the lab to process our film and take care of the accompanying administrative chores before heading out to the field again. Not so for many of the grunts; their rear areas were usually on some hill out in Indian country that was frequently mortared or attacked. The best they could hope for was to be assigned to guard a bridge for a week or so.

As photographers we were given free rein when out in the field, but you were expected to come back with good photos, which meant self-reliance was the norm. After completing a few operations, you would receive little in the way of direction other than the unit you had been assigned to cover. Even that was more of a suggestion than an order, as once in the field, the photographer would be expected to join up with the units that were actively engaged in the fighting.

I mentioned Robert Capa's quote earlier: "If your pictures aren't good enough, you aren't close enough." He died following his own advice during the First Indochina War when he stepped on a land mine while trying to get closer to the action. Good combat photography requires you to be where the action is; our photographers not only knew how to do this, but did it day after day. The cost of that dedication to our mission at 1st Division was two photographers killed in action, and nearly everyone who went out in the field was wounded at least once.

Yet the work of military photographers seldom made its way into civilian publications. All our work was filtered through the ISO office, which determined what photos could be released to the public. They operated under guidance from Division

Headquarters on what types of photos were releasable to the media. For example, as photographers we could not release photos to our hometown newspaper without having them cleared through the ISO office. Consequently, very little of our work was seen during the war.

The biggest contribution of the military photographers was to create a visual body of work for future generations that depicts the courage, hardships, and suffering of our men at war. There are no monuments, parks, or places set aside to remember the combat photographers who suffered, bled, and died in the performance of their duties. Their legacy is the images they captured.

## Acknowledgments

As a first-time author, bringing my story to print seemed like an insurmountable task. That road was smoothed with support and advice from many people along the way. My wife, Mary Fisher, has provided a level of compassion and understanding about my need to share this story I find hard to put into words. She has always been there for me, especially in the years when I first returned from Vietnam, when many tragedies of that time were still fresh in my mind. Her love and devotion has been the keystone of my life.

My family provided tremendous support throughout this project, and their contributions helped mold this manuscript into something worthy of sharing with the outside world. Dr. Julie Fisher, daughter and historian/author with NARA, reviewed some of my early work and provided a wealth of helpful hints on basic writing style to get me started; and my brother, author Keith Fisher, provided additional suggestions on style and sentence structure to try and keep me from making too many rookie mistakes.

Dr. Joanna Fisher, daughter and naturopathic doctor, has always honored my service and that of other veterans. She has helped me to set up exhibits, has listened to some of my presentations, and encouraged me to get my story and photos into print. Further encouragement over the years from my sister Harriette "Elizabeth" Carey and brother Richard Fisher helped to solidify my resolve to finally put pen to paper.

No acknowledgments would be complete without singling out several of my comrades in arms, men with whom I served, who shared all the rigors of combat photojournalism. First would be R. J. "Del" Del Vecchio, best friend and fellow combat photographer in the 1st Marine Division, with whom I shared many adventures in Vietnam. He is a scholar of the Vietnam War and founder of the Vietnam Healing Foundation that supports disabled South Vietnam soldiers. Del has helped refresh my memory with firsthand accounts of operations we participated in during 1968. Next is Earl Gerheim, a friend and Marine Corps combat correspondent with whom I shared the coverage of many combat operations. His stories and unerring recall of names helped me piece together parts of this narrative, especially Operations No Name II and Allen Brook.

Dr. Mark Moyar, author of several works on Vietnam, and the William P. Harris Chair of Military History at Hillsdale College, put me in touch with the right person to get this project off the ground. Without his help in making that critical first step, I might yet be pursuing a publishing house.

I am forever grateful to Michael "Lee" Lanning, author of twenty-six books on Vietnam, who served as an army officer and infantry platoon leader in that war. His encouragement, advice, and support were critical to the success of this book. He provided a recommendation for me to his publisher that opened the door for this project. Sadly, Lee lost his battle with cancer and did not live to see the completion of this work.

Special thanks to the folks at the National Archives and Records Administration, Still Picture Branch, for helping me locate and scan negatives that I had submitted back during the war. William "Billy" Wade, the branch chief, not only made me feel welcome, but made sure I had everything I needed to complete this task. Archivist Sarah Bseirani kept in email contact with me and provided a wealth of information to help me prepare. From the moment I arrived at the front desk and was greeted by archivist Cecilia Figliuolo, until I finished my scanning, I never wanted for anything. She and archives technician Heather Sulier brought everything to one of the research tables and helped me get set up. I continue to collaborate with Cecilia on a number of photo projects with NARA, including a critically received blog about my combat photography that she authored.

Last but certainly not least, I want to acknowledge David Reisch, author and editor. Dave knows a good story when he sees one and had confidence that my memoir and photographs were worthy of sharing with the world. I will be forever grateful for his editorial skills and for shepherding me through the world of publishing. Preparing the final manuscript would not have been possible without the help of production editor Felicity Tucker and copy editor Melissa Hayes, who guided me through that process with the deftness of true professionals. No book is complete without a cover, and Piper Wallis provided an eye-catching design and layout. The tightly cropped action photo and bold fonts are sure to entice readers for a closer look.

It is indeed an honor having this manuscript brought to life by Stackpole Books, with their ninety-plus-year history of bringing military books to press. I am grateful for their support and being counted as one of their authors.

# Glossary

| | |
|---|---|
| **AA form** | Administrative action form. |
| **AIT** | Advanced infantry training. |
| **Amtrac** | Short for "amphibious tractor"; the LVTP-5 (landing vehicle, tracked, personnel Mark 5) was the variant most often seen in Vietnam. |
| **Arc Light** | Operation Arc Light was the name for B-52 bombing missions in South Vietnam conducted out of Anderson AFB on Guam. |
| **ARVN** | Army of the Republic of Vietnam; military force of South Vietnam. |
| **assault pouch** | An olive-drab cloth pouch with carrying strap containing a one-hundred-round belt of 7.62mm ammunition for use in the M60 machine gun. |
| **bennie** | Short for "benefit." |
| **Blooper** | M79 40mm grenade launcher that acquired this name from the sound it made when fired. |
| **CG** | Commanding general. |
| **CH-46** | Sea Knight medium-lift tandem-rotor transport helicopter. |
| **CH-53** | Sea Stallion heavy-lift helicopter. |
| **ChiCom** | Chinese Communist. |
| **church key** | Jargon for a combination bottle and beverage can opener. |
| **CMC** | Commandant of the Marine Corps. |
| **CO** | Commanding officer. |
| **corpsman** | US Navy medical personnel that served in hospitals and in the field on combat operations with the Marines. |
| **CP** | Command post; can refer to a fixed facility in the rear or a mobile command staff group in the field. |

**Cpl.**　　Abbreviation for enlisted rank of corporal, E-4.

**crapshoot**　　Reference to the dice game, meaning that one never knew how things would turn out.

**C-rations**　　Combat rations. Officially known as Meal, Combat Individual, or MCI. A big letter C on the case of rations led to them being called C-rations.

**CS**　　CS gas (2-chlorobenzylidene malononitrile) is one of the most commonly used tear gases and was widely used in Vietnam. The name "CS" is derived from the surnames of the scientists who synthesized the compound, Ben Corson and Roger Stoughton.

**deuce and a half**　　Nickname for the M35 series 2.5-ton, 6×6 cargo truck used by all branches of the military to transport both personnel and material.

**ditty bag**　　A small bag to carry personal items; in the States they would have been called gym bags.

**DMZ**　　Demilitarized zone that separated North and South Vietnam.

**EE-8 field telephone**　　A battery-powered wired telephone that could transmit up to seven miles; used primarily in rear areas.

**enlisted ranks**　　Marine enlisted ranks in order of seniority: private, private first class, lance corporal, corporal, sergeant, staff sergeant, gunnery sergeant, master sergeant, first sergeant, master gunnery sergeant, sergeant major, and sergeant major of the Marine Corps.

**EOD**　　Explosive ordnance disposal.

**E-tool**　　Entrenching tool; a small folding shovel carried by infantrymen.

**Freedom Bird**　　Jargon for the commercial airliners that transported many Marines home after their tour was completed in Vietnam.

**Gunny**　　Short for "gunnery sergeant."

**HE**　　High explosives.

**H&Is**　　Harassment and interdiction artillery fire was employed to disrupt enemy movement at night.

**hooch**　　Generally referred to a sixteen-by-thirty-two-foot wooden building that served as living quarters in the rear areas.

**HQMC**　　Headquarters Marine Corps.

**H-34**　　Model designation of a single-rotor helicopter used to transport men and equipment.

**intel**　　Short for "intelligence"; any information about the enemy that would be useful to the Marines in conducting the war.

**Intel**            Short for intelligence team, US Marine Corps.

**ISO**            Information Services Office.

**KA-BAR**            The KA-BAR was the Marines' fighting knife. It had a seven-inch blade with an overall length of nearly a foot and a stacked leather washer handle. The Marine Corps adopted it during World War II, and it was still in use during Vietnam. It served as both a fighting tool and a general-purpose knife.

**KIA**            Killed in action.

**LAW**            The M72 LAW was a 66mm one-shot throwaway light anti-armor weapon that replaced the rifle grenade as an individual antitank weapon; also used against fortified positions.

**LCM**            Landing craft, mechanized; a World War II–vintage landing craft used to carry vehicles or troops.

**L/Cpl.**            Lance corporal.

**Looky-loo**            A person who views something for sale with no genuine intention of buying.

**LP**            Listening post.

**LRPs**            Long-range patrol rations.

**LZ**            Landing zone.

**M1**            The M1 carbine is a lightweight semiautomatic carbine chambered in the .30 carbine.

**M2**            Browning .50 caliber machine gun.

**M3A1 grease gun**            A .45 caliber submachine gun.

**M14**            Standard US battle rifle used during the early years of the Vietnam War that fired the 7.62mm NATO round.

**M16**            Standard US battle rifle that fired the 5.56mm NATO round and replaced the older M14.

**M26**            A type of fragmentation grenade in common use early in the Vietnam War, later replaced by the M33 baseball-type grenade.

**M-37 Personnel Carrier**            The Dodge M-37 was a ¾-ton four-wheel-drive vehicle similar to the commercially available Dodge Power Wagon. It had wooden fold-down bench seats in the back and was used to transport men and equipment.

**M48**  The Patton tank, which served as the Marines' main battle tank in Vietnam, weighed forty-five tons and had a 90mm main gun; a flame-throwing version was also used in Vietnam.

**M60**  Military designation for a medium-caliber machine gun, which fired the 7.62mm NATO round; in the jargon of the day, it was called "the pig."

**M79**  A 40mm grenade launcher commonly called a blooper by the Marines, from the sound it made when fired.

**MACV**  Military Assistance Command Vietnam, pronounced "Mac-Vee," was a joint-service command responsible for coordinating all US military operations in South Vietnam during the Vietnam War.

**Ma Deuce**  Slang for the Browning M2 .50 caliber machine gun.

**MCI**  Meal, combat, individual; aka, C-rations.

**MEDCAP**  Medical civic action program.

**MFB**  Main force battalion.

**MIA**  Missing in action.

**midrats**  Short for "midnight rations."

**Mighty Mite**  The M422 Mighty Mite was a quarter-ton vehicle that replaced the Jeep in the US Marine Corps.

**mopic**  Short for "motion picture."

**MOS**  Military occupational specialty; usually expressed as a four-digit number, such as "4631," which denoted a still photographer.

**MPC**  Military payment certificate; paper money used by the military in Vietnam to help prevent destabilization of local economies that would have resulted from widespread use of the US dollar.

**MRE**  Meals ready to eat.

**Mustang**  Military slang for a commissioned officer who began their career as an enlisted service member; they tended to be older and more experienced than their counterparts.

**Nam**  Vietnam; Marines seldom referred to the country by its proper name, instead using "Nam" or "the Nam" (i.e., "How long have you been in the Nam?").

**NARA**  National Archives and Records Administration.

**NCO**  Noncommissioned officer; included all enlisted ranks of corporal (E-4) and above.

**NVA**  North Vietnamese Army; now called the PAVN, or People's Army of Vietnam.

| | |
|---|---|
| **OCS** | The Officer Candidate School was a training program designed to prepare civilians and enlisted personnel for commissioning as officers in the Marine Corps. |
| **OD** | Depending on usage, it could refer to the Officer of the Day or the olive drab color used by the military on uniforms and equipment. |
| **OIC** | Officer in charge. |
| **122mm rockets** | Rocket artillery supplied to the enemy by the Russians; aka, grad or katyusha rockets. |
| **OP** | Outpost. |
| **Otter** | The M76 Otter was a tracked amphibious vehicle used for transporting men and cargo. |
| **PC** | Personnel carrier. |
| **PFs** | Popular forces. |
| **PFC** | Private first class. |
| **Phonetic alphabet used in Vietnam** | Alfa, Bravo, Charlie, Delta, Echo, Foxtrot, Golf, Hotel, India, Juliet, Kilo, Lima, Mike, November, Oscar, Papa, Quebec, Romeo, Sierra, Tango, Uniform, Victor, Whiskey, X-ray, Yankee, Zulu. |
| **pig** | Jargon for the M60 machine gun. |
| **pogue** | "Pogue" or "office pogue" was a derogatory term for non-combat rear-echelon personnel. |
| **PRC-25** | The AN/PRC-25, or "Prick 25" as the Marines called it, was a field portable, battery-powered radio communications set. It had a range of about five miles and was extensively used in Vietnam. |
| **PSP** | Perforated steel planking. |
| **P-38** | A small, lightweight, disposable, foldable alloy steel can opener issued with canned US military rations. |
| **PX** | Post exchange; a place on military bases where servicemen can shop, varying in size and selection of merchandise. |
| **quad-50** | M45 towed antiaircraft gun with four .50 caliber machine guns mounted on an elevation over azimuth revolving pedestal; some units were dismounted from their trailer and installed in the back of trucks to protect convoys. |
| **REMF** | A rear echelon motherfu*ker; derogatory term for non-combat personnel who served in rear areas. |
| **rocket belt** | An area surrounding Da Nang between 9,000 and 11,000 meters distant used by the enemy to fire rockets at the military bases there. |

| | |
|---|---|
| **RPD** | Ruchnoy Pulemyot Degtyaryova machine gun. |
| **RTO** | Radio telephone operator; more commonly called a radioman in the field, he carried the PRC-25 radio that was used for field communications. |
| **782 gear** | Equipment issued to individual Marines which included pack, canteen, poncho, ammo pouch, etc., used when in the field; "782" referred to the DD form signed when the gear was issued. |
| **Sgt.** | Abbreviation for sergeant, E-5. |
| **snafu** | "Situation normal, all fouled up"; normally applied to things that have gone wrong within our own military. |
| **SOG** | Studies and Observation Group. |
| **soup (verb)** | Jargon for processing film. |
| **SSgt.** | Abbreviation for staff sergeant, E-6. |
| **TAOR** | Tactical area of responsibility. |
| **TFX** | Task Force X-Ray; a unit comprised of the 1st and 3rd Battalions of the 5th Marine Regiment and the 1st Battalion, 3rd Marine Regiment, Battalion Landing Team that provided added support and manpower to other units during combat operations. |
| **Top** | Master sergeants were sometimes referred to informally as "Top," referring to their rank as the top sergeant in a unit. |
| **UH-34** | Medium helicopter used for various roles, including troop transport, combat assault, search and rescue, and medical evacuation. |
| **USNS** | United States Naval Ship; a noncommissioned ship owned by the US Navy, in this case, the *Hugh J. Gaffey*, a troop transport ship. |
| **VC** | Viet Cong; Communist fighters recruited from the South Vietnamese population; also known as Victor Charlie, Charlie, or Charles by the Marines. |
| **vill** | Short for "village," commonly used by Marines to denote a small village or hamlet. |
| **Willie Pete** | Military radio pronunciation of the letters "WP"; white phosphorus munition used primarily to mark the location of mortar and artillery shell impacts for targeting purposes. |
| **WO** | Warrant officer. |

# About the Author

Dennis Irwin Fisher was born in Latrobe, Pennsylvania, grew up in nearby Ligonier, and now resides in Battle Ground, Washington, with his wife Mary. He has two daughters, Dr. Julie Fisher and Dr. Joanna Fisher. He enlisted for three years in the US Marine Corps in 1966 and served nineteen months in Vietnam as an infantry rifleman and combat photographer, attaining the rank of sergeant.

Dennis enjoyed a post–Marine Corps career that has spanned more than fifty-eight years as a still photographer, cinematographer, range instrumentation optics engineer, and optics consultant. His career began in 1965 at the University of Miami in Florida. There he studied photojournalism under the mentorship of Mr. Wilson Hicks, the former executive editor of *Life* magazine, and Mr. William Retskin, the photo editor of the *Hurricane* newspaper. The knowledge, skills, and abilities acquired there led to his work as a USMC combat photographer in Vietnam.

After his discharge from the Marines, Dennis worked for Pratt & Whitney Aircraft's Florida Research and Development Center, going on to complete his photographic education with a BA in commercial and scientific technical photography from the prestigious Brooks Institute of Photography in Santa Barbara, California. A career in photography followed, shooting photojournalism assignments around the world with the US Air Force's Aerospace Audiovisual Service, the Defense Audiovisual Agency, and finally, serving as chief of technical service/optics for the Western Test Range at Vandenberg AFB in California. Following his retirement from federal service in 2006, he began a successful consulting career in applied optics, serving many commercial, aerospace, and defense companies.

www.ingramcontent.com/pod-product-compliance
Lightning Source LLC
Chambersburg PA
CBHW080446030726
47592CB00011B/2992